The
AMAZING
BOOK
of
LISTS

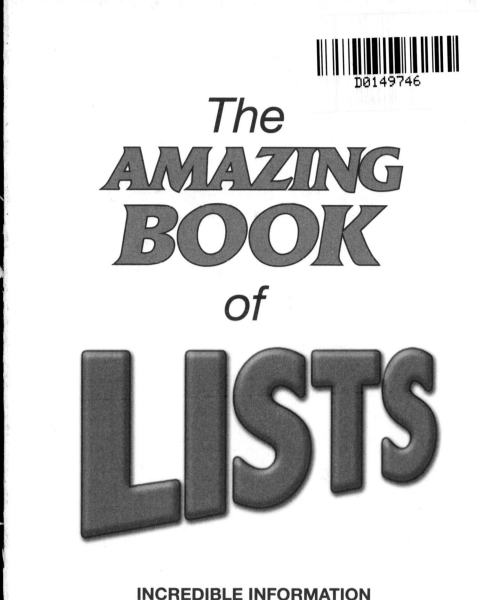

INCREDIBLE INFORMATION
AND TIDBITS OF TRIVIA

Publications International, Ltd.

D0149746

Contributing writers: Helen Davies, Marjorie Dorfman, Mary Fons, Deborah Hawkins, Martin Hintz, Linnea Lundgren, David Priess, Julie Clark Robinson, Paul Seaburn, Heidi Stevens, and Steve Theunissen

Mary Fons makes her living as a freelance writer, creating snazzy content for clients such as Jellyvision and Content That Works. She also works as a slam poet, actress, and ensemble member of Chicago's longest-running theater show, the Neo-Futurist's *Too Much Light Makes the Baby Go Blind.* Check out www.maryfons.com for more about Mary and to read her juicy blog, PaperGirl.

Julie Clark Robinson is the award-winning author of *Live in the Moment.* She's also the editor of the *General Hospital* and *The Bold and the Beautiful* pages on www.Soaps.com. Her works have been published in *A Cup of Comfort* books and *Family Circle* magazine. Peruse her inspirational tidbits about everyday joy at www.nabbw.com or www.julieclarkrobinson.com.

Paul Seaburn is a comedy writer and teacher. His television credits include *The Tonight Show* and *Comic Strip Live,* and he's also the head writer for *Taylor's Attic,* a family comedy. He is the author of *Jestercises & Gamestorms,* and he teaches "Creative Thinking Through Comedy," a program for gifted students.

Front and back cover: **PhotoDisc Collection**

Louis Weber, CEO
Publications International, Ltd.
7373 North Cicero Avenue
Lincolnwood, Illinois 60712

Permission is never granted for commercial purposes.

ISBN-13: 978-1-4127-5298-5
ISBN-10: 1-4127-5298-1

Manufactured in U.S.A.

8 7 6 5 4 3 2 1

CONTENTS

✳ ✳ ✳ ✳

Chapter 3—Animals

� ✳ ✳ ✳

Chapter 4—Fun, Games, and Pop Culture

✳ ✳ ✳ ✳

Chapter 5—Music

✳ ✳ ✳ ✳

Chapter 6—Around the World

✳ ✳ ✳ ✳

Chapter 7—Religion, Folklore, and the Paranormal

✳ ✳ ✳ ✳

Chapter 8—Death

Chapter 9—Health, Fitness, and the Human Body

✳ ✳ ✳ ✳

Chapter 10—People

✳ ✳ ✳ ✳

Chapter 11—Law & Disorder

Chapter 12—Food & Drink

✵ ✵ ✵ ✵

Chapter 13—Television

✵ ✵ ✵ ✵

Chapter 14—Science & Nature

※ ※ ※ ※
Chapter 15—Money & Business

※ ※ ※ ※
Chapter 16—This & That

LIST-EN UP!

✳ ✳ ✳ ✳

In the words of journalist H. Allen Smith, "The human animal differs from the lesser primates in his passion for lists." In today's hectic world, when vast quantities of information are thrown at us from various outlets—television, radio, print media, and the Internet—we often feel a bit overwhelmed by information overload. So we use lists to help us focus, keep track of things, and basically hold on to our sanity. How many people could remember all the items they need to buy at the grocery store without making a handy list?

Although it won't help you remember what you need at the store, once you've read *Armchair Digest™: The Amazing Book of Lists,* you'll impress your friends and family with all the interesting insights and tantalizing tidbits of trivia you'll soak up.

Here are some of the captivating tales you'll find inside:

- Mysterious Disappearances in the Bermuda Triangle

- 12 Dropouts Who Made It Big

- Freaky Facts About the Human Body

- 13 Facts You Didn't Know About Bats

- 9 Fictional Bands and Their Hits

- And much, much more

Once you start reading *Armchair Digest™: The Amazing Book of Lists,* you'll find it hard to stop. There's no need to start at the beginning, either—you can open up to any page you like and dive into a virtual cornucopia of lists.

P.S. If you have thoughts, questions, or ideas concerning this book, or if you would like more information about our other titles, please contact us.

(Chapter 1)
MOVIES

✳ ✳ ✳ ✳

YOU WOULD HAVE BEEN PERFECT IN THAT MOVIE!
Stars Who Turned Down Juicy Roles

*It seems that the actors cast in our favorite movies are perfect
for the part, but they're often not the director's first choice. Most
celebs have turned down more roles than they've taken, some
with regrets but many with thanks to their lucky stars.*

1. Brad Pitt
Brad Pitt has had hunky roles in many films including *Troy* (2004),
Legends of the Fall (1994), and *Thelma & Louise* (1991). But he
turned down a role in *Apollo 13* (1995) to make the movie *Se7en*
(1995), which won an MTV Movie Award for Best Movie, beating
out *Apollo 13*. But *Apollo 13* received nine Academy Award nominations and won two Oscars, leaving *Se7en* in the dust.

2. Mel Gibson
Mel Gibson has had a blockbuster career as an actor, starring in
both the *Mad Max* and *Lethal Weapon* series, and as a director,
winning an Academy Award for *Braveheart* (1995), in which he also
starred. Gibson turned down the lead role in *The Terminator* (1984),
which went to Arnold Schwarzenegger instead. Gibson was also
offered the lead in the first *Batman* movie (1989) (which went to
Michael Keaton), but he was already committed to *Lethal Weapon
2* (1989). Later, he turned down the part of villain Two-Face in
Batman Forever (1995), which went to Tommy Lee Jones.

3. Sean Connery
A star with a career as long as Sean Connery's is bound to make
both good and bad decisions. The good ones include roles in *Indiana Jones and the Last Crusade* (1989), *The Hunt for Red October*
(1990), seven James Bond movies, and his Academy Award-winning

role in *The Untouchables* (1987). But one questionable decision was turning down the 007 role in *Live and Let Die* (1973), which became a great career move for his replacement, Roger Moore. Connery later turned down the role of Gandalf in the *Lord of the Rings* trilogy, which went to Ian McKellen, and the role of Morpheus in *The Matrix* films, which went to Laurence Fishburne—two decisions that he admitted regretting.

4. Al Pacino

Al Pacino rose to fame playing Michael Corleone in *The Godfather* movies and has since starred in many great movies, including *Scarface* (1983), *Donnie Brasco* (1997), and *Scent of a Woman* (1992), for which he won an Oscar. But can you imagine Big Al as Han Solo in *Star Wars* (1977), the role that started the career of Harrison Ford? Pacino also turned down the lead role in *Close Encounters of the Third Kind* (1977), which instead went to Richard Dreyfuss. But the actor Pacino has had the most close encounters with is Dustin Hoffman. Pacino turned down starring roles in *Midnight Cowboy* (1969), *Marathon Man* (1976), and *Kramer vs. Kramer* (1979), all of which went to Hoffman.

5. Rock Hudson

Rock Hudson, a favorite leading man of the 1950s and 1960s, starred in films such as *Come September* (1961), *Send Me No Flowers* (1964), and *Pillow Talk* (1959), the first of several films that costarred Doris Day. He signed on to play the lead in *Ben Hur* (1959), but when contract negotiations broke down, the part went to Charlton Heston instead, an outcome that would ultimately be Hudson's only career regret.

6. Will Smith

Will Smith began his showbiz career as half of the hip-hop duo DJ Jazzy Jeff & the Fresh Prince, who won the first ever Grammy in the Rap category in 1988. Smith was nearly bankrupt by 1990, when he was hired to star in the sitcom *The Fresh Prince of Bel-Air*, which became a huge success. His movies include *Independence Day* (1996), *Men in Black* (1997), and *Ali* (2001). He was also offered the lead role in *The Matrix* (1999). Despite the film's phenomenal success, Smith later said that he didn't regret turning down the role because Keanu Reeves "was brilliant as Neo." Smith also originally passed on *Men in Black*, but his wife convinced him to reconsider.

Birth Names of 26 Vintage Movie Stars

✳ ✳ ✳ ✳

1. Fred Astaire . . . . Frederic Austerlitz
2. Jack Benny . . . . Benjamin Kubelsky
3. Milton Berle . . . . Milton Berlinger
4. George Burns . . . . Nathan Birnbaum
5. Eddie Cantor . . . . Edward Israel Iskowitz
6. Gary Cooper . . . . Frank James Cooper
7. Joan Crawford . . . . Lucille Fay LeSueur
8. Bing Crosby . . . . Harry Lillis Crosby
9. Tony Curtis . . . . Bernard Schwartz
10. Bette Davis . . . . Ruth Elizabeth Davis
11. Doris Day . . . . Doris Kappelhoff
12. Dale Evans . . . . Frances Smith
13. Judy Garland. . . . . Frances Gumm
14. Cary Grant . . . . Archibald Leach
15. Rita Hayworth . . . . Margarita Cansino
16. William Holden . . . . William Beedle
17. Al Jolson . . . . Asa Yoelson
18. Boris Karloff. . . . . William Henry Pratt
19. Jerry Lewis . . . . Joseph Levitch
20. Bela Lugosi. . . . . Béla Blaskó
21. Dean Martin. . . . . Dino Crocetti
22. Marilyn Monroe . . . . Norma Jean Baker
23. Roy Rogers . . . . Leonard Slye
24. Barbara Stanwyck. . . . . Ruby Stevens
25. Lana Turner . . . . Julia Jean Turner
26. John Wayne. . . . . Marion Morrison

ROLES OF A REBEL
James Dean's 6 Movie Roles

✳ ✳ ✳ ✳

This Indiana boy lived only 24 years, but his legend as an American icon continues to thrive. He began his showbiz career in a Pepsi commercial, standing around a jukebox with a group of teens singing "Pepsi-Cola hits the spot." Within a decade, Dean had two Oscar nominations. Sadly, both were posthumous. In 1955, Dean bought a Porsche Spyder, bragging that it could reach speeds of 150 miles per hour. Upon hearing this, actor Alec Guinness told him not to set foot inside the car because he would be dead before the week was out. Six days later, Dean's body was pulled from the twisted wreckage of his new car on a stretch of California highway. Dean's career was cut short, but his legacy lives on in the movies he left behind.

1. *Fixed Bayonets* (1951)

James Dean's first movie role was far from "cushy." This Korean War film was the first to depict the violence of combat. Director Samuel Fuller was given free reign to portray the grisly "kill or be killed" premise of the film, and he took it! Actors and camera crews were pushed to their physical limits, including lead actors Richard Basehart, Gene Evans, and Michael O'Shea. Twenty-year-old Dean was uncredited in the film and had only one line, which was cut in the final production.

2. *Sailor Beware* (1952)

Dean's next film was a nice departure from Korean combat. With Dean Martin and Jerry Lewis at the helm, production must have been more pleasant. This Paramount film took only five weeks to film, and even though it technically deals with the military, the plot centers around a good-natured bet between sailors that involves kissing girls. Dean went uncredited again, playing a guy in the locker room, but at least his line wasn't cut this time.

3. *Has Anybody Seen My Gal?* (1952)

Rock Hudson carried this film about a wealthy older man trying to decide if the family of his former love is worthy of inheriting his estate. James Dean remained one of many guys with a bit part. Specifically, he's on a bar stool at a soda fountain without any lines. He's listed as "youth at soda fountain" in the credits.

4. *East of Eden* (1955)

Dean's first major film role gave him top billing along with Julie Harris, Raymond Massey, and Burl Ives. Dean played Cal Trask, who competes with his brother for their father's love. This was Dean's only major film released while he was alive. The role landed him an Oscar nomination for Best Actor, although it came posthumously. However, Ernest Borgnine won for his role in *Marty*.

5. *Rebel Without a Cause* (1955)

This is the film for which James Dean is best remembered. It came out just a month after his tragic death, and costarred teens Natalie Wood and Sal Mineo. Dean played the new kid in town, Jim Stark, who finds trouble when searching to replace the love that is lacking in his family life. A daring commentary on tough teenage existence, this movie pitted boys against each other in knife fights that used real switchblades. The actors wore chest protectors under their shirts, but Dean still ended up with a cut on his ear.

6. *Giant* (1956)

Rock Hudson worked one last time with James Dean, and this time legendary star Elizabeth Taylor rounded out the top billing. Dean played Jett Rink, a ranch hand who became a Texas oil tycoon. The actor finished shooting his scenes just days before he died, but a few voice-over lines still needed to be recorded, so actor Nick Adams stepped to the microphone to read the part of Jett Rink. Dean received a second posthumous Oscar nomination for Best Actor for this role. Rock Hudson was also nominated, but the award went to Yul Brynner for his role in *The King and I*.

13 Steven Spielberg-Directed Films

✳ ✳ ✳ ✳

As a child, Cecil B. DeMille's production of The Greatest Show
on Earth *was the first movie Steven Spielberg ever saw, marking
the beginning of his love affair with the world of film.
Spielberg began making home movies at an early age, and, at 14,
he won an award for a 40-minute war movie he called* Escape
to Nowhere. *Spielberg attended Long Beach University
but dropped out to pursue his dream of a career in film.
Television assignments followed, but it wasn't until his 1971
direction of a Richard Matheson television adaptation
called* Duel *that Spielberg's burgeoning reputation as
a superb filmmaker was cemented.*

1. *Amistad* (1997)

This film relates the true story of mutiny aboard the slave ship
Amistad in 1839. The slaves revolted, murdered the crew, and
remained adrift for weeks. After discovery by some American
marine officers, the slaves were tried for murder. A few noble
people stood to defend them—no matter what the cost—to end the
dehumanizing institution of slavery in the New World. Those few
are the strength of *Amistad,* which means "friendship" in Spanish.
Starring Morgan Freeman, Anthony Hopkins, Nigel Hawthorne,
and newcomer Djimon Hounsou, *Amistad* was nominated for four
Academy Awards and grossed more than $44 million.

2. *Catch Me If You Can* (2002)

Based on a true story, this movie stars Leonardo DiCaprio as Frank
Abagnale, Jr., a con artist who, in the 1960s, passed more than
$2.5 million in fake checks in 26 countries and also posed as a pilot,
pediatrician, and attorney, all by age 21. Tom Hanks plays FBI
agent Carl Hanratty, who pursued Abagnale for years. The film
earned two Oscar nods and grossed more than $164 million at the
box office. Incidentally, Abagnale is now a multimillionaire who
advises businesses on fraud detection and prevention.

3. *Close Encounters of the Third Kind* (1977)

This unique UFO story tells the tale of an electrician (Richard Dreyfuss) who is drawn to an isolated area in the wilderness where an alien spaceship has landed. It is not a terror-filled tale of alien conflict or hostility, and therein lies its remarkable difference from other films of this ilk. Instead, it is a compelling story of contact and communication, foreshadowing the power of *E.T.* a few years later. The special effects were dazzling, and the movie garnered many Oscar nods, including a win for Best Cinematography.

4. *The Color Purple* (1985)

Based on Alice Walker's Pulitzer Prize-winning novel, this 1985 production chronicles the life of a young African American woman named Celie (Whoopi Goldberg), who lives in the South at the turn of the 20th century. She is a poor mother of two with an abusive husband (Danny Glover) whom she fears so greatly that she calls him "Mister." Often criticized as being compelling but too careful and slick, *The Color Purple* still grossed more than $98 million at the box office and was nominated for 11 Oscars, although it did not win any.

5. *E.T. (The Extra Terrestrial)* (1982)

If Spielberg struck gold with *Close Encounters of the Third Kind,* he struck platinum with *E.T.* A classic film that appeals to all age groups, the story centers around a cute but very odd alien who gets marooned on Earth. He chances upon a boy named Elliot (Henry Thomas), and the two form a powerful bond. The film captivates and enthralls with its message of friendship, love, and generosity. *E.T.* was critically acclaimed and became one of the biggest money-makers in box office history, grossing more than $435 million in the United States alone, followed by a marketing frenzy that ensued from the sale of *E.T.* memorabilia.

6. *Hook* (1991)

This adaptation of J. M. Barrie's classic story is a film of élan and rambunctious spirit. According to the story line, an adult Peter Pan (Robin Williams) must regain his youthful spirit and confront his old enemy Captain Hook (Dustin Hoffman), who has kidnapped Peter's children. Julia Roberts plays Tinkerbell, who accompanies Peter on his return to Neverland and helps him become "Peter Pan" again. Although Spielberg himself admitted that he was disappointed with the final version of the movie, it still grossed more than $119 million and garnered five Oscar nominations.

7. Jaws (1975)

Based on the Peter Benchley novel, this horror film was released just in time for beach season. The villain was a very homicidal great white shark that attacked people in a quiet coastal town. But the film, which Spielberg calls the most difficult he's made, often played on the power of suggestion, proving that what the mind conjures in the imagination can sometimes be more powerful than an actual image. *Jaws* banked on that, earning more than $260 million in the United States and setting a record at the time for box office gross. The film also won Oscars for editing, sound, and original score.

8. Jurassic Park (1993)

Written by Michael Crichton, *Jurassic Park*—the book and subsequent movie—generated so much interest in dinosaurs that the study of paleontology increased dramatically and has been at an all-time high ever since. The setting is a remote island where a wealthy businessman has secretly created a theme park featuring live dinosaurs cloned from prehistoric DNA found encased in amber. As preposterous as this may sound, it works, and there is genuine suspense, especially when the prehistoric creatures break free. The special effects are dazzling and eye-popping, earning the film three Oscars—Best Effects (Sound Effects), Best Effects (Visual), and Best Sound. *Jurassic Park* held the box office record gross of $357,067,947 before it was beaten by *Titanic* in 1997.

9. *Munich* (2005)

Nominated for five Oscars, including Best Picture, this film, based on a book by George Jonas, is one of courage and conscience. It relates the true story of 11 Israeli athletes who were murdered during the 1972 Olympics by the Palestinian terrorist group Black September, and the retaliation that followed. One of the actors, Guri Weinberg, plays his own father, Moshe Weinberg, who was one of the athletes killed in the massacre. *Munich* grossed more than $47 million in the United States and $127 million worldwide.

10. *Raiders of the Lost Ark* (1981)

Spielberg struck pure gold in 1981 with the release of this movie, which was written by George Lucas and Philip Kaufman. Set in the 1930s, the film stars Harrison Ford as archaeologist and adventurer Indiana Jones and follows his breathtaking journey in search of the Ark of the Covenant, which is said to hold the Ten Commandments. He must find it before the Nazis do because, according to the story, Hitler has plans to use the Ark as a weapon. The film received glowing reviews and grossed more than $242 million.

11. *Saving Private Ryan* (1998)

Based on a true story, this war drama centers around a group of U.S. soldiers trying to rescue paratrooper Ryan, a comrade who is stationed behind enemy lines during World War II. Spielberg's camera is graphic and wild, deliberately evoking the reality of war. The opening scene is mayhem and chaos mingled with blood, vomit, and tears. In one memorable moment a soldier has his arm blown off, then he bends over and picks it up as if it were a fallen handkerchief. Starring Tom Hanks and Matt Damon, the film grossed more than $481 million worldwide, raking in $30 million in its opening weekend. *Saving Private Ryan* also took home five Oscars, including Best Director and Best Cinematography.

12. *Schindler's List* (1993)

This masterpiece, based on the true horrors of the Holocaust, is quite possibly Spielberg's finest achievement. The plot concerns a greedy Czech-born businessman, Oskar Schindler (Liam Neeson), who is determined to make his fortune in Nazi Germany by exploiting cheap Jewish labor. Despite his fervent affiliation with the Third Reich, Schindler turns his factory into a refuge for Jews—working in a factory guaranteed longer life to those slated for extermination in the barbaric concentration camps. Although Schindler ended up penniless, he single-handedly saved about 1,100 Jews from certain death. *Schindler's List* won seven Academy Awards including Best Picture and Best Director, and the film grossed more than $321 million worldwide.

13. *Sugarland Express* (1974)

Sugarland Express marked the big-screen directorial debut of Steven Spielberg. Starring Goldie Hawn, Ben Johnson, and William Atherton, this movie, based on a true story, revolves around a young woman who helps her husband escape from prison so they can kidnap their child who's been placed in foster care. Along the way, they take a policeman hostage, and the movie becomes a madcap escape caper. The film grossed more than $12 million and won Best Screenplay at the Cannes Film Festival.

Early Roles of 9 Hollywood Stars

❋ ❋ ❋ ❋

The hair is big, and the script is bad, but everyone has to start somewhere. In showbiz, a job is a job and young actors take what they can get. These stars might be famous today, but they weren't born on the A-list. They worked their way up through bit parts and the strange, often painfully mediocre jungle of Hollywood. Here are some of the early films of today's red-carpet royalty.

1. Julia Roberts in *Firehouse* (1987)

Julia Roberts got super famous relatively early in her career, so there wasn't too much time for clunkers. But there were a few. *Firehouse* is a raunchy comedy à la *Police Academy* that used the tagline, "When the fire's out... the heat is on!" Roberts plays a character named Babs, but doesn't do enough in the film to even get a screen credit. Roberts filmed another movie entitled *Blood Red* before *Firehouse,* but it wasn't released until 1989, making this lowbrow farce her big-screen debut.

2. Keanu Reeves in *One Step Away* (1985)

The man who cracked *The Matrix* and was half of the cultural phenomenon known as *Bill and Ted's Excellent Adventure* (he was Ted), Reeves did some TV work before his role in this troubled-teen flick produced by the National Film Board of Canada. He plays a kid with tough choices to make in a world that has stacked the odds against him. *One Step Away* is a couple steps away from being a good movie, but the future *Speed* star showed promise.

3. Tom Cruise in *Endless Love* (1981)

The only people to benefit commercially from this story of two star-crossed lovers (played by Brooke Shields and Martin Hewitt) were Diana Ross and Lionel Richie, who sang the hit song of the same name. The movie itself, directed by Franco Zefferelli, was pretty much a disaster. Tom Cruise makes a quick appearance as Billy—he auditioned for the lead but was beat out by Hewitt. Not only did Cruise, the future *Top Gun* hunk/Oscar nominee/media magnet, make his big-screen debut in this sappy teen flick, James Spader, Jamie Gertz, and Ian Ziering were also rookies in *Endless Love.*

4. Nicole Kidman in *BMX Bandits* (1983)

Before the Chanel campaign, even before Tom, there was *BMX Bandits.* Nicole Kidman filmed several movies in 1983, but this one stands out. Hilarity ensues when two BMX bikers and their friend (Kidman) become entangled with a group of bank robbers. The Aussie has said this is one of her favorite films from the early days, and while it's no *Moulin Rouge,* the reviews weren't that bad.

5. Chris Rock in *Beverly Hills Cop II* (1987)

Surely no one on the set of *Beverly Hills Cop II* looked at the young actor playing "Playboy Mansion valet" and thought, "That kid's going to be hosting the Academy Awards someday!" Chris Rock has made a name for himself as one of the most brilliant voices in stand-up comedy, but before his own original material opened doors at HBO and network television, Rock was opening car doors for Eddie Murphy in this classic '80s comedy.

6. Courtney Cox in *Masters of the Universe* (1987)

Life was pretty sweet while playing Monica in NBC's megahit sitcom, *Friends,* but in 1987 Courtney Cox was running for her life from characters named Gildor and Karg. Cox had done a Bruce Springsteen video and television work before this He-Man movie, and she completed other film projects in 1987, but this role made her a favorite among the sci-fi set and possibly foretold her future work in kitschy movies such as the 1996 thriller *Scream.*

7. Jack Nicholson in *The Cry Baby Killer* (1958)

One of the better-known and most-respected screen actors of our time, Jack Nicholson has won three Oscars and has been nominated for many more. But before that he had to pay the rent. At age 21, Nicholson got a part in *The Cry Baby Killer,* a super low-budget, not-yet-ready-for-prime-time movie about an unstable young man who finds himself in dire circumstances. Nicholson plays Jimmy, the "cry baby killer," and does a good job with a weak script. But if you want to see Jack at his best, check out *One Flew Over the Cuckoo's Nest, The Shining,* or *The Departed.*

8. Madonna in *A Certain Sacrifice* (1985)

In 1985, when it was clear the world had a pop icon on its hands, the creators of *A Certain Sacrifice* released this low-budget movie, much to Madonna's chagrin. In the movie, filmed in New York in the late '70s, Madonna portrays a streetwise teen who gets in over her head with some unsavory characters. Madonna may not be known as a great actor, but *A Certain Sacrifice* shows she had star appeal long before she ruled MTV.

9. Tom Hanks in *He Knows You're Alone* (1980)

Long before he made us laugh in *Big,* before he made us cry in *Forrest Gump,* and way before he made mega-blockbusters like *The Da Vinci Code,* Tom Hanks was in a simple teen horror flick called *He Knows You're Alone*. The tagline of the movie was: "Every girl is frightened the night before her wedding, but this time... there's good reason!" A young bride-to-be is being stalked while her future husband is out of town. Hanks plays the grieving boyfriend of another victim. Maybe the promise of a shelf full of Oscars would have cheered him up.

24 Comic Books that Jumped to the Big Screen

✳ ✳ ✳ ✳

1. *Batman*
2. *Blade*
3. *Casper*
4. *The Crow*
5. *Daredevil*
6. *Dick Tracy*
7. *The Fantastic Four*
8. *Flash Gordon*
9. *The Green Hornet*
10. *The Incredible Hulk*
11. *Iron Man*
12. *Josie and the Pussycats*
13. *The Mask*
14. *Men in Black*
15. *Popeye*
16. *Richie Rich*
17. *Spawn*
18. *Spider-Man*
19. *Superman*
20. *Swamp Thing*
21. *Teenage Mutant Ninja Turtles*
22. *Timecop*
23. *The Transformers*
24. *X-Men*

20 Films Directed by the Master of Suspense, Alfred Hitchcock

✳ ✳ ✳ ✳

Perhaps no other director in the history of film has had a greater impact on the industry than Alfred Hitchcock. "Hitch" made more than 65 full-length movies that have defined cinema for generations. Nicknamed "the Master of Suspense," the rotund, gravelly-voiced man (who never won a Best Director Oscar) made films that put viewers on the edge of their seats time and time again. Strong characterization, symbolism, surprise endings, and extended chase scenes were a few of Hitch's trademarks. Here are some of his most memorable movies.

1. *The Birds* (1963)

Alfred Hitchcock will forever be known as "the Master of Suspense" because of his ability to take the everyday and make it terrifying. Hotels, heights, neighbors, women, and birds were benign until Hitch got ahold of them. *The Birds* is the ultimate example of this—any shred of avian cuteness is obliterated when swarms of birds attack a northern California town. Tippi Hedren plays the doomed blonde alongside handsome Rod Taylor. Hitch said the characters in *The Birds* "are the victims of Judgment Day," making the film an acceptably horrifying follow-up to *Psycho*.

2. *To Catch a Thief* (1955)

Hitch was among the first to film the engaging story of the reformed thug. Cary Grant plays John Robie, a retired cat burglar who lives a quiet life in the plush Riviera. Naturally, when a rash of burglaries explodes in the area, Robie is suspected. To clear his name, he sets out to catch the thief himself. He is aided by Grace Kelly, an American heiress initially convinced that Robie is guilty. Look for a long Hitch cameo in this film—he plays an unassuming bus passenger for about ten minutes.

3. *Dial "M" for Murder* (1954)

The first of Hitch's so-called "blonde films," this double-crossing plot is among the filmmaker's best. Grace Kelly is a woman torn between her handsome but murderous husband (Ray Milland) and her new dashing but philandering love (Robert Cummings). When Milland learns of the affair, he decides to blackmail an old acquaintance into murdering his wife. Things go a bit haywire, so Milland switches plans and attempts to frame his wife for the murder of the would-be assassin. Everything seems to be going according to Plan B, until an inspector starts snooping around. This film was originally done in 3-D, but switched to 2-D soon after. The 3-D version of this thriller is now available as a reissue.

4. *Family Plot* (1976)

Hitch's final film uses both humor and suspense to tell a tongue-in-cheek tale of a rich lady's eccentric foibles and the trouble they cause. Stars abound in this film, including Bruce Dern and William Devane, but Hitch had originally wanted the likes of Liza Minnelli and Al Pacino in the picture. If you look closely, there is a street sign in *Family Plot* that reads "Bates Ave.," a nod to *Psycho,* one of the many films that made this director one of the most influential men of the 20th century.

5. *Frenzy* (1972)

Stop the presses! *Frenzy* was the first Hitch film to earn an R rating with the new ratings system that took effect in 1968. This ultra-dark comedy about an innocent man on the run was filmed in England, putting Hitch back home for the first time in nearly 20 years. Jon Finch, Alec McCowen, and Barry Foster make up the strong cast in this gallows-humor story that incorporates many trademark Hitchcock touches—bathrooms, continuous camera shots, and criminals around every corner.

6. *Lifeboat* (1944)

Long before *Survivor* and *Lost,* there was *Lifeboat.* Two World War II ships crash at sea and a group of survivors have to figure out how to stay afloat and reach safety with limited options. The group in the cramped boat includes a journalist, a radio operator, a businessman, and a nurse, among others. Many in the cast suffered from pneumonia during filming, but the set's chilly conditions created tension and incredible atmosphere for this fan favorite.

7. *The Man Who Knew Too Much* (1956)

One of Hitch's favorite leading men, Jimmy Stewart stars opposite Doris Day as a naive American couple vacationing in Morocco. When a French spy dies in Stewart's arms and the couple's son is kidnapped, a tense international espionage story plays out. Stewart is chased by the bad guys, since he knows too much about an assassination set to be carried out in London. The scene known as "The Albert Hall Scene" is about 12 minutes long and contains no dialogue whatsoever, delighting film students and cinephiles the world over—it's a risky filmmaking move and a Hitchcock masterstroke.

8. *Marnie* (1964)

Tippi Hedren is back as Marnie, a compulsive thief, in this rock-solid psychological thriller. Sean Connery plays the dashing leading man who tries to get Marnie to confront her schizophrenia. Long scenes and heavy dialogue kept this picture from having the mass appeal of *Psycho* or *The Birds,* but the suspense is every bit as potent. Hitch originally wanted Grace Kelly to play the lead role, but she had recently married the Prince of Monaco, and his people weren't thrilled about their new princess portraying such an unstable character.

9. *Mr. & Mrs. Smith* (1941)

Leave it to Hitchcock to surprise everyone by making a movie with no murder and no mystery at all. Lighthearted and purely entertaining, *Mr. & Mrs. Smith* stars Carole Lombard and Robert Montgomery as a couple with a rather odd relationship. When the two find out that they might not be married at all, their strained commitment is given new life. It was Lombard who is said to have convinced Hitch to do this beloved departure movie.

Sadly, she wouldn't live to see its long-standing success: Lombard died in a plane crash outside of Las Vegas in 1942. In 2005, Brad Pitt and Angelina Jolie starred in another movie of the same title, but it bore little resemblance to the original.

10. *North by Northwest* (1959)

This movie sold itself as "A 3,000 mile chase scene!" with a star-studded cast that included Cary Grant, Eva Marie Saint, and James Mason. The chase reaches its climax on Mount Rushmore. Hitch wanted to film on location, but the powers that be didn't want an attempted murder taking place on a national monument, so the entire set was constructed on a soundstage instead. The film was nominated for three Oscars and is often touted by critics as one of the best movies of all time.

11. *Psycho* (1960)

Hitchcock didn't use his usual, expensive production unit for this cultural juggernaut, opting instead to use his TV crew because he wanted *Psycho* to look like "a cheap exploitation film." Anthony Perkins stars as Norman Bates, a creepy mama's-boy innkeeper who offers Marion Crane (Janet Leigh) a place to stay for the night. Hitchcock chose to shoot in black and white to resemble the news-reels of the time—and also because the gory nature of the film would be too much in living color. *Psycho* is truly Hitchcock's masterpiece, a must-see for anyone who has ever wanted to be entertained—or scared out of their mind.

12. *Rear Window* (1954)

One of the most acclaimed suspense films of all time features Hitch favorites Grace Kelly and Jimmy Stewart. Stewart stars as Jeff, a snoop who believes he's seen a murder take place in his neighbor's house while looking out his window. Jeff's apartment was the set for the movie and except for one or two exterior shots, all shooting was done there—at the time, the largest set Paramount had ever constructed. The suspenseful ending is one of the more gripping finales ever committed to celluloid.

13. *Rebecca* (1940)

This early Hitchcock film tells the spooky tale of Rebecca (played by Joan Fontaine), the naive second wife of a rich widower (portrayed by Sir Laurence Olivier). It becomes abundantly clear that Rebecca's husband and the servants in his mansion aren't totally over the death of his first wife, and Rebecca is driven mad. Winner of the Academy Award for Best Picture, this movie was tied up in legal trouble over the rights to the script for several years before and after its release.

14. *Rope* (1948)

The first picture Hitch made with his own production company, Transatlantic Pictures, was also his first film in color. Two young men murder for fun and play cat and mouse with a former teacher, played by Jimmy Stewart. This movie, which was based on a true story, is noted for its incredibly long takes—the film often goes seven or eight minutes without an edit.

15. *Saboteur* (1942)

This Hitchcock film tells the tale of Barry Kane, a factory worker who sees a Nazi agent blow up his plant. Robert Cummings plays the leading man-on-the-run (though it's rumored that Hitch wanted Cary Grant in the role), and lots of classic Hitchcock moments ensue—cross-country chases, a lovely blonde, a slimy antagonist, and a big finish. Although it's not one of Hitchcock's top ten, it's definitely a thrilling film.

16. *Shadow of a Doubt* (1943)

Who knew Thornton Wilder, the playwright who penned *Our Town*, had it in him to write such a murderous tale? Hitchcock, ever the innovator, teamed up with Wilder to create this tale starring Joseph Cotten as Uncle Charlie and Teresa Wright as his niece. Uncle Charlie seems to be a mild-mannered guy, but his loving niece finds out something sinister about him and has to make some tough, dangerous decisions about how to handle the sticky situation. Hitch often said that *Shadow* was his favorite of all his films.

17. *Topaz* (1969)

A tense Cold War adventure, *Topaz* is based on a Leon Uris novel about the Cuban Missile Crisis. John Forsythe is a CIA agent who hires a French operative to investigate rumors of missiles in Cuba and a shady NATO spy known as "Topaz." True to Hitchcock form, much intrigue, double-crossing, and death transpire. Hitch admitted that *Topaz* was one of his more experimental films and had elements that didn't totally work, but true fans still appreciate the film as a risky but important fixture in the Hitchcock arsenal.

18. *Torn Curtain* (1966)

Nothing is what it appears to be in this "trust no one" thriller set during the Cold War. Paul Newman and Julie Andrews star as a young couple caught up in an international mystery in which everyone is a suspect. This would be the last picture that Hitch and composer and longtime collaborator Bernard Herrmann would work on together. Universal Pictures convinced Hitch that the score Herrmann penned wasn't upbeat enough, so the director cut the score and a brilliant, 11-year relationship came to an end.

19. *The Trouble with Harry* (1955)

Fans either love or hate *The Trouble with Harry,* a suspenseful satire starring Jerry Mathers, Academy Award-winner Edmund Gwenn, John Forsythe, and Shirley MacLaine (in her first film role). They all try to solve the problem—Harry is dead and no one knows what to do with the body. This comedy revealed the range that Hitch was capable of, even though many wondered where his dark, foreboding side had gone.

20. *Vertigo* (1958)

Based on a French novel, Jimmy Stewart and Kim Novak star in this megahit movie—filmed in "VistaVision" color. The dark story is set in San Francisco and features Stewart as an obsessive man who falls for a girl who kills herself. Novak plays two roles in the film. This is said to be Hitch's most "confessional" movie, dealing directly with how he feared women and tried to control them. Stewart is essentially playing Hitchcock himself.

Hollywood's Hunks

✳ ✳ ✳ ✳

Match the Hollywood hunk to one of his most memorable roles.

1. John Travolta
2. Patrick Swayze
3. Kevin Bacon
4. Tom Cruise
5. Keanu Reeves
6. Mel Gibson
7. Denzel Washington
8. Al Pacino
9. Robert De Niro
10. Brad Pitt
11. James Dean
12. George Clooney
13. Kevin Costner
14. Johnny Depp
15. Andy Garcia
16. Mark Wahlberg
17. Russell Crowe
18. Harrison Ford
19. Richard Gere

a. Jim Stark (*Rebel Without a Cause*)
b. Michael Green (*When a Man Loves a Woman*)
c. Crash Davis (*Bull Durham*)
d. Dirk Diggler (*Boogie Nights*)
e. Danny Zuko (*Grease*)
f. Jim Braddock (*Cinderella Man*)
g. Johnny Castle (*Dirty Dancing*)
h. Han Solo (*Star Wars*)
i. Jack Sparrow (*Pirates of the Caribbean*)
j. Sgt. Martin Riggs (*Lethal Weapon*)
k. Michael Corleone (*The Godfather*)
l. Officer Jack Traven (*Speed*)
m. Jake LaMotta (*Raging Bull*)
n. Zack Mayo (*An Officer and a Gentleman*)
o. Ren McCormack (*Footloose*)
p. Tristan Ludlow (*Legends of the Fall*)
q. Lincoln Rhyme (*The Bone Collector*)
r. Maverick (*Top Gun*)
s. Danny Ocean (*Ocean's Eleven*)

Answers: 1. e; 2. g; 3. o; 4. r; 5. l; 6. j; 7. q; 8. k; 9. m; 10. p; 11. a; 12. s; 13. c; 14. i; 15. b; 16. d; 17. f; 18. h; 19. n

15 Films Based on Stephen King Short Stories

✳ ✳ ✳ ✳

Stephen King sold numerous short stories to magazines before Doubleday published his full-length novel Carrie *in 1973, launching a career that has spanned decades. As King churned out hit books like* Christine *and* The Green Mile, *Hollywood clamored for the opportunity to turn his prose into box office gold. More than 50 King stories have been filmed for the big screen or TV so far, and there's no sign of stopping.*

1. *Carrie* (1976)

This story about a young girl named Carrie (Sissy Spacek) has a spot in the hallowed halls of classic horror movies. Carrie's over-protective mother shelters her so much that when she gets taunted mercilessly by her classmates, they learn that teasing Carrie is a bad idea—the girl's got a few nasty tricks up her sleeve. The movie, which also stars Piper Laurie and John Travolta, grossed more than $33 million. This was the first film adaptation of a King novel and years later, the first Broadway adaptation, too. *Carrie,* the musical, was one of the biggest theater flops ever, closing after just five performances and losing around $7 million.

2. *Children of the Corn* (1984)

This tale of terror came from a book of short stories entitled *Night Shift,* which also included future adaptations such as *The Lawnmower Man* and *Graveyard Shift.* The children of Gatlin, a little town in Nebraska, are called to murder by a preacher-boy named Isaac. A young couple gets in the way of their plans and creepy shots of wigged-out kids follow. Peter Horton and Linda Hamilton star as the doomed couple Burt and Vicky. In one scene, a copy of *Night Shift* can be seen on the dashboard of their car. This movie was universally panned, but that didn't stop it from spawning seven sequels. Most of them are as weak as the original, but the seventh film, released in 2001, is reportedly the best (and scariest) of the bunch.

3. *Christine* (1983)

Stephen King was so popular in the early 1980s that *Christine* the book wasn't even published before preproduction began on the movie version. Producers took a chance on his latest story about a boy and his car. That's right—Christine is a car, not a girl. Arnie Cunningham, who might have been played by Kevin Bacon if he hadn't chosen *Footloose* instead, is a high-school nerd who falls in love with a 1958 Plymouth Fury. The car is possessed and threatens to kill anyone who tries to get in its way. The story and the film are well known but not regarded as King's best. The author has the uncanny ability to tap into people's basic fears (rejection, clowns, ghosts, etc.), but his portrayal of a fearsome car didn't terrorize audiences as much as some of his other menaces.

4. *Cujo* (1983)

Here, doggie-doggie! Here, doggie—AAAAGGGGH! That pretty much sums up the plot behind this King adaptation. Dee Wallace plays Donna Trenton, a mom with marital problems, and a young Danny Pintauro (of *Who's the Boss?* fame) stars as her son Tad. The two find themselves in big trouble when their car breaks down miles from town and the family dog appears to be very, very ill. Cujo, a Saint Bernard, has been bitten by a rat and is none too friendly for most of the film. It took five different dogs, a mechanical head, and a guy in a dog suit to get the shots of Cujo's raging—perhaps that's why this film has a slight cheese factor. The movie might not have nabbed any awards, but it remains a horrifying tale.

5. *The Dead Zone* (1983)

A talented cast including Christopher Walken, Tom Skerritt, and Martin Sheen plays out this story of a schoolteacher involved in an auto accident that puts him in a coma for five years. When he awakens, he's got a knack for seeing the future, which is not as fun as it sounds. The story is loosely based on the life of famous psychic Peter Hurkos. Although this film hasn't reached the cult status of some other King adaptations, the Academy of Science Fiction, Fantasy & Horror named it the Best Picture of the year.

6. *Dolores Claiborne* (1995)

This psychological thriller tells the story of Dolores, a maid who works for a wealthy woman in Maine, the setting for many of King's stories. When the rich woman is murdered, Dolores's daughter comes in from New York to sort out all the details. Lots of flashbacks about the family's domestic problems ensue and a cast that includes Kathy Bates and Jennifer Jason Leigh plays out the vivid drama with engaging results and a suspenseful ending with a twist. The movie received excellent reviews, especially for the performances by the leading ladies. It did well at the box office, too, pulling in almost $25 million.

7. *Firestarter* (1984)

College students beware: Those medical tests you participate in to earn money for rent could result in serious trouble later in life. So it goes with Andy and Vicky McGee, who were given doses of a nasty chemical in college that would adversely affect their future daughter, played by a cute but dangerous Drew Barrymore. A TV miniseries entitled *Firestarter: Rekindled* was produced in 2002, possibly because King is rumored to have hated the original, something filmmakers have to be wary of when working with him.

8. *The Green Mile* (1999)

The Green Mile was based on King's series of six short books of the same name. In one of King's most successful movie adaptations, Tom Hanks stars as Paul Edgecomb, a cynical death row prison guard. Michael Clarke Duncan, Oscar-nominated for his role in the film, plays John Coffey, a prisoner accused of murdering two children. The movie grossed $136 million at the box office and DVD sales are still strong. King reportedly came to the set and asked to sit in the electric chair being used in the film. He didn't like how "Old Sparky" felt and asked to be released right away.

9. *Misery* (1990)

King often centers his stories on a protagonist who bears a striking resemblance to himself. *Misery* is one of these. Novelist Paul Sheldon finds himself being nursed back to health by Annie Wilkes after crashing his car in the Colorado mountains. Annie is Paul's self-proclaimed number one fan and relishes the opportunity to help her favorite author. Kathy Bates won an Oscar for her role as Annie—she's terrifyingly good as the obsessed, isolated woman. If you're paying attention, you'll catch a reference to another King adaptation, *The Shining.* At one point, the odd couple discusses the "guy who went mad in a hotel nearby."

10. *Needful Things* (1993)

This adaptation was a bit of a clunker, collecting more negative reviews than ticket sales. The movie didn't make much more than $15 million at the box office, which isn't too hot in terms of movie sales. The Faustian story, however, based on the King novel of the same name, is a strong one. Satan has a shop in a small New England town and gladly sells his customers whatever they need—for a price. The best-known actor in the movie is Ed Harris, who plays doomed Sheriff Alan Pangborn.

11. *Pet Sematary* (1989)

When the Creed family's cat gets smooshed on the highway, an elderly neighbor instructs Mr. Creed to bury the cat in the "pet sematary" and watch what happens. The cat comes back, but he's a little different this time around. When Mr. Creed's son dies, guess what bright idea daddy has? Watch for a King cameo in the funeral scene. This campy, but intensely creepy, movie did well at the box office and got decent reviews for a horror movie. It also generated a sequel three years later, but it didn't do as well as the original.

12. *The Running Man* (1987)

What other Stephen King screen adaptation can boast a cast that included not one but two future U.S. governors? Only *The Running Man,* which stars Arnold Schwarzenegger as the lead and Jesse Ventura in a smaller role. The story, based on the novel of the same name written under King's nom de plume Richard Bachman, is set in the year 2017. America is a police state where criminals have the opportunity to run for their freedom on a weirdly ahead-of-its-time reality show. The movie did well when it was released, earning almost $40 million, and reviews were decent, especially for a story that King reportedly penned in less than three days.

13. *The Shawshank Redemption* (1994)

Taken from King's *Different Seasons* short story collection, *The Shawshank Redemption* may be King's most critically-acclaimed adaptation, garnering seven Oscar nods and grossing nearly $30 million at the box office. Morgan Freeman and Tim Robbins star as Red and Andy, two prison inmates who strive to reconcile their fates in different ways. This story is effectively frightening not because of supernatural events but because of the terror of watching one's life pass by.

14. *The Shining* (1980)

The term *cult classic* doesn't really cover what *The Shining* is to American pop culture. Starring Jack Nicholson and Shelley Duvall and directed by Stanley Kubrick, *The Shining* is essentially a story about cabin fever—really, really, bad cabin fever in a haunted cabin where tidal waves of blood occur from time to time and a force called "the shining" possesses little kids. There is an element of camp that can't be denied about this particular adaptation, but King intensely disliked what Kubrick did with the story. Nevertheless, the movie spawned a dozen catchphrases, including, "Heeeeere's Johnny!" and "Redrum! Redrum!"

15. *Stand By Me* (1986)

The *Different Seasons* collection also included a story called "Fall from Innocence: The Body." *Stand By Me*, one of King's greatest movie successes, was based on this story. A group of preteen boys go on an adventure to find the body of a classmate who is missing and presumed dead. They are tailed by bullies and must make very grown-up decisions throughout the course of the film, which garnered an Oscar nod for Best Adapted Screenplay. A critical and box office success, *Stand By Me* starred teen heartthrobs River Phoenix, Wil Wheaton, and Corey Feldman and is one of the most widely enjoyed King films to date, perhaps due to the focus on tension among humans rather than killer clowns or deadly cars.

Chapter 2
THIS IS AMERICA

✳ ✳ ✳ ✳

IT'S A LONG WAY FROM THE BRAIN TO THE MOUTH
8 Political Slips of the Tongue

*Presidents and other politicians have a lot to say and not much
time to say it; in their haste, the message often gets lost on its way
from the brain to the mouth and comes out in funny, embarrassing, and memorable quotes. Here are some favorites.*

1. George W. Bush

Reflecting about growing up in Midland, Texas, President George W.
Bush said in a 1994 interview, "It was just inebriating what Midland
was all about then." Back in those days, Dubya was known to be a
heavy drinker, so misspeaking the word *invigorating* was a real Freud-
ian slip. During his time in the White House, the junior Bush had
enough malaprops to give a centipede a serious case of foot-in-the-
mouth syndrome.

2. George H. W. Bush

With Dan Quayle as his vice president, the bloopers of President
George H. W. Bush sometimes got overlooked, but he still managed
some zingers. While campaigning in 1988, he described serving
as Ronald Reagan's vice president this way, "For seven and a half
years I've worked alongside President Reagan. We've had triumphs.
Made some mistakes. We've had some sex...uh...setbacks." With
presidents 41 and 43, the slip doesn't fall far from the tongue.

3. Dan Quayle

Before President George W. Bush took over the title, Dan Quayle
was the reigning king of malaprops. Serving as vice president from
1989 to 1993, Quayle's slips of the tongue made him an easy but

well-deserved target for late-night talk shows. His most famous blunder came in 1992 when, at an elementary school spelling bee in New Jersey, he corrected a student's correct spelling of *potato* as p-o-t-a-t-o-e. Quayle didn't really help the campaign for reelection when, at a stop in California, he said, "This president is going to lead us out of this recovery."

4. Texas House Speaker Gib Lewis

A true slow-talkin' Texan, many of Gib Lewis's famous bloopers may have influenced his colleague, future president George W. Bush. While closing a congressional session, Lewis's real feelings about his peers slipped out when he said, "I want to thank each and every one of you for having extinguished yourselves this session." He tried to explain his problems once by saying, "There's a lot of uncertainty that's not clear in my mind." He could have been describing his jumbled reign as Texas speaker when he commented, "This is unparalyzed in the state's history."

5. Richard J. Daley

Mayor Richard J. Daley served the city of Chicago during the turbulent 1960s. The Democratic National Convention was held there in August 1968, but with the nation divided by the Vietnam War and the assassinations of Martin Luther King, Jr., and Robert F. Kennedy fueling animosity, the city became a battleground for antiwar protests, which Americans witnessed on national television. When confrontations between protesters and police turned violent, Daley's comment reflected the opinion of many: "The police are not here to create disorder, they're here to preserve disorder."

6. Richard Nixon

Richard M. Nixon, who served as president of the United States from 1969 to 1974, is the only U.S. president to have resigned from office. Famous for telling reporters, "I am not a crook," Nixon once gave this advice to a political associate, "You don't know how to lie. If you can't lie, you'll never go anywhere." Nixon couldn't cover up Watergate and he couldn't cover up bloopers like that either.

7. Al Gore

Al Gore served as vice president under Bill Clinton from 1993 to 2001. During the 1992 campaign, he asked voters skeptical of change to remember that every Communist government in Eastern Europe had fallen within 100 days, followed by, "Now it's our turn here in the United States of America." Gore has often been incorrectly quoted as saying that he invented the Internet, but his actual comment in 1999 was, "During my service in the United States Congress, I took the initiative in creating the Internet."

8. Ronald Reagan

As president, Reagan sometimes veered from his carefully written speeches with disastrous results. In 1988, when trying to quote John Adams, who said, "Facts are stubborn things," Reagan slipped and said, "Facts are stupid things." Not known as an environmentalist, Reagan said in 1966, "A tree is a tree. How many more do you have to look at?" His most famous blooper came during a microphone test before a 1984 radio address. Unaware that he was on the air at the time, Reagan joked, "My fellow Americans, I am pleased to tell you I just signed legislation which outlaws Russia forever. The bombing begins in five minutes."

America's Defining Monuments

✳ ✳ ✳ ✳

The United States has a penchant for building. As such, there are numerous buildings and other structures that represent the freedom and opportunity expressed in the American dream. Here are a few of those landmarks that define the American Way.

1. White House

The history of the White House began when President George Washington and city planner Pierre L'Enfant chose the site for the presidential residence, now listed at 1600 Pennsylvania Avenue. Irish-born architect James Hoban's design was chosen in a competition to find a builder of the "President's House."

Although Washington oversaw the construction of the house, which began in October 1792, he never lived in it. When the White House was completed in 1800, President John Adams and his wife, Abigail, moved in as the first residents. Since then, the house has survived a fire at the hands of the British during the War of 1812 and another blaze in the West Wing in 1929 when Herbert Hoover was president. Harry Truman gutted and renovated the building during his time in office. Encompassing approximately 55,000 square feet, the White House has 132 rooms, including 35 bathrooms and 16 family and guest rooms. It is the world's only private residence of a head of state that is open to the public.

2. Statue of Liberty

The Statue of Liberty is perhaps the most enduring symbol of America and has become a universal symbol of freedom and democracy. Located on a 12-acre island in New York Harbor, the Statue of Liberty was a friendly gesture from the people of France to the people of the United States. The statue, designed by French sculptor Frédéric Auguste Bartholdi, was dedicated on October 28, 1886, designated a national monument in 1924, and underwent a face-lift for its centennial in 1986. Lady Liberty stands 305 feet 6 inches high, from the ground to the tip of her torch.

3. Sears Tower

In 1969, retail giant Sears, Roebuck and Company wanted to consolidate its employees working in offices around the Chicago area. Designed by chief architect Bruce Graham and structural engineer Fazlur Khan of Skidmore, Owings and Merrill architects, construction on Chicago's Sears Tower began in 1970. The colossal structure opened in 1973, making it the world's tallest building. In 1998, it was surpassed by the Petronas Towers in Malaysia, but it is still the tallest building in the United States. With 110 stories, the distance to the roof is 1,450 feet 7 inches. However, in 1982, two television antennas were added, increasing its total height to 1,707 feet. To improve broadcast reception, the western antenna was extended in 2000, bringing the total height to 1,725 feet. In only 45 seconds, an express elevator takes passengers to the Skydeck observatory on the 103rd floor. At 1,353 feet, sightseers can see Illinois, Indiana, Michigan, and Wisconsin on a clear day.

4. Empire State Building

The Empire State Building is the crown jewel of the New York City skyline. Designed by William Lamb, the art deco structure was the world's tallest building when it opened in 1931, soaring 1,454 feet from the ground to the top of its lightning rod. More than 3,000 workers took less than 14 months to build the structure, with the framework erected at a pace of 4.5 stories per week. Today, visitors still marvel at the breathtaking views visible from the observatory, which on a clear day offers glimpses of five states.

5. Vietnam Veterans Memorial

The Vietnam Veterans Memorial in Washington, D.C., honors the men and women who served in the Vietnam conflict, one of America's most divisive wars. The memorial was intended to heal the nation's emotional wounds and was designed to be neutral about the war itself. Three components comprise the memorial: the Wall of Names, the Three Servicemen Statue and Flagpole, and the Vietnam Women's Memorial. The Wall was built in 1982 and designed by 21-year-old Maya Lin, who submitted the winning sketch. Visitors descend a path along two walls of black granite with one wing pointing at the Washington Monument a mile away and the other at the Lincoln Memorial about 600 feet away. When viewed closely, the names of the more than 59,000 soldiers killed or missing in action dominate the structure.

6. St. Louis Arch

The St. Louis Arch on the bank of the Mississippi River marks the city as the "Gateway to the West." Thomas Jefferson's vision of freedom and democracy spreading from "sea to shining sea" inspired architect Eero Saarinen's contemporary design for a 630-foot stainless steel memorial. Construction began in 1963 and was completed on October 28, 1965. The Arch's foundation is set 60 feet into the ground and is built to withstand earthquakes and high winds. A 40-passenger train takes sightseers from the lobby to the observation platform, where on a clear day the view stretches for 30 miles.

7. Lincoln Memorial

"In this temple, as in the hearts of the people for whom he saved the Union, the memory of Abraham Lincoln is enshrined forever." Beneath these words rests the Lincoln Memorial on the National Mall in Washington, D.C. Designed by architect Henry Bacon, sculptor Daniel Chester French, and artist Jules Guerin, the monument was completed in 1922 to honor the sixteenth president of the United States. The structure resembles a Greek Doric temple ringed by 36 columns, each representing a state in the Union at the time of Lincoln's death. Seated within the monument is a sculpture of Lincoln, and inscriptions from the Gettysburg Address and his second inaugural address adorn the walls. The Lincoln Memorial served as the site of Martin Luther King, Jr.'s famous, "I Have a Dream" speech on August 28, 1963.

8. Golden Gate Bridge

San Francisco's Golden Gate Bridge, named for the Golden Gate Strait, which it spans, was the vision of chief engineer Joseph B. Strauss, who was told by contemporaries that such a bridge could not be built. Nevertheless, construction began on January 5, 1933. Nearly four and a half years, $35 million, and 11 worker fatalities later, the 1.7-mile-long and 90-foot-wide bridge was finally opened to an estimated 200,000 pedestrians on May 27, 1937, and to vehicles the next day. The suspension span was the longest in the world until New York City's Verrazano Narrows Bridge opened in 1964.

The bridge has two principal cables passing over the tops of the two main towers. If laid end to end, the total length of wire in both main cables would total 80,000 miles. The Golden Gate Bridge is painted "International Orange," making it more visible to ships and the 38 million vehicles that cross it annually in the lingering and persistent fog.

9. Washington Monument

The Washington Monument, a 555-foot-high white obelisk situated at the west end of the National Mall in Washington, D.C., honors George Washington as the first president of the United States and a Revolutionary War hero. Comprised of 36,491 marble, granite, and sandstone blocks, the structure was designed by Robert Mills, a prominent American architect. Construction began in 1848, but due to the outbreak of the Civil War and lack of funding, it took nearly 40 years to complete. It is clearly visible where work resumed in 1876 by the difference in the marble's shading, about 150 feet up the obelisk. The monument was dedicated on February 22, 1885, Washington's birthday, but did not officially open to the public until October 9, 1888, after the internal construction was complete. At the time it was the world's tallest structure, a title it held only until 1889, when the Eiffel Tower was completed in Paris.

10. World Trade Center

A list of some of the nation's iconic structures would be incomplete without mentioning the 110-story Twin Towers and five smaller buildings of the World Trade Center in New York City, which were destroyed by a terrorist attack on September 11, 2001. Located in lower Manhattan, the Twin Towers opened in 1973. Tower One was 1,368 feet tall, and Tower Two was 1,362 feet tall. Of the approximately 50,000 people who worked in the 13.4 million square foot complex, 3,000 died when hijackers slammed two passenger jets into the buildings' upper floors on that fateful day. Construction is underway to rebuild the World Trade Center complex, with an expected completion date in 2012.

10 Fastest-Growing Cities in the United States*

✳ ✳ ✳ ✳

1. Austin, Texas
2. Cape Coral–Ft. Myers, Florida
3. Atlanta, Georgia

4. Seattle, Washington
5. San Francisco, California
6. Dallas–Ft. Worth, Texas
7. San Jose, California
8. Houston, Texas
9. Orlando, Florida
10. Palm Bay–Melbourne–Titusville, Florida

° *Populations over 500,000*
Source: Forbes

THE MOTHER LODE ON THE MOTHER ROAD
11 Vintage Stops Along Historic Route 66

✳ ✳ ✳ ✳

*This 2,400-mile stretch of Americana, dubbed "The Mother Road"
by John Steinbeck, is dotted with iconic saloons, motels, and
kitschy pit stops. In the early 1920s, when the national highway
system was in its infancy, Oklahoma highway commissioner
Cyrus Stevens Avery envisioned a superhighway linking Chicago
and Los Angeles by way of small, rural towns. Route 66 opened in
1927, but the Federal Highway Act of 1956 led to its demise with
the creation of several new interstates, and, by 1985, Route 66 had
been formally decommissioned, though most of the winding route
from Illinois to California can still be traveled today. Ready for a
road trip? Here are some places you may want to stop.*

1. Buckingham Fountain (Chicago, Illinois)
Located in Chicago's Grant Park, Buckingham Fountain is where
Route 66 began. The fountain, which represents Lake Michigan, is
adorned with sculptures of four sea horses that symbolize the states
bordering the lake—Illinois, Indiana, Michigan, and
Wisconsin. The fountain's 134 jets shoot 14,000 gallons
of water (per minute) 150 feet into the air for a mag-
nificent display, which incorporates music and a light
show in the evening.

2. The Cozy Dog Drive-In (Springfield, Illinois)

Anyone who's ever been to a county fair has probably had a corn dog—a breaded hot dog on a stick. While working at an army base in the early 1940s, Illinois native Ed Waldmire was toying with the idea of wrapping hot dogs in corn bread. A friend suggested that he try frying the meat in the batter. Originally called crusty curs, Waldmire changed the name and opened his first cozy dog stand in Springfield in 1946, after being discharged from the army. The Cozy Dog Drive-In continues to be a popular family-run business.

3. 66 Drive-In Theater (Carthage, Missouri)

In 1949, when drive-in movies were as hot as buttered popcorn, the 66 Drive-In Theater was a new attraction. Along with most drive-in theaters across the country, it fell into disrepair until the Goodman family bought it and returned it to its former glory in the late '90s. During the summer months, feature films are still shown under the stars. Today, there are less than 400 drive-in theaters still operating in the United States out of about 5,000 that existed in the '50s and '60s.

4. Ed Galloway's Totem Pole Park (Foyil, Oklahoma)

What better place to stretch your legs on a road trip than at the park that boasts the world's largest totem pole? It's 90 feet tall, made of 200 carved pictures, and was sculpted by Ed Galloway between 1937 and 1948. This tribute to Native American culture, which contains 28 tons of cement, 6 tons of steel, and 100 tons of sand, was added to the National Register of Historic Places in 1999.

5. Lucille's (Hydro, Oklahoma)

Lucille's is currently one of only two porch-style gas stations still operating on Oklahoma's portion of Route 66. In 1941, Lucille Hamons and her husband bought the structure, which was built in 1927 and originally known as Provine Station. She operated it herself until she died in 2000. Lucille was known as "the Mother of the Mother Road" because of her many stories of the people who stopped by for a tank of gas or a snack.

6. Cadillac Ranch (Amarillo, Texas)

Artists and auto enthusiasts alike will appreciate the beauty of ten Cadillacs buried halfway into the ground nose first. Passersby are encouraged to add a personal touch by wildly decorating the vehicles, which span the model years 1949 to 1963. In fact, the cars are frequently painted over to create a fresh canvas for road-weary artists. Created in 1974 by the Ant Farm, a San Francisco art collective, Cadillac Ranch has become part of the nation's kitschy culture. The unusual attraction was the subject of a Bruce Springsteen song and was even depicted in the 2006 animated film *Cars*.

7. Tee Pee Curios Trading Post (Tucumcari, New Mexico)

Tucumcari has a five-mile stretch of pure Route 66 nostalgia in the form of motels, diners, and curiosity shops. One neon sign after another tempts motorists to put on the brakes and kick around for a while. One of the famed shops is Tee Pee Curios Trading Post, which was built in the early 1940s as a gas station that sold groceries and novelty items. When the road was widened in the 1950s Tee Pee got rid of its gas pumps and focused solely on the fun stuff.

8. The Wigwam Village Motels (Holbrook, Arizona, and Rialto, California)

Frank Redford built the first of several Wigwam Village motels in 1934 near popular tourist spot Mammoth Cave in Kentucky. Two more opened out west by the mid-1950s—one in Holbrook, Arizona, and one in Rialto, California. Each wigwam featured a guest room that was naturally suited to the southwestern stretch of Route 66. The Arizona, California, and Kentucky locations are still in business, with the marquee in front of the Holbrook location posing the question: "Have you slept in a wigwam lately?"

9. Jackrabbit Trading Post (Joseph City, Arizona)

In 1949, James Taylor (not the folksinger) converted a simple shack into one of the most popular souvenir shops along the Mother Road. To attract the growing throngs of tourists passing through town, Taylor painted dancing American Indians on the facade and lined the rooftop with 30 jackrabbits that appear to hop along the top of the building. Inside, he sold turquoise jewelry and south-western souvenirs. And to ensure that the road weary noticed his shop among the many, he and another local retailer traveled from Arizona to Springfield, Missouri, and dotted more than 1,000 miles of roadside with billboards of jackrabbits and dancing cowgirls!

10. Roy's (Amboy, California)

During the 1930s, Roy and Velma Crowl owned the café, motel, and service station that comprised most of Amboy, a tiny town on a desolate stretch of Route 66. Years later, Roy's daughter Betty and her husband, Buster Burris, took over the business and continued the tradition of caring for road-weary travelers. In fact, Buster was still changing tires for folks when he retired in 1995, well into his eighties. Today, the entire 690-acre town and all of its contents are owned by Albert Okura, founder of the Juan Pollo restaurant chain. Okura plans to restore the famous gas station, convenience store, diner, motel, and cottages to their 1950s-era charm.

11. Georgian Hotel (Santa Monica, California)

The Santa Monica Pier is literally the end of the road, not only for Route 66, but for the contiguous United States as well. Within walking distance is the Georgian Hotel, a luxurious art deco hotel steeped in history since opening its doors in 1933. The hotel, which served as a speakeasy during Prohibition, has also been a hideaway for the famous and infamous. Clark Gable and Carole Lombard hid from the press at the Georgian, and you might find today's Holly-wood royalty doing the same.

Slowest-Growing Cities in the United States*

❊ ❊ ❊ ❊

1. St. Louis, Missouri
2. Cincinnati, Ohio
3. Boston, Massachusetts
4. Detroit, Michigan

5. New Orleans, Louisiana
6. Cleveland, Ohio
7. Pittsburgh, Pennsylvania
8. Toledo, Ohio
9. Buffalo, New York
10. Baltimore, Maryland
11. Milwaukee, Wisconsin

° *Populations over 250,000, from 7/1/04–7/1/05*
Source: U.S. Census Bureau

CAN I CHANGE MY VOTE?
Political Scandals

✳ ✳ ✳ ✳

Political scandals in the United States have been around since the birth of the nation and don't show any signs of going away, much to the satisfaction of late-night comedians and talk show hosts. Who needs soap operas when real life in Washington is so scandalous? Check out these infamous political scandals.

1. The Keating Five

After the banking industry was deregulated in the 1980s, savings and loan banks were allowed to invest deposits in commercial real estate, not just residential. Many savings banks began making risky investments, and the Federal Home Loan Bank Board (FHLBB) tried to stop them, against the wishes of the Reagan administration, which was against government interference with business. In 1989, when the Lincoln Savings and Loan Association of Irvine, California, collapsed, its chairman, Charles H. Keating, Jr., accused the FHLBB and its former head Edwin J. Gray of conspiring against him. Gray testified that five senators had asked him to back off on the Lincoln investigation. These senators—Alan Cranston of California, Dennis DeConcini of Arizona, John Glenn of Ohio, Donald Riegle of Michigan, and John McCain of Arizona—became known as the Keating Five after it was revealed that they received a total of $1.3 million in campaign contributions from Keating. While an investigation determined that all five acted improperly, they all claimed this was a standard campaign funding practice. In August 1991, the Senate Ethics Committee recommended censure for Cranston and criticized the other four for "questionable conduct." Cranston had already decided not to run for reelection in 1992. DeConcini and Riegle served out their terms but did not run for reelection in 1994. John Glenn was reelected in 1992 and served until he retired in 1999. John McCain continues his work in the Senate following his unsuccessful bid for the 2008 presidential nomination.

2. Watergate

Watergate is the name of the scandal that caused Richard Nixon to become the only U.S. president to resign from office. On May 27, 1972, concerned that Nixon's bid for reelection was in jeopardy, former CIA agent E. Howard Hunt, Jr., former New York assistant district attorney G. Gordon Liddy, former CIA operative James W. McCord, Jr., and six other men broke into the Democratic headquarters in the Watergate Hotel in Washington, D.C. They wiretapped phones, stole some documents, and photographed others. When they broke in again on June 17 to fix a bug that wasn't working, a suspicious security guard called the Washington police, who arrested McCord and four other burglars. A cover-up began to destroy incriminating evidence, obstruct investigations, and halt any spread of scandal that might lead to the president. On August 29, Nixon announced that the break-in had been investigated and that no one in the White House was involved. Despite his efforts to hide his involvement, Nixon was done in by his own tape recordings, one of which revealed that he had authorized hush money paid to Hunt. To avoid impeachment, Nixon resigned on August 9, 1974. His successor, President Gerald Ford, granted him a blanket pardon on September 8, 1974, eliminating any possibility that Nixon would be indicted and tried. *Washington Post* reporters Bob Woodward and Carl Bernstein helped expose the scandal using information leaked by someone identified as Deep Throat, a source whose identity was kept hidden until 2005, when it was revealed that Deep Throat was former Nixon administration member William Mark Felt.

3. Chappaquiddick

Since being elected to the Senate in 1962, Edward M. "Ted" Kennedy has been known as a liberal who champions causes such as education and health care, but he has had less success in his personal life. On July 18, 1969, Kennedy attended a party on Chappaquiddick Island in Massachusetts. He left the party with 29-year-old Mary Jo Kopechne, who had campaigned for Ted's late brother Robert. Soon after the two left the party, Kennedy's car veered off a bridge and Kopechne drowned. An experienced swimmer, Kennedy said he tried to rescue her but the tide was too strong. He swam to shore, went back to the party, and returned with two other men. Their rescue efforts also failed, but Kennedy waited until the next day to report the accident, calling his lawyer and Kopechne's parents first, claiming the crash had dazed him. There was speculation that he tried to cover up that he was driving under the influence, but nothing was ever proven. Kennedy pleaded guilty to leaving the scene of an accident, received a two-month suspended jail sentence, and lost his driver's license for a year. The scandal may have contributed to his failed presidential bid in 1980, but it didn't hurt his reputation in the Senate. In April 2006, *Time* magazine named him one of "America's 10 Best Senators."

4. Teapot Dome Scandal

The Teapot Dome Scandal was the largest of numerous scandals during the presidency of Warren Harding. Teapot Dome is an oil field reserved for emergency use by the U.S. Navy and is located on public land in Wyoming. Oil companies and politicians claimed the reserves were not necessary and that the oil companies could supply the Navy in the event of shortages. In 1922, Interior Secretary Albert B. Fall accepted $404,000 in illegal gifts from oil company executives in return for leasing the rights to the oil at Teapot Dome to Mammoth Oil without asking for competitive bids. The leases were legal but the gifts were not. Fall's attempts to keep the gifts secret failed, and, on April 14, 1922, *The Wall Street Journal* exposed the bribes. Fall denied the charges, but an investigation revealed a $100,000 no-interest loan in return for leases that Fall had forgotten to cover up. In 1927, the Supreme Court ruled that the oil leases had been illegally obtained, and the U.S. Navy regained control of Teapot Dome and other reserves. Fall was found guilty of bribery in 1929, fined $100,000, and sentenced to one year in prison. He was the first cabinet member imprisoned for his actions while in office. President Harding was not aware of the scandal at the time of his death in 1923, but it contributed to his administration being considered one of the most corrupt in history.

5. Wilbur Mills

During the Great Depression, Wilbur Mills served as a county judge in Arkansas and initiated government-funded programs to pay medical and prescription drug bills for the poor. Mills was elected to the House of Representatives in 1939 and served until 1977, with 18 of those years as head of the Ways and Means Committee. In the 1960s, Mills played an integral role in the creation of the Medicare program, and he made an unsuccessful bid for president in the 1972 primary. Unfortunately for Mills, he's best known for one of Washington's juiciest scandals. On October 7, 1974, Mills's car was stopped by police in West Potomac Park near the Jefferson Memorial. Mills was drunk and in the back seat of the car with an Argentine stripper named Fanne Foxe. When the police approached, Foxe fled the car. Mills checked into an alcohol treatment center and was reelected to Congress in November 1974. But just one month later, Mills was seen drunk onstage with Fanne Foxe. Following the incident, Mills was forced to resign as chairman of the Ways and Means Committee and did not run for reelection in 1976. Mills died in 1992, and despite the scandal, several schools and highways in Arkansas are named after him.

6. The Iran-Contra Affair

On July 8, 1985, President Ronald Reagan told the American Bar Association that Iran was part of a "confederation of terrorist states."

He failed to mention that members of his administration were secretly planning to sell weapons to Iran to facilitate the release of U.S. hostages held in Lebanon by pro-Iranian terrorist groups. Profits from the arms sales were secretly sent to Nicaragua to aid rebel forces, known as the contras, in their attempt to overthrow the country's democratically-elected government. The incident became known as the Iran-Contra Affair and was the biggest scandal of Reagan's administration. The weapons sale to Iran was authorized by Robert McFarlane, head of the National Security Council (NSC), in violation of U.S. government policies regarding terrorists and military aid to Iran. NSC staff member Oliver North arranged for a portion of the $48 million paid by Iran to be sent to the contras, which violated a 1984 law banning this type of aid. North and his secretary Fawn Hall also shredded critical documents. President Reagan repeatedly denied rumors that the United States had exchanged arms for hostages but later stated that he'd been misinformed. He created a Special Review Board to investigate. In February 1987, the board found the president not guilty. Others involved were found guilty but either had their sentences overturned on appeal or were later pardoned by George H. W. Bush.

18 Statue of Liberty Facts

❄ ❄ ❄ ❄

1. The statue's real name is "Liberty Enlightening the World."

2. Lady Liberty was sculpted by Frédéric Auguste Bartholdi; Alexandre Gustave Eiffel was the structural engineer.

3. Construction of the statue began in France in 1875 and was completed in June 1884.

4. The statue was given to America on July 4, 1884, then reassembled and dedicated in the United States on October 28, 1886.

5. The model for the face of the statue is reputed to be the sculptor's mother, Charlotte Bartholdi.

6. A smaller-scale bronze replica of Lady Liberty was erected in Paris in 1889 as a gift from Americans living in the city. The statue stands about 35 feet high and is located on a small island in the River Seine, about a mile south of the Eiffel Tower.

7. There are 25 windows and 7 spikes in Lady Liberty's crown. The spikes are said to symbolize the seven continents.

8. The inscription on the statue's tablet reads: July 4, 1776 (in Roman numerals).

9. More than four million people visit the Statue of Liberty each year.

10. Symbolizing freedom and the opportunity for a better life, the Statue of Liberty greeted millions of immigrants as they sailed through New York Harbor on their way to nearby Ellis Island.

11. Lady Liberty is 111 feet 6 inches tall from her heel to the top of her head and 305 feet 6 inches tall from the ground to the tip of her torch.

12. The statue's hand is 16 feet 5 inches long and her index finger is 8 feet long. Her fingernails are 13 inches long by 10 inches wide and weigh approximately 3.5 pounds each.

13. Lady Liberty's eyes are each 2 feet 6 inches across, she has a 35-foot waistline, and she weighs about 450,000 pounds (225 tons).

14. Lady Liberty's sandals are 25 feet long, making her shoe size 879.

15. The statue functioned as an actual lighthouse from 1886 to 1902. There was an electric plant on the island to generate power for the light, which could be seen 24 miles away.

16. The Statue of Liberty underwent a multimillion dollar renovation in the mid-1980s before being rededicated on July 4, 1986. During the renovation, Lady Liberty received a new torch because the old one was corroded beyond repair.

17. The Statue of Liberty's original torch is now on display at the monument's museum.

18. Until September 11, 2001, visitors were able to climb the winding staircase inside the statue to the top of her crown for a spectacular view of New York Harbor. Lady Liberty is still open to the public, but now guests cannot go above her pedestal.

25 Peculiar Presidential Nicknames

✳ ✳ ✳ ✳

President	Nickname
1. James Monroe	Last Cocked Hat
2. John Quincy Adams	Old Man Eloquent
3. Martin Van Buren	The Little Magician; Martin Van Ruin
4. John Tyler	His Accidency
5. Zachary Taylor	Old Rough and Ready
6. James Buchanan	The Bachelor President; Old Buck
7. Andrew Johnson	King Andy; Sir Veto
8. Ulysses S. Grant	Useless; Unconditional Surrender
9. Rutherford B. Hayes	Rutherfraud Hayes; His Fraudulency
10. James Garfield	The Preacher; The Teacher President
11. Grover Cleveland	Uncle Jumbo; His Obstinacy
12. Benjamin Harrison	Little Ben; White House Iceberg
13. Woodrow Wilson	The Schoolmaster
14. Warren Harding	Wobbly Warren
15. Herbert Hoover	The Great Engineer
16. Harry Truman	The Haberdasher
17. John F. Kennedy	King of Camelot
18. Lyndon B. Johnson	Big Daddy
19. Richard M. Nixon	Tricky Dick
20. Gerald Ford	The Accidental President

President	Nicknam...
21. Jimmy Carter	The Peanut Farmer
22. Ronald Reagan	Dutch; The Gipper; The Great Communicator
23. George H. W. Bush	Poppy
24. Bill Clinton	Bubba; Slick Willie; The Comeback Kid
25. George W. Bush	Junior; W; Dubya

8 Kooky North American Festivals

✳ ✳ ✳ ✳

Looking for somewhere wacky to have a good time? Festivals, no matter how quirky, bring out the best in creativity. A festival-goer can celebrate animals, insects, foods, historical events, and just about any other topic under the sun. It's easy to fill your calendar with events; just check out these examples.

1. Frozen Dead Guy Days (Nederland, Colorado)

The fun at the annual Frozen Dead Guy Days festival heats up Nederland during Colorado's typically frosty March. The fest commemorates a cryogenically-preserved Norwegian who has been kept in a shed by his grandson since late 1993. Visitors are encouraged to dress as a frozen or dead character and attend the Blues Masquerade Ball. Coffin races and a parade featuring antique hearses are among the liveliest attractions, along with salmon tossing and a polar plunge into a frozen pond. The event started in 2002 and annually attracts about 7,000 visitors.

2. Faux Film Festival (Portland, Oregon)

For anyone who loves fake commercials or movie trailers, Portland's Faux Film Festival is the ticket to a surreal filmic never-never land. Mockumentaries and other celluloid spoofs are among the dozens of goofy entries shown in the historic 460-seat Hollywood Theatre. Past viewings have included the silly classic, *It Came from the Lint rap* and the quirky *The Lady from Sockholm*, a film noir featuring sock puppets. The fest is usually staged at the end of March, with a packed house at each screening.

3. Rattlesnake Roundup (Freer, Texas)

Billed as the biggest party in Texas, the Freer Rattlesnake Roundup held each May features nationally known country and Tejano artists… and loads and loads of snakes. In addition to daredevil snake shows, snake twirling displays, a carnival, arts and crafts, and fried rattlesnake to chaw, prizes are given out for the longest and smallest rattlesnakes, and for the greatest number of nonvenomous snakes brought to the fest by one person.

4. Contraband Days Pirate Festival (Lake Charles, Louisiana)

Legend has it that buccaneer Jean Lafitte buried an enormous treasure somewhere along the sandy shoreline of Lake Charles. Each May since 1958, Contraband Days Pirate Festival, which attracts more than 100,000 people, has been honoring that legend. Perhaps one of the funniest sights of the festival is when the mayor is made to walk the plank after pirates take over the town. The plucky civic chief is naturally rescued quickly, then is free to enjoy the rest of the fest with its carnival, arm-wrestling competition, sailboat regatta, and bed races. With an eclectic selection of nearly 100 different events, Contraband Days is frequently chosen by the American Bus Association as a Top 100 Event in North America.

5. Secret City Festival (Oak Ridge, Tennessee)

The annual Secret City Festival highlights the important role Oak Ridge played in World War II. In the 1940s, researchers there developed the top secret atomic bomb—hence the city's nickname—and today visitors can tour Manhattan Project sites to see where the bomb was devised. One of the country's largest World War II reenactments is also a popular draw, with roaring tanks, motorcycles, and other vintage military gear. Each June, the event draws about 20,000 people to Oak Ridge, which is nestled between the picturesque Cumberland and Great Smoky Mountains.

6. Nanaimo Marine Festival (Nanaimo, British Columbia)

At the Nanaimo Marine Festival held in mid-July, up to 200 "tubbers" compete in the Great International World Championship Bathtub Race across a 36-mile course. Contestants use just about any conceivable watercraft, most of which at least vaguely resemble a bathtub, and make their way to Vancouver's Fisherman's Cove across the Straits of Georgia. The first race was held in 1967 and activities have expanded since to include a food fair, craft show, Kiddies' Karnival, and waiters' race.

7. Barnesville Potato Days (Barnesville, Minnesota)

Up to 14,000 visitors head to west-central Minnesota for Barnesville Potato Days in late August when this small town celebrates the lowly spud with a great menu of activities. The Potato Salad Cook-off attracts onlookers eager to compare the year's winning recipe with how Grandma used to make this popular picnic dish. Things can get messy during mashed potato wrestling, but the Miss Tator Tot pageant is much more refined. Of course, there is plenty of food to sample, including Norwegian lefse, potato pancakes, potato sausage, potato soup, and traditional German potato dumplings. On Friday, there's even a free French Fry Feed. Barnesville, tucked away in the fertile Red River Valley, has been honoring the crop of choice of many nearby farmers with this festival since 1938.

8. BugFest (Raleigh, North Carolina)

Billed as the nation's largest single-day festival featuring insects, BugFest attracts around 25,000 people to Raleigh each September. The event started in 1997 and now covers beekeeping demonstrations, a flea circus, and roach races. The festival features many exhibits on insects, from live spiders and centipedes, to displays on how bugs see. At Café Insecta, festivalgoers can sample Buggy Bean Dip with Crackers, Quivering Wax Worm Quiche, Stir-fried Cantonese Crickets over rice, and Three Bug Salad, among other aptly named goodies that actually include worms, ants, and related critters raised for cooking.

Chapter 3
ANIMALS
✳ ✳ ✳ ✳
11 Famous Pooches

If you're a dog owner, you're probably convinced that you've got the greatest dog in the world. But does your dog bring home a paycheck? Whether they've stolen our hearts, made us laugh, or scared us silly, no one can deny that the dogs listed here are one of a kind.

1. Benji

In the 1970s and 1980s, several feature films centered around the adventures and loving personality of Benji, a terrier with an uncanny ability to sniff out trouble just in the nick of time. Created by Joe Camp, the films were produced in Texas starting in 1974. The dog that played Benji in the original film was actually named Higgins. Other Benjis have come and gone over the course of nine feature-length films, the most recent which was released in 2004.

2. Blue

In 1994, Nickelodeon's parent company, Viacom, decided to commit more than $60 million to new programming, and *Blue's Clues* was born. The formula for the show, marketed toward preschoolers, was simple: A blue puppy places clues around her world for the kids watching. Through these clues, the kids can figure out what Blue wants to do. As it turned out, kids wanted to do whatever Blue wanted to, and computer games, live tours, books, DVDs, apparel, and food products prove that Blue is still one popular puppy.

3. Buck

The main character in Jack London's *The Call of the Wild*, Buck is a St. Bernard–Scots shepherd mix that lives a comfortable, somewhat pampered life in northern California, in the late 19th century. But his life is turned upside down when he is kidnapped, sold as a sled dog, and shipped off to the Yukon Territory in the upper reaches of northwestern Canada. Buck quickly learns to survive on his own and discovers basic instincts he didn't know he had.

4. Cujo

No human fear has been left untouched by horror writer Stephen King, so when he turned his attention to dogs in the 1981 book *Cujo*, the results were terrifying. The story, which was later made into a movie, tells of a friendly St. Bernard that contracts a nasty case of rabies. Disaster, death, and mayhem ensue, and the main characters—a mother and her asthmatic son—are held hostage by the drooling, psychotic dog.

5. Eddie

In 1993, the world was introduced to Eddie on the hit sitcom *Frasier*. The rascally Jack Russell terrier was intelligent, adorable, and more than a little prone to taunting Kelsey Grammer's character, Dr. Frasier Crane. Eddie was played by a father and son team—Moose was the original Eddie, then when he retired, his son Enzo stepped in to play the role. Eddie rounded out the cast of the popular *Cheers* spin-off, which ran for 11 seasons.

6. Goofy

Disney's lovably stupid dog first appeared in a 1932 cartoon short as an audience member watching Mickey onstage. Goofy was originally known by the even less dignified moniker Dippy Dawg. The tall mutt in overalls had an incredibly dopey laugh, supplied by Disney writer, musician, and former circus clown Pinto Colvig. When Disney heard Colvig's laugh, he decided that Goofy should get a little more face time. Soon, Goofy was appearing in his own cartoons and has been a favorite ever since.

7. Lassie

Author Eric Knight's original short story entitled "Lassie Come Home" tells the story of a young boy and his loyal collie. After being separated under dire circumstances, Lassie crosses hundreds of miles to find her master. The story first appeared in *The Saturday Evening Post* in 1940, and, in 1954, *Lassie* the TV show made its debut. The show ran for 20 years, using nine different dogs to portray the faithful pooch.

8. Rin Tin Tin

Rin Tin Tin was one of America's first doggie stars. American serviceman Lee Duncan found Rin in a bombed-out dog kennel in France during World War I. Duncan took the German shepherd home with him to California and taught him how to do tricks and perform in dog shows. More showbiz opportunities followed, including a role as a wolf in a 1922 motion picture. For the next decade, Rin had parts in 26 films, making him as big a star as any of his human counterparts. Rin Tin Tin was honored with a star on the Hollywood Walk of Fame, and, during the 1950s, his offspring portrayed him on the television show, *The Adventures of Rin Tin Tin.*

9. Rowlf the Dog

Muppets come in every shape, color, and size, but the biggest stars are the basic characters: the frog, the pig, and the dog. Originally created by Jim Henson and Don Sahlin for a Purina Dog Chow commercial, Rowlf quickly became an in-demand dog. Rowlf was a perfect sidekick for Jimmy on the popular *Jimmy Dean Show,* making him the first Muppet to have a regular gig on a network TV show. In 1976, Rowlf made a career change—he joined the cast of *The Muppet Show* as the in-house pianist. Rowlf favored Beethoven and the standards, but he was so amiable and friendly, we're guessing he was okay with taking requests, too.

10. Snoopy

Once upon a time, on a sunny day at the Daisy Hill Puppy farm, a litter of seven adorable beagles was born, including a particularly mischievous puppy named Snoopy. *Peanuts*, the classic cartoon strip created by Charles M. Schulz in 1950, still runs in newspapers around the world despite Schulz's passing in 2000. Snoopy, Charlie Brown's faithful dog, is one of the most recognized dogs in history.

Heavy on personality but light on words, the feisty beagle was a foil or friend to every character in the *Peanuts* pantheon. The popular pooch even has his own attraction—Camp Snoopy—at several major theme parks across the country.

11. Toto

In L. Frank Baum's classic tale *The Wonderful Wizard of Oz,* a terrier named Toto accompanies Dorothy on her adventures and eventually saves the day. The movie adaptation, which starred Judy Garland, made the story—and the dog—cultural icons. The dog that played Toto in the movie reportedly received $125 per week—more than twice as much as the people playing the Munchkins.

19 Odd Names for Animal Groups

✳ ✳ ✳ ✳

1. A *shrewdness* of apes
2. A *battery* of barracudas
3. A *kaleidoscope* of butterflies
4. A *quiver* of cobras
5. A *murder* of crows
6. A *charm* of finches
7. A *skulk* of foxes
8. A *smack* of jellyfish
9. A *mob* of kangaroos
10. An *exaltation* of larks
11. A *troop* of monkeys
12. A *parliament* of owls
13. An *ostentation* of peacocks
14. A *rookery* of penguins
15. A *prickle* of porcupines
16. An *unkindness* of ravens
17. A *shiver* of sharks
18. A *pod* of whales
19. A *zeal* of zebras

Celebrity Cat Club

✶ ✶ ✶ ✶

They say, "Dogs have masters, cats have staff." That certainly rings true for these famous felines. Some are real, some are fictional, but either way, they don't answer to anyone.

1. Socks: The First Cat

Socks knew a good thing when he saw it. The eventual First Cat joined the Clinton family in 1991 when he jumped into Chelsea's arms at her piano teacher's house in Little Rock, Arkansas. Socks, a black-and-white kitty, spent eight years in the White House and became a star in his own right, appearing on an episode of *Murphy Brown* and inspiring two books: *Socks Goes to Washington: The Diary of America's First Cat* and *Dear Socks, Dear Buddy: Kids' Letters to the First Pets.* When the Clintons left the White House in 2001, Socks was given to Clinton's secretary, Betty Currie. Socks still lives with the Curries in Maryland.

2. Garfield

A cat that eats lasagna? That would be Garfield, the star of the most widely syndicated comic strip in the world. Created by Jim Davis in 1978, *Garfield* now appears in more than 2,500 newspapers, as well as movies, TV specials, and video games. The pudgy orange and black feline is best known for his love of Italian food, his disdain for Mondays, and his constant tormenting of canine pal Odie.

3. The Cheshire Cat

The Cheshire cat first appeared—and disappeared—in Lewis Carroll's children's story, *Alice's Adventures in Wonderland.* The cat pops in and out of Alice's adventure, often turning her innocent queries into philosophical discussions. But the scene that forever seals the Cheshire cat's place in history is when he makes the rest of his body gradually disappear, leaving only his smile behind, hence the phrase "grinning like a Cheshire cat" to describe someone with a mischievous grin.

4. Morris

Rescued from a Hinsdale, Illinois, shelter in 1968, Morris, the 15-pound, orange-striped tabby went on to earn fame and fortune as the "spokescat" for 9Lives cat food. He also starred opposite Burt Reynolds in 1973's *Shamus* and even ran for president in 1988 and 1992 on the Finicky Party platform.

5. Puss in Boots

Puss in Boots began life as a boot-wearing hero that used his feline wiles to gain wealth for his impoverished master in a collection of Mother Goose fairy tales published in 1697. He went on to become the star of a 1913 opera by Cesar Cui and made numerous film appearances, including a 1922 animated short by Walt Disney, a 1969 Japanese anime feature, and Antonio Banderas's character in the *Shrek* sequels.

6. Orangey

Audrey Hepburn won an Emmy, a Grammy, an Oscar, and a Tony. But did she ever win a Patsy? Nope, that honor belongs to her *Breakfast at Tiffany's* costar Orangey. The orange and black tabby that portrayed Holly Golightly's lazy cat in the 1961 classic actually broke onto the Hollywood scene in 1951's *Rhubarb,* a movie about an eccentric millionaire who adopts a feral cat. Orangey won his first Patsy (Picture Animal Top Star of the Year) for the *Rhubarb* role, so awards were old hat by the time he shared a screen with Hepburn. Orangey also appeared in *Gigot* (1962) alongside Jackie Gleason and in the 1950s sitcom *Our Miss Brooks.*

7. The Cat in the Hat

The Cat in the Hat is a whimsical creation of Dr. Seuss. This troublemaking yet lovable cat attempts to entertain two children who are stuck inside on a rainy day. He wreaks a bit of havoc and torments the family goldfish incessantly, but all ends well. The black-and-white cat, with his signature red-and-white striped top hat and red bow tie, first appeared in the classic tale in 1957. He has since appeared in numerous books, TV specials, and in the 2003 live-action movie of the same name, which starred Mike Myers.

8. Catwoman

Don't mess with Catwoman, as Halle Berry will attest. When the Oscar-winning actress portrayed the infamous comic book character in 2004's *Catwoman*, she received critical pans and a Razzie Award for worst actress. Catwoman first appeared in the *Batman* comic book series in 1940 as an expert burglar with above-average agility. She's been portrayed by actresses such as Julie Newmar, Eartha Kitt, and Michelle Pfieffer, all of whom remained fairly true to the original character's signature traits. But when Berry's character departed from the *Batman* story line, the claws came out.

13 Facts You Didn't Know About Bats

✳ ✳ ✳ ✳

It isn't easy being a bat. With Dracula, a few cases of rabies, their pointy teeth, and the fact that they hang upside down to sleep, bats inspire fear in many people. But as you'll see, bats are amazing creatures, even though they eat bugs . . . and sometimes blood.

1. Vampire bats don't suck blood. They lap it up.

Calm down. There are only three species of vampire bats in the whole world. If you are traveling in Central or South America, however, you might see a vampire bat bite a cow and then lick blood from the wound—no sucking involved.

2. Fewer than 10 people in the last 50 years have contracted rabies from North American bats.

Due to movies and television, bats are thought to be germ machines, bringing disease and toxins to innocent victims. Not true. Bats *avoid* people. If you are bitten by a bat, go to the doctor, but don't start making funeral arrangements—you'll probably be fine.

3. Bats wash behind their ears.

Bats spend more time grooming themselves than even the most image-obsessed teenager. They clean themselves and each other meticulously by licking and scratching for hours.

4. Bats make up a quarter of all mammals.

Yep, you read that right. A quarter of all mammals are bats. There are more than 1,100 species of bats in the world. That's a lot of bats!

5. A single brown bat can catch around 1,200 mosquito-size insects in one hour.

It's estimated that the 20 million Mexican free-tailed bats that live in Bracken Cave, Texas, eat about 200 tons of insects... each night.

6. Bats don't have "fat days."

The metabolism of a bat is enviable—they can digest bananas, mangoes, and berries in about 20 minutes.

7. Bats are the only mammals able to fly.

And you thought it was the winged marmoset! Bats are exceptional in the air. Their wings are thin, giving them what is called, in flight terms, "airfoil." The power bats have to push forward is called "propulsion."

8. Bats use echolocation to get around in the dark.

Bats don't see very well and do a lot of living at night, so they have to rely on navigational methods other than sight. Bats send out beeps and listen for variations in the echoes that bounce back at them and that's how they get around. Bats are nocturnal, mostly because it's easier to hunt bugs and stay out of the way of predators when it's dark. Bats do use their eyesight to see things in the daytime, but most bat business is done under the blanket of darkness for convenience.

9. Cold night? Curl up next to a bat!

Inside those drafty caves they like so much, bats keep warm by folding their wings around themselves, trapping air against their bodies for instant insulation.

10. The average bat will probably outlive your pet dog or cat.

The average lifespan of a bat varies, but some species of brown bat can live to be 30 years old. Considering that other small mammals live only two years or so, that's impressive.

11. Bats have only one pup a year.

Most small mammals have way more offspring than that. Think cats, rabbits, and rats.

12. An anticoagulant found in vampire bat saliva may soon be used to treat human cardiac patients.

The stuff that keeps blood flowing from vampire bats' prey seems to keep blood flowing in humans, too. Scientists in several countries are trying to copy the enzymes found in vampire bat saliva to treat heart conditions and stop the effects of strokes in humans.

13. More than 50 percent of bat species in the United States are either in severe decline or are listed as endangered.

You don't know what you've got until it's gone. Industry, deforestation, pollution, and good old-fashioned killing have wiped out many bats and their habitats. For information on how to help keep bats around, contact your local conservation society.

ROVER-ACHIEVERS
8 Dogs Who Are Tops in Their Class

❊ ❊ ❊ ❊

Everyone who has ever loved a dog feels that their dog is the best dog ever. We're not about to get between a man (or woman) and their best friend, but here are a few dogs that truly stand out in a crowd of canines.

1. The Oldest Dog: Bluey

The oldest dog reliably documented was an Australian cattle dog named Bluey. After 29 years and 5 months of faithful service, Bluey was put to rest in 1939. We can only hope that now Bluey is chasing cows in the big cattle ranch in the sky.

2. The Heaviest (and Longest) Dog: Zorba

In Kazantzakis' famous novel, Zorba the Greek tackled spiritual and metaphysical quandaries; Zorba the dog apparently tackled his dinner. Zorba, an Old English mastiff, was the world's heaviest and longest dog ever recorded. Zorba weighed 343 pounds and, from nose to tail, was eight feet three inches long.

3. Smallest Dog: Tiny Tim

Measuring three inches tall at the shoulder and four inches long from wet nose to wagging tail, Chihuahua and shih tzu mix Tiny Tim of London holds the record (as of 2004) for being the tiniest dog ever. The little guy weighs just over a pound.

4. Coolest Dog on the Playground: Olive Oyl

In 1998, Russian wolfhound Olive Oyl of Grayslake, Illinois, made the *Guinness Book of World Records* when she skipped rope 63 times in one minute.

5. The Quietest Dog: The Basenji

A yip or a yap, a whine or a woof—if you don't want a barking dog, consider a basenji. The favorite dog of ancient Egyptians, this breed is incapable of barking, instead uttering a sound called a yodel, which makes them perfect for those living in an apartment with thin walls or touchy neighbors.

6. Dog Most Likely to Help You with Your Algebra Homework: The Border Collie

Border collies are widely regarded as the smartest of dogs, since they have been bred to work closely with humans for centuries. Again, different dogs are better at certain tasks and are more apt to thrive in different environments. However, collies can appear hyper and less-than-brilliant if they're not given enough stimulation.

7. The Dog that Might Score Low on an IQ Test: A Hound

We couldn't bring ourselves to say *dumbest,* but it looks like the hound group is given this reputation most often. Hounds weren't bred for taking IQ tests, or doing much of anything except hunting and following scents, so expecting them to quickly learn how to sit or stay is a big mistake. It's just not in their nature, so have patience with your hound—they're not dumb, they're just different.

8. Most Courageous Dogs: September 11 Search and Rescue Dogs (SAR Dogs)

Okay, so any dog serving its country as a SAR dog gets the "Most Courageous Dog" distinction, but the SAR dogs that waded into the rubble in the wake of the terrorist attacks on September 11, 2001, get an extra gold star. Hundreds of SAR dogs scoured the debris and braved the chaos in the days after the attack. While German shepherds are often trained for SAR duties, any working, herding, or sporting breed can be trained to be a hero.

Animals that Use Camouflage to Protect Themselves

✳ ✳ ✳ ✳

The animal kingdom is a wild, wacky place where animals have to be clever in order to survive. One of the most amazing techniques for survival is animal camouflage. Animals have the ability to mimic plants, ground cover, or even other animals in order to hide or hunt. The following is a list of some animals that are particularly gifted in the art of invisibility.

1. Arctic Owls

Ah, the Arctic tundra: cold, barren, and totally white. Arctic owls have a coat of snow-white feathers to keep them warm and safe from predators, such as foxes and wolves.

2. Bark Bugs

For most bugs, birds are the bad guys. For bark bugs, which hang out on trees around the world, this is especially true. In order to hide and stay alive, bark bugs appear to be part of the tree itself.

3. Chameleons

Contrary to popular belief, chameleons only change color when in imminent danger. Their everyday skin color, a light khaki, keeps them hidden from enemies during those not-so-dangerous times. Nearly half the world's chameleon species live in Madagascar, but they're also found in Africa, the Middle East, and southern Europe.

4. Dragon Lizards

Spiders, snakes, birds, and even other lizards all want a piece of the dragon lizard, so they have some of the most effective camouflage around. Not only do dragon lizards look nearly invisible when hanging out on a tree branch, they keep extraordinarily still, knowing that their predators react to the smallest movements. It doesn't make for an exciting life, but at least they live to tell about it.

5. Flower Mantises

Careful—that flower you're thinking about smelling might have a flower mantis hiding inside. The flower mantis of western Africa uses colorful, pistil-and-stamen-like camouflage to trick smaller insects into smelling the roses, then snap—lunch is served.

6. Gaboon Vipers

In order to hide from their prey, gaboon vipers—among the most venomous snakes on Earth—make the most of their brownish-gray, mottled scales. These big snakes hide in the layer of dead leaves that carpet the African rain forest. They also like to snuggle into forest floor peat and sneak up on unsuspecting prey.

7. Leaf Butterflies

Complete with fake leaf stalk, fake leaf veins, and perfect dead-leaf coloring, leaf butterflies have the whole camouflage thing down pat. Birds pass them by without a second glance since these insects from southeast Asia look more like dead leaves than butterflies.

8. Leopards

Whether their coats are spotted (useful for hiding in sun-dappled areas in the African outback) or black (perfect for nighttime stalking or lurking in shadows), these elegant and deadly cats are born with fashionable camouflage. Rabbits,

young buffalo, and monkeys don't stand a chance when a hidden leopard makes a surprise attack.

9. **Ornate Wobbegongs**
   If you're ever swimming in the shallow waters off Australia or New Guinea, look for the ornate wobbegong—though you probably won't be able to see it! This shark's body flattens out on the seafloor where its spots and blotchy lines resemble rock and coral. Wobbegongs take camouflage a step further with a little "beard" under their chins that looks like seaweed. Prey that swim in front of their mouths are gobbled up without knowing what hit them.

10. **Polar Bears**
    Other bears and human poachers are the biggest threats to the majestic polar bear, but by blending in to the blindingly white snow of the Arctic with equally white fur coats, some danger can be avoided. Only a polar bear's nose and foot pads are without fur.

11. **Turtles**
    If you're a fish, you better look twice before resting near that big rock... it could be a snapping turtle. There are hundreds of species of turtles and tortoises that use camouflage to blindside their prey and hide from large predators like alligators. Sadly, camouflage can't protect turtles from the poacher's fishnet.

9 Fabulous Felines

Some people are cat people. They take pictures of their cats, tell stories about their cats, and feed their cats designer food. For a cat lover, even the most unremarkable cat is special, but the following cats have been singled out for extra-noteworthy achievements or distinctions.

1. **First Cat: The Eocene Kitty**
   Fossils from the Eocene period show that cats roamed the earth more than 50 million years ago. Sure, they looked a little different,

but these remains show that today's domestic cats have a family tree that goes way, way back.

2. Cat Most in Need of a Babysitter: Bluebell

Bluebell, a Persian cat from South Africa, gave birth to 14 kittens in one litter. She holds the record for having the most kittens at once, with all of her offspring surviving—rare for a litter so large.

3. Big Mama: Dusty

In 1952, a seemingly ordinary tabby cat gave new meaning to the term "maternal instinct." Texas-born Dusty set the record for birthing more kittens than any other cat in history. Dusty had more than 420 kittens before her last litter at age 18.

4. Oldest Cat: Cream Puff

More than 37 years old at the time of her death, Cream Puff, another Texan, is recognized as the oldest cat to have ever lived. In human years, she was about 165 years old when she died.

5. Cat Most in Need of a Diet: Himmy

According to the *Guinness Book of World Records,* the heaviest cat in recorded history was an Australian kitty named Himmy that reportedly weighed more than 46 pounds in 1986. If the data is accurate, Himmy's waistline measured about 33 inches. Guinness has removed this category from their record roster, so as not to encourage people to overfeed their animals.

6. Most Itty-Bitty Kitty in the Whole World: Tinker Toy

Though this kitty died in 1997, it still holds the record for being the smallest cat ever. Tinker Toy was just 2.75 inches tall, 7.5 inches long, and weighed one pound eight ounces.

7. Best-dressed Cat: The Birman

The Birman cat breed originally came from Burma (now Myanmar) where these longhairs were bred as companions for priests. A Birman cat can be identified by its white "gloves." All Birmans have four white paws, which give them that oh-so-aristocratic look.

8. Most Aloof Cat: Big Boy

When Hurricane George hit Gulfport, Mississippi, in 1998, Big Boy was blown up into a big oak tree. In 2001, Big Boy's owner claimed the cat never left the tree. The feline eats, sleeps, and eliminates in the tree and climbs from branch to branch for exercise.

9. Most Ruthless Killer: Towser

In Scotland, a tortoiseshell tabby named Towser was reported to have slain 28,899 mice throughout her 21 years—an average of about four mice per day. Her bloodlust finally satiated, Towser died in 1987. (The mice of Scotland are rumored to celebrate her passing as a national holiday.)

Lost Pets that Found Their Way Home

✳ ✳ ✳ ✳

Salmon follow the smell of their home waters.
Birds and bees appear to navigate by the sun, stars, and moon.
We can't really explain how so many lost dogs and cats magically
seem to find their way back to their owners over great distances,
so we'll just tell you about them instead.

1. Tony the mutt finds his family.

When the Doolen family of Aurora, Illinois, moved to East Lansing, Michigan, nearly 260 miles away, they gave away their mixed-breed dog Tony. Six weeks later, who came trotting down the street in East Lansing and made himself known to Mr. Doolen? That's right—Tony. Doolen recognized a notch on Tony's collar that he'd cut while still living in Illinois.

2. Troubles finds his way through ten miles of jungle.

Troubles, a scout dog, and his handler William Richardson were taken via helicopter deep into the war zone in South Vietnam in the late 1960s. When Richardson was wounded by enemy fire and taken to a hospital, Troubles was abandoned by the rest of the unit. Three weeks later, Troubles showed up at his home at the First

Air Cavalry Division Headquarters in An Khe, South Vietnam. But he wouldn't let anyone near him—he was on a mission! Troubles searched the tents and eventually curled up for a nap after he found a pile of Richardson's clothes to use for a bed.

3. Misele the farm cat goes to the hospital.

When 82-year-old Alfonse Mondry was taken to a hospital in France, his cat Misele missed him greatly. So she took off and walked across cattle fields, rock quarries, forests, and busy highways. She entered the hospital—where she had never been before—and found her owner's room. The nurses called the doctor right away when they found Mondry resting comfortably with his cat purring on his lap.

4. Howie the Persian cat crossed the Australian outback.

The Hicks family wanted their cat to be lovingly cared for while they went on an extended vacation overseas. So, they took him to stay with relatives who lived more than 1,000 miles away. Months later, when they returned to retrieve Howie, they were told that he had run away. The Hicks were distraught, assuming that because Howie was an indoor cat, he wouldn't have the survival skills to make it on his own. A year later, their daughter returned home from school one day and saw a mangy, unkempt, and starving cat. Yep, it was Howie. It had taken him 12 months to cross 1,000 miles of Australian outback, but Howie had come home.

5. Emily the cat went across the pond.

Lesley and Donny McElhiney's home in Appleton, Wisconsin, wasn't the same after their one-year-old tabby Emily disappeared. But she didn't just disappear, she went on a 4,500-mile adventure! It seems Emily was on her evening prowl when she found herself on a truck to Chicago inside a container of paper bales. From there she was shipped to Belgium, finally arriving in France where employees at a laminating company found her thin and thirsty. Because she was wearing tags, it didn't take long for Emily to be reunited with her family, compliments of Continental Airlines.

Chapter 4
FUN, GAMES, AND POP CULTURE

✳ ✳ ✳ ✳

GEE, THAT POODLE SKIRT SURE IS SWELL!
Fads of the Fabulous '50s

If you were around in the 1950s, you probably remember the Korean War and McCarthyism. But that's not the fun stuff to visit on Memory Lane. It's much more fun to remember the fads, the crazes, and the pop culture sensations that emerged in an age when moms still made dinner every night and a car with fins could get you a date. The following is a list of some of the most decade-defining fads and trends of the '50s. Don't get too excited, though—nice boys and girls never do.

1. Sock Hops

Those 1950s teens were so thoughtful! Informal high school dances were named "sock hops" because students would remove their shoes to avoid scuffing the floor while they danced. And they really liked to dance! Elvis made his famous appearance on *The Ed Sullivan Show* in 1956, and youngsters across the country were moving to the beat of the neat, new sound of rock 'n' roll. The always chaperoned sock hops were hugely popular—where else could you show off your hand-jive, bop, stroll, or box step?

2. Beatniks

Every generation has a rebellion and the "beats" emerged from the 1950s underground. While good girls and boys were heading to sock hops, these writers, artists, and musicians were pushing cultural expectations and embracing taboo subject matter. Writers Jack Kerouac and Allen Ginsberg were admired by this group of largely New York City-based artists. Today, the beatnik has been reduced to an image of a guy with a goatee wearing sunglasses and a beret and beating bongo drums. That's not exactly what the beats had in mind, but many were intrigued by their acts of "spontaneous creativity" that blended words and music, and they continue to influence poetry and music today.

3. 3-D Movies

Just as the proliferation of downloadable music sent the record industry scrambling at the turn of this century, the advent of television spooked movie executives. Would anyone go to the movies if they could be entertained at home? In an attempt to offer something unique, studios like Warner Brothers released movies in "3-D." Watching a flick while wearing the funky, paper glasses created a three-dimensional effect. Early 1950s titles included *Bwana Devil* and *House of Wax*. In 1953, there were more than 5,000 theaters in the United States equipped to show 3-D movies.

4. Poodle Skirts

The poodle skirt was one of the most iconic fashion trends of the 1950s. The long, swingy, often pastel-hued skirts had a motif appliquéd below the knee. Some common images were musical notes, flowers, and, of course, poodles. Dancing to the new rock 'n' roll music was popular, but it required dancers to wear clothes that allowed them to move. Since women rarely wore pants at the time, A-line poodle skirts were a must-have!

5. The Conical Bra

Although it was invented in 1943, the cantilevered brassiere really came into the spotlight in the 1950s. Jane Russell sported one of the bras in *The Outlaw,* and her lifted and separated bosom caused quite a sensation. The new silhouette was invented by none other than director, eccentric, and ladies' man Howard Hughes, who directed Russell in the movie. The look became popular and heavy-duty brassieres stuck around—at least until women started burning them a decade later.

Fads of the Groovy '60s

✳ ✳ ✳ ✳

Free love, flower power, hippies, psychedelic drugs, and political mayhem—these were the trends of a decade that saw the upheaval of social mores and cultural behaviors. As The Beatles rocked and Bob Dylan rolled, the world saw changes in the political climate (war protests, the sexual revolution, civil rights), the fashion world (the miniskirt), and even in the realm of food (the mighty processed cheese slice). Read on to learn about some of the most iconic fads of the decade that just wanted everyone to get along.

1. Go-go Boots and Miniskirts

The postwar baby boom had produced 70 million teenagers by the time the 1960s rolled around. All of those hormones dictated some changes in the fashion world. Long gone was the poodle skirt. Skirts in the '60s got shorter—much, much shorter. Miniskirts and minidresses often came up four to five inches above the knee in the United States and an eye-popping seven to eight inches above the knee in the UK. While skirts got shorter, boots got taller. The most popular boot was the go-go boot, which was often white patent leather and went almost to the knee. Singer Nancy Sinatra and TV's *The Avengers* helped popularize the look.

2. Surfing

What better place than a sunny beach to spread peace, goodwill, and free love? Polynesians had been surfing for centuries, but when lightweight surfboards became affordable in the late 1950s, anyone near the ocean could grab a board and hang ten. By the early 1960s, the fad had really caught a wave, and movies like *Beach Party* and *Beach Blanket Bingo* helped popularize surfing and beach culture.

3. Fallout Shelters

With the Cold War in full force and the Cuban Missile Crisis exposed, many people in the early 1960s decided that building a fallout shelter wasn't such a paranoid notion. After all, how else would they safeguard their family against a nuclear attack? Kits began at around $100 (flashlight, shortwave radio, can opener), but a family could spend thousands on special basements equipped with board games, gas masks, and escape hatches.

4. The Twist

This dance craze of the early 1960s came as the result of Chubby Checker's number one song of the same name. The Twist was the first modern dance style that did not require a partner, and couples did not have to touch each other while dancing. Checker said, "It's like putting out a cigarette with both feet, [or] coming out of a shower and wiping your bottom with a towel to the beat of the music." It seemed like everyone was jumping on the bandwagon with a Twist record. Checker also recorded "Let's Twist Again," and Joey Dee and The Starliters reached number one with "The Peppermint Twist," while Sam Cooke was "Twistin' the Night Away."

5. Hippies

U.S. troops were sent to Vietnam in 1954 and, by the 1960s, thousands of soldiers had died fighting a war that was growing more and more unpopular by the day. The cry "Make Love, Not War" was a mantra among the hippies—the antiestablishment, counterculture of America. Hippies were easily spotted: both men and women sported long hair and ethnic-inspired clothes, dabbled in Eastern religions, used words like *groovy*, and referred to "the Man" when talking about the flawed government. They were known to experiment with mind-altering drugs and hang out in places such as Greenwich Village in New York City and the Haight-Ashbury section of San Francisco. The hippie movement sparked music, art, and cultural dialogue that continues well into the 21st century.

6. Peace Symbol

Thanks to British graphic designer Gerald Holtom, no hippie had to go without a peace symbol talisman. Holtom, who was hired to create an image for the Campaign for Nuclear Disarmament, claimed his inspiration for the symbol came from the shape of the letters *N* and *D* in the semaphore alphabet. The hippies adopted the icon, and it remains as popular today as it was when protests and antiwar marches were daily events.

7. Tie-Dye

The ancient fabric dyeing method of *shibori* began in Japan centuries ago, but it became a fashion trend symbolic of the 1960s. By wrapping fabric around sticks or gathering and securing it with rubber bands, then submerging it in a bucket of dye, a funky, almost hallucinogenic pattern emerges when the sticks or rubber bands are removed. This homemade method became popular with hippies, providing living color to the ethnic look that so many embraced during the era of free love and liberation. Tie-dyed clothing is still pretty much the standard uniform for peaceniks today.

8. Lava Lamp

Invented by Edward Craven Walker, this novelty lighting instrument featured a glass lamp full of wax and oil with a coil in the metal base. When the lamp was turned on, the coil would heat up and globs of wax would bubble around in the oil, producing a "lava" effect. Some claim the lava lamp was meant to simulate the hallucinogenic visuals from the drugs that were popular in this era.

Off to an Early Start

✳ ✳ ✳ ✳

The people on this list made a name for themselves early in life and probably don't intend to fade away any time soon. The good news—maybe your kid will be on the list one day! The bad news—if you're over 20 and you're not on a list like this, we recommend shooting for the "Oldest" list.

1. Youngest Person with a Stethoscope

No, it's not Doogie Howser. After graduating from New York University in 1991 at age 13 and Mount Sinai's School of Medicine at 17, Balamurali Ambati became the youngest doctor in the world in 1995 according to the *Guinness Book of World Records.* His list of awards and honors is lengthy, and he currently teaches and does research in ophthalmology.

2. Youngest Person to Win an Oscar
In 1974, at age ten, actor Tatum O'Neal became the youngest person to win an Academy Award for her role in *Paper Moon,* costarring her father Ryan O'Neal. Her career didn't exactly take off after that, but she has recently returned to acting with several TV roles.

3. Youngest Microsoft Employee
Arfa Karim Randhawa of Pakistan has become a pal of Bill Gates since she passed her Microsoft Certified Professional examinations at age nine. She asked for a job, but Gates told her she should stay in school a while longer, offering her an internship instead.

4. Youngest Billionaire

The Thurn und Taxis family of Germany created Europe's first mail service back in the 16th century and has scads of profitable business ventures to this day. Prince Albert von Thurn und Taxis inherited a fortune at age seven when his father died, but he couldn't touch the money until he turned 18 in 2001. Still, he was the world's youngest billionaire at the time. According to a 2007 report by *Forbes* magazine, he's worth a cool $2.3 billion.

5. Youngest Tibetan Buddhist Monarch
In southern Asia, there's a tiny, mountainous country called Bhutan. In 1972, Jigme Singye Wangchuck became the "Druk Gyalpo," or "Dragon King," of the tiny country at age 17, making him the youngest monarch in the world. He remained in power until December 2006, when he handed the throne to his eldest son.

6. Youngest Person to Sail Solo Across the Atlantic Ocean
Michael Perham, a 14-year-old chap from Hertfordshire, England, completed the 3,500-mile trek across the Atlantic Ocean in his yacht, the *Cheeky Monkey,* in January 2007, after six weeks at sea.

7. Youngest College Student at Oxford

At 11 years old, child prodigy Ruth Elke Lawrence passed the Oxford entrance exam in mathematics and, in 1981, became the youngest person ever to attend the prestigious university. Her father accompanied her to classes, and she graduated with a bachelor's degree in two years instead of the usual three. Now in her thirties, Lawrence teaches at Hebrew University in Jerusalem.

8. Youngest Person to Climb Mount Everest

Temba Tsheri, a Nepalese boy traveling with a French hiking group, reached the summit of Mount Everest in 2001 at age 16. It's no easy task—Everest is approximately 29,035 feet high and claims more than a few lives each year.

FOR THRILLS 'N' CHILLS
8 of the World's Best Roller Coasters

✳ ✳ ✳ ✳

In the late 1880s, the first American roller coasters were created at New York's Coney Island. One of the pioneer coasters, the Flip-Flap Railway, had the unfortunate problem of snapping riders' necks due to the extreme g-forces experienced when accelerating through its circular loop. Engineering innovations and steel construction have made coasters safer, and now the sky's the limit. Here are some of today's biggest thrillers.

1. Kingda Ka

As of 2008, Kingda Ka, at Six Flags Great Adventure in Jackson, New Jersey, was the tallest and fastest roller coaster on the planet. Reaching 128 miles per hour in 3.5 seconds, the train rockets straight up to the 456-foot apex before plummeting straight down into a hair-raising descent through a spiral twist at speeds of more than 100 miles per hour. Riders then face a 129-foot tall hill that bounces them out of their seats for a few seconds before bringing them back to home base a mere 59 seconds after takeoff.

2. Top Thrill Dragster

Top Thrill Dragster located at Cedar Point, America's roller coaster capital, in Sandusky, Ohio, is labeled an "accelerator coaster" with trains shaped like rip-roaring dragsters. But the ride feels more like a jaw-tightening space launch. Reaching a speed of 120 miles per hour in just four seconds, passengers are thrust to the top of a 420-foot peak before plunging straight down 400 feet, while at the same time twisting and turning through 270-degree spirals.

3. Dodonpa

When it first opened in 2001 at Fuji-Q Highland in Japan, Dodonpa was the world's fastest steel coaster. But by 2006, it had slipped to third place. It still retains the title for the world's fastest acceleration, reaching top speeds of 106.8 miles per hour in just 1.8 seconds! At speeds like that, ride time is only 55 seconds, but that seems like an eternity when plummeting 170 feet at a 90-degree angle.

4. Steel Dragon 2000

Steel Dragon 2000, located at Nagashima Spa Land Amusement Park in Japan, represents "The Year of the Dragon." It boasts the longest track of any coaster in the world, hurtling its riders along at speeds up to 95 miles per hour for 8,133.17 feet. With a peak at 318.25 feet, it is also the world's tallest coaster to use a chain lift: Two chains are utilized, one for the bottom half and one for the top half because a single chain would be too long and heavy. For earthquake protection, more steel was used in this $50 million machine than in any other coaster in the world.

5. Son of Beast

Son of Beast, built in 2000 at Kings Island near Cincinnati, Ohio, is touted as the world's tallest and fastest wooden coaster, with a 218-foot apex and speeds up to 78 miles per hour. At the time of its construction, Son of Beast was also the world's only looping wooden roller coaster, although in 2007, the loop was removed. Son of Beast's daddy, The Beast, was constructed at King's Island in 1979 and holds the title as the longest wooden roller coaster, at 7,400 feet.

6. Apollo's Chariot

Apollo's Chariot, a steel coaster at Busch Gardens in Williamsburg, Virginia, holds the world record for a gulping 825 feet of drops on a coaster. The ride starts with a 170-foot lift hill, then hits a maxi-  mum speed of 73 miles per hour. At the peak, riders drop down a few teasing feet before the cars swoop down 210 feet to graze a water-filled gully at a 65 degree angle. Riders then soar up a second hill and back down a 131-foot drop. Then, the coaster screams through a short tunnel and takes off up a third incline, before screeching around a curved 144-foot plunge. The ride slows down with a series of bunny bumps before returning to the station.

7. Magnum XL-200

Opened in 1989 at Cedar Point in Sandusky, Ohio, Magnum XL-200 is a steel roller coaster that was the first constructed circuit roller coaster to break the 200-foot barrier, with its 205-foot peak and 194.67-foot drop. The view of Lake Erie from the pinnacle is breathtaking, with plenty of opportunity to see the countryside along the nearly mile-long track. That is, if passengers can keep their eyes open while speeding along at 72 miles per hour. Expert riders prefer the third row of seats in the first car because of numerous, intense airtime moments.

8. Superman—Ultimate Flight

If you've ever wanted to fly like a superhero, this is the ride for you! Located at Six Flags theme parks in Illinois, New Jersey, and Georgia, this ride's specially designed cars tilt passengers facedown into a flying position, so that they're suspended horizontally from the track above. Riders get a bird's-eye view at the top of a 109-foot hill, before sailing through the air at 60 miles per hour in a series of loops, spirals, turns, and rolls. And with the first-of-its-kind pretzel-shape loop, this truly is a unique thrill ride.

Fads of the Swinging '70s

✳ ✳ ✳ ✳

In the wake of the political upheaval and social reform of the 1960s, the '70s may seem fairly frivolous. Sure, there were discos, polyester suits, and gold chains, but there was much cultural and political change happening as well. The second wave of feminism, the end of the Vietnam War, Roe v. Wade—many ideas that are de rigueur today were introduced in the 1970s. Read on to learn about the crazes that made this decade so far-out.

1. Mood Rings

Who knew a thermochromic liquid crystal could foretell the mood of humans? Joshua Reynolds didn't really believe it could, but he did figure that he could sell the idea to the general public as a novelty item. That's exactly what he did in 1975 with the mood ring, which was invented in the late 1960s by Marvin Wernick. Heat from the wearer's hand would cause crystals in the ring to warm up, making the face of the ring change from black to green to blue to purple. Reynolds sold more than a million dollars worth of mood rings within three months of their debut, and everyone checked in with their mood rings with nearly religious fervor.

2. Leisure Suits

If you were a hip dude in the '70s, you had at least one leisure suit. Made popular by TV shows such as *Charlie's Angels* and movies like *Saturday Night Fever,* these polyester suits were marked by flamboyant colors, wide pockets, and winged collars. Bands like the Bay City Rollers used satiny fabric in their suits, too, a trend that trickled down into the mainstream—for better or worse.

3. Afros

The Black Power movement of the late '60s and early '70s claimed the mantra "Black is Beautiful," and the Afro was one way to show solidarity among black people. Rather than continue to straighten their hair, African Americans let their textured, kinky manes grow unhindered. The effect was a kind of halo or ball shape around the head. Anyone with curly hair could achieve this style, made popular by '70s stars such as Angela Davis and the Jackson 5, but it was generally reserved for the "Black is Beautiful" set.

4. Pet Rock

California entrepreneur Gary Dahl was joking around with friends one night in 1975 about the perfect pet. It wouldn't eat, make noise, or need to be potty trained. Dahl joked that a rock would fit the bill. Everyone laughed, but within two weeks, he had written *The Pet Rock Training Manual* and had marketed the idea at a trade show. A story in *Newsweek* and an appearance on *The Tonight Show* followed, and, within a few months, a million pet rocks had sold for $3.95 a piece. Dahl made a dollar for each rock sold, making him an instant millionaire.

5. Roller Skates

Way back in the 18th century, people were hip to the idea of attaching wheels to their feet to get around faster. But not until the 1970s did roller-skating become enmeshed in American culture. As mate-

rials and technology advanced, wheels and skates became slicker and faster, and roller-skating really took off. By the mid-1970s, thousands of roller rinks had opened across the United States. Most rinks combined disco with skating, so patrons could skate under the mirror ball and groove to the music of KC and the Sunshine Band while they strutted their stuff.

6. Disco

In the 1970s, disco arrived armed with keyboards, drum machines, sugary lyrics, and extended dance breaks. Artists such as the Bee Gees, ABBA, and Donna Summer crooned their way into the hearts of people in America, Europe, and beyond. Bell-bottom pants, feathered hair, and big sunglasses were all disco accessories. Most people knew the lyrics to "Stayin' Alive" whether they liked it or not, thanks to disco movies like *Saturday Night Fever* (yes, that one again). Disco music, disco dancing, and disco culture usually get a bad rap for being frivolous and over-the-top, but today's pop, techno, and club music all have their roots in disco.

7. Punk Rock

Not everyone in the '70s was feeling the love. Disillusioned youth in the UK were forgoing the Hustle for the fast, hard, raw power of what they called "punk." Bands such as The Sex Pistols, The Ramones, and The Clash showcased their anger, frustration, and disregard for authority in songs such as "God Save the Queen," "I Wanna Be Sedated," and "London Calling." Just as disco laid the groundwork for later dance genres like techno and house, grunge and heavy metal are rooted in the riotous sounds of punk rock.

8. CB Radio

Before chat rooms, there were CB radios. Citizens' Band radios were (and still are) largely used by truckers on the road to communicate with other drivers in their range. However, in the 1970s and into the early '80s, people across the United States, the UK, and Australia took back the meaning of "citizens' radio" and began to use the low-frequency radio waves to chat with other CB users. They had their own special slang terms and nicknames, and First Lady Betty Ford even got into the action. She was known by the CB handle "First Mama" when she crackled over the airwaves. That's a big 10–4…over and out.

Aging Gracefully

✳ ✳ ✳ ✳

Western culture has become so age-obsessed that people in their thirties are trying to recapture that youthful glow. Well, outta the way, kiddies! There's something to be said for withstanding the tests of time, so this list pays homage to the old.

1. Oldest Person

Some come close, but so far, no one's been officially recognized as having lived longer than Jeanne Louise Calment, who died at age

122 in Arles, France. Calment was born in February 1875, a year before Alexander Graham Bell invented the telephone. She met Vincent Van Gogh at age 13 and was known for her wit, famously saying, "I've only ever had one wrinkle and I'm sitting on it."

2. Oldest City

In 2001, archaeologists found signs of an ancient city in the Gulf of Cambay in western India. In the 5.6-mile stretch of submerged city, carbon dating found evidence going back to 7500 B.C., making the city about 4,500 years older than what were believed to be the first cities, located in the Sumer Valley of Mesopotamia.

3. Oldest Professional Chorus Line

When the Tivoli Lovelies of Melbourne, Australia, entered *Guinness World Records* in 2004, the ten dancers had a combined age of 746 years and some change. The geriatric ladies still kicked as high and wore the sequins of younger chorus girls, and they certainly had more experience.

4. Oldest Male Stripper

Until he passed away in 2007, Bernie Baker was America's oldest male stripper. In 2000, after a bout with prostate cancer, Baker reinvented himself as an erotic dancer at the tender age of 60. Baker had plenty of loyal fans and racked up many awards.

5. Oldest Company

Headquartered in Osaka, Japan, Kongo Gumi Co., Ltd., has continuously operated for more than 1,400 years. Its business? Construction. Since A.D. 578, when the company built the still standing Shitennoji Temple, Kongo Gumi has had a hand in building other famous Japanese buildings and temples, including Osaka Castle. In 2006, the company had financial trouble and liquidated its assets, but it still maintains its identity and continues to function in Japan as a wholly owned subsidiary of the Takamatsu Corporation.

6. Oldest Tavern in America

Established in 1795, Boston's Bell in Hand Tavern is the longest continuously running tavern in America. Founded by town crier

Jimmy Wilson, the Bell in Hand still serves frosty mugs and food to an often full house. Famous customers have included Paul Revere and President McKinley.

7. Oldest Person to View Earth from Space

John Glenn was a U.S. pilot during World War II and, in 1967, became a national hero as the first American and third person to orbit Earth when he rode in the *Friendship 7*, a NASA space capsule that successfully circled the globe three times. In 1998, Glenn went back into the great beyond at age 77, making him the oldest person to travel into space. The reason? To test the effects of space travel on the elderly, of course.

ARE THOSE PANTS MADE OUT OF A PARACHUTE?
Totally Awesome Fads of the '80s

In the 1980s, the hair was big, the clothes were big (i.e., shoulder pads), the music was big, and the political climate was grandiose, too (Reaganomics, Star Wars). With cellular phones and cable television hitting the masses, this decade triggered much of the tech boom that would really get cooking in subsequent decades. With the ever-increasing range and scope of the media, music- and electronics-based fads got bigger and faster in the '80s. Here are a few fads that took the country by storm and helped define the generation that just wanted its MTV.

1. The Walkman

Though the technology looks ancient to us today, we wouldn't have the beloved iPod if it wasn't for the Walkman. In 1979, Sony introduced its first portable music player in Japan. By 1980, America had jumped on the bandwagon, and there were dozens of portable cassette players on the market. They were heavy, didn't deliver great sound quality, and initially cost upwards of $150, but it didn't matter—they were delivering tunes to the masses, one tape at a time.

2. Atari

The name of the gaming system that started them all loosely translates from Japanese as "prepare to be attacked." Thus, it's fitting that some of the earliest video games were simple shooting games or games such as Frogger, which required players to move a frog across a busy road without getting squished. Atari, Inc., was formed in 1972, and five years later one of the most successful gaming consoles of all time—the Atari 2600—was released. By the mid-1980s, millions of consumers were spending hours per day glued to the TV set, playing Q*Bert, Pac-Man, and Space Invaders. The Atari company consolidated a few years ago but still has a hand in shaping today's much more advanced gaming world.

3. "Valspeak"

Did you, like, realize that in the '80s, like, everyone totally got pulled into this thing called Valspeak? Seriously! The old way of talking with, like, specificity and declarative statements was, like, super lame-o! Like, whatever! So, like, the San Fernando Valley in California was, like, the place where it started. But soon it was a nationwide, like, trend. Can you even stand it? And it's totally still, like, a thing? You know, like, a totally awesome way of speaking. And, like, you thought Valley Girls were a passing fad. Whatever!

4. Break Dancing

When DJ Kool Herc took the dance break sections off vinyl records and remixed them to create a longer, funkier song, break dancing was born. These extended breaks gave New York City street dancers all the time in the world to showcase their gravity-defying moves, including the pop and lock, the windmill, the freeze, the moonwalk, the worm, and the closing "suicide." It's believed that the first break dancing trend occurred among rival gang members who used the dance style to settle disputes. As the media attention grew for this competitive, visually exhilarating dance style, so did its popularity. The fashion, the music, and the dance moves themselves became hallmarks of '80s youth culture.

5. Parachute Pants

If you're thinking about break dancing, you'd be wise to consider your outfit—you need to look "fresh" and "fly," but you also need to be able to slip, slide, and spin on a dance floor, and regular pants just won't do. Baggy in the thigh and narrow at the ankle, parachute pants increased mobility for dancers who needed more flexible clothing. The pants were often made of synthetic materials (you can backspin way better in a poly-blend than you can in cotton) and usually came in bright colors. As break dancing became cooler, the clothes of these street dancers became the "in" fashion trend and even kids in the suburbs were donning parachute pants.

6. Swatch Watches

In 1983, executives at Swatch Group, Ltd., of Switzerland had an idea. They thought that watches could be less of a financial investment for the stuffy and time-conscious and more of a disposable, funky accessory. Their idea was a big hit. Swatch watches came in hundreds of different colors and styles, and some were even scented! Many people chose to wear several styles at once, loading up two, three, even six Swatches on their wrists at the same time. If you wanted to know what time it was in the 1980s, you probably got your information from a Swatch watch. Swatch Group is still the largest watch company in the world, although it is hard to find someone using a Swatch as a ponytail holder these days.

7. Hair Bands

The heavy-metal music of the 1980s was typified by a heavy, guitar-and-drums-centered sound with highly amplified distortion, fairly raunchy lyrics (for the time), and plenty of dramatic builds. The heavy-metal lifestyle was known for wild parties, girls, leather, and really big hair. As the music got louder and bolder from groups like Warrant, Mötley Crüe, and Poison, the hair got bigger and fluffier—and we're not just talking about the girls. These "hair bands" were so named because of the wavy, full-bodied, and teased tresses swung around by the men onstage.

8. Preppies

While some kids were break-dancing, and others were coiffing their hair sky-high with hair spray and mousse, preppies were busy wearing chinos and loafers, talking about sailboat races, and working with their financial advisors. *Preppy* was a word used to describe the clean-cut teens, twenty- and thirtysomethings of the '80s who could usually be spotted wearing pink and playing tennis. With the release of the tongue-in-cheek (but frighteningly accurate) *Official Preppy Handbook* in 1980, it was easy to spot a preppy—or a preppy wannabe—anywhere.

The Birth of 12 Modern Advertising Icons

✳ ✳ ✳ ✳

Who knows what makes some images endure while others slip through our consciousness quicker than 50 bucks in the gas tank. In any case, you'll be surprised to learn how some of our most endearing "friends" made their way into our lives.

1. Ronald McDonald

Perhaps the most recognizable advertising icon in the world, this beloved clown made his television debut in 1963, played by future *Today* weatherman Willard Scott. Nicknamed the "hamburger-happy clown," Ronald's look was a bit different back then: He had curly blond hair, a fast-food tray for a hat, and a paper cup for a nose. Ronald's makeover must have been a hit because McDonald's serves more than 52 million customers around the globe each day.

2. Joe Camel

Looking for a way to revamp Camel's image from an "old-man's cigarette" in the late 1980s, the R. J. Reynolds marketing team uncovered illustrations of Old Joe in their archives. (He was originally conceived for an ad campaign in France in the 1950s.) In 1991, the new Joe Camel angered children's advocacy groups when a study revealed that more kids under the age of eight recognized Joe than Mickey Mouse or Fred Flintstone.

3. The Coppertone Girl

It was 1959 when an ad for Coppertone first showed a suntanned little girl's white buttocks being exposed by a puppy. "Don't be a paleface!" was the slogan, and it reflected the common belief of the time that a suntan was healthy. Artist Joyce Ballantyne Brand created the pig-tailed little girl in the image of her three-year-old daughter Cheri. When the campaign leapt off the printed page and into the world of television, it became Jodie Foster's acting debut. As the 21st century beckoned, and along with it changing views on sun exposure and nudity, Coppertone revised the drawing to reveal only the girl's lower back.

4. Alfred E. Newman, the face of *Mad* magazine

Chances are you're picturing a freckle-faced, jug-eared kid, right? The character's likeness, created by portrait artist Norman Mingo, was first adopted by *Mad* in 1954 as a border on the cover. In 1956, the humor magazine used a full-size version of the image as a write-in candidate for the presidential election. Since then, several people have been said to be "separated at birth" from Mr. Newman, namely Ted Koppel, Jimmy Carter, and George W. Bush.

5. Betty Crocker

Thousands of letters were sent to General Mills in the 1920s, all asking for answers to baking questions. So, to give the responses a personal touch, managers created a fictional character. The surname Crocker was chosen to honor a retired executive, and Betty was selected because it seemed "warm and friendly." In 1936, artist Neysa McMein blended the faces of several female employees to create a likeness. Crocker's face has changed many times over the years. She's been made to look younger, more professional, and now has a more multicultural look. At one point, a public opinion poll rating famous women placed Betty second to Eleanor Roosevelt.

6. The California Raisins

Sometimes advertising concepts can lead to marketing delirium. In 1987, a frustrated copywriter at Foote, Cone & Belding was working on the California Raisin Advisory Board campaign and said,

"We have tried everything but dancing raisins singing 'I Heard It Through the Grapevine.'" With vocals by Buddy Miles and design by Michael Brunsfeld, the idea was pitched to the client. The characters plumped up the sales of raisins by 20 percent, and the rest is Claymation history!

7. Juan Valdez

This coffee lover and his trusty donkey have been ensuring the quality of coffee beans since 1959. Back then, the National Federation of Coffee Growers of Columbia wanted to put a face on the thousands of coffee growers in the industry. The Doyle Dane Bernback ad agency found their man! By 1981, Valdez's image was so well known that it was incorporated into the Federation's logo. Originally played by Jose Duval, the role was taken over by Carlos Sanchez from 1969 to 2006. In his spare time, Sanchez manages his very own small coffee farm in Columbia.

8. Mr. Whipple

The expression "Do as I say, not as I do" took on a persona in the mid-1960s—Mr. Whipple, to be specific. This fussy supermarket manager (played by actor Dick Wilson) was famous for admonishing his shoppers by saying, "Ladies, *please* don't squeeze the Charmin!" The people at Benton & Bowles Advertising figured that if, on camera, Mr. Whipple was a habitual offender of his own rule, Charmin toilet paper would be considered the cushiest on the market. The campaign included a total of 504 ads and ran from 1965 until 1989, landing it a coveted spot in the *Guinness Book of World Records.* A 1979 poll listed Mr. Whipple as the third most recognized American behind Richard Nixon and Billy Graham.

9. The Gerber Baby

Contrary to some popular beliefs, it's not Humphrey Bogart, Elizabeth Taylor, or Bob Dole who so sweetly looks up from the label of Gerber products. In fact, the face that appears on all Gerber baby packaging belongs to mystery novelist Ann Turner Cook. In 1928, when Gerber began its search for a baby face to help promote its new brand of baby food, Dorothy Hope Smith submitted a simple charcoal sketch of the tot—promising to complete it if chosen. That wasn't necessary because the powers that be at Gerber liked it just the way it was. In 1996, Gerber updated its look, but the new label design still incorporates Cook's baby face.

10. The Pillsbury Doughboy

Who can resist poking the chubby belly of this giggling icon? This cheery little kitchen dweller was "born" in 1965 when the Leo Burnett advertising agency dreamt him up to help Pillsbury sell its refrigerated dinner rolls. The original vision was for an animated character, but, instead, agency producers borrowed a unique stop-action technique used on *The Dinah Shore Show*. After beating out more than 50 other actors, Paul Frees lent his voice to the Doughboy. So, if you've ever craved Pillsbury rolls while watching *The Adventures of Rocky and Bullwinkle*, it's no wonder... Frees was also the voice for Boris Badenov and Dudley Do-Right.

11. The Aflac Duck

A duck pitching insurance? Art director Eric David stumbled upon the idea to use a web-footed mascot one day when he continuously uttered, "Aflac... Aflac... Aflac." It didn't take him long to realize how much the company's name sounded like a duck's quack. There are many fans of the campaign, but actor Ben Affleck is not one of them. Not surprisingly, he fields many comments that associate his name with the duck and is reportedly none too pleased.

12. Duke, the Bush's Baked Beans Dog

Who else to trust with a secret recipe than the faithful family pooch? In 1908, A. J. Bush and his two sons founded Bush Brothers & Company. A few generations later, A. J.'s grandson Condon runs the company. In 1995, the advertising agency working for Bush's Baked Beans decided that Jay Bush (Condon's son) and his golden retriever, Duke, were the perfect team to represent the brand. But the real Duke is camera shy, so a stunt double was hired to portray him and handle all the gigs on the road with Jay. In any case, both dogs have been sworn to secrecy.

Funky Fads of the '90s

✳ ✳ ✳ ✳

*In the 1990s, the World Wide Web was born, grunge reigned over
the music scene, and O. J. took off in his Bronco. For many,
the 1990s were a golden era. The tech boom made many people
rich, the fashion scene was much less ridiculous, and hip-hop
hit the mainstream. Despite the slacker attitude, the last decade
of the 20th century had its fair share of fads, too.
Here are a few that stand out.*

1. Hypercolor T-shirts

Clothing manufacturer Generra created these fad-ready T-shirts in
the late '80s, but they really caught on in the '90s. The shirts were
dipped in temperature-sensitive pigment, which meant that when
heat was applied to the fabric, the color would change. Shirts would
turn vague shades of blue, yellow, pink, and gray depending on
the level of heat they received, working much like the body-heat
activated fad of a previous decade—the mood ring.

2. Hip-Hop Fashion

When hip-hop music became more mainstream in the early '90s,
its fashion style became a trend as well. Rappers such as The Fresh
Prince, Kid 'N Play, and Left Eye of TLC sparked a trend in wearing brightly colored, baggy clothing and baseball caps. Often the
jeans were so baggy that they hung down several inches below the
waist, making the question, "Boxers or briefs?" irrelevant. An off-
shoot of the hip-hop fashion was the fad of wearing clothes back-
wards, which was popularized by teen rappers Kris Kross.

3. Grunge

After the glitz and glamour of disco and the excess and pomp of
hair bands, it was inevitable that the music pendulum would swing.
That shift created grunge—a genre of music categorized by disso-
nant harmony, lots of guitars, and cynical lyrics. Grunge was initially
delivered by young men and women from the Pacific Northwest

who dressed in flannel shirts and ripped jeans. Groups like Nirvana and Pearl Jam were the first to emerge on the scene around 1991, but when the indie scene exploded into the mainstream, groups like Soundgarden, Alice in Chains, and Stone Temple Pilots became household names.

4. The Macarena

"Macarena," a catchy tune from Spanish group Los del Rio, became a worldwide phenomenon in 1996, smashing records by staying at number one on *Billboard*'s Hot 100 chart for an astonishing 14 weeks. The jovial, bouncy tune (that repeats itself over and over and over again) had its own dance, making it two fads in one. The group remains popular in their home country, but once the Macarena had played itself out a year later, the song and the two men behind it were only a distant memory in America.

5. The Waif Look

While they weren't exactly "full-figured," 1980s supermodels like Cindy Crawford were zaftig compared to the half-starved, heroin-chic look embodied by models like Kate Moss, who weighed in at barely 100 pounds. The super-skinny look was a worldwide trend in fashion and came with some serious backlash. Girls everywhere were literally starving to look like the women in the fashion magazines. The waif look garnered much criticism and controversy, but it only fueled the fire. Not until the 2000s did the pendulum begin to swing to the "real women are beautiful" direction—in the 1990s, thin was definitely "in."

6. Tattoos and Piercing

Human beings have many pierceable body parts: ears, noses, lips, tongues, eyebrows, and bellybuttons, just to name a few. In the last decade of the 20th century, no cartilage was safe from the needle of a piercing gun. If you had your fill of metal rings and studs, you could move on to some ink and round out your counterculture look. Both tattooing and piercing were all the rage in the 1990s and many people today have the tats and scars to prove it.

MULLETS AND BEEHIVES AND FLIPS, OH MY!
Hairstyles that Defined Their Generation

✳ ✳ ✳ ✳

Some hairstyles stand the test of time while others do not.
No matter the latest trends, hairstyles are a reflection of who we
are as individuals and as a culture on the whole. Below is a selec-
tion of hairstyles from the 1930s and beyond, for better or worse.

1. The Finger Wave

Often hailed as the most tasteful decade, the '30s found women
styling themselves after the stars of the burgeoning Hollywood
film industry. Think Greta Garbo, Katharine Hepburn, and Carole
Lombard, who all kept their hair short to mid-length, wavy, and
styled for maximum sex appeal.

2. The Veronica Lake

The smoky, alluring look of this 1940s screen siren was identifiable
by miles of long, wavy blonde hair that covered one eye. This
was the hairstyle of a star; everyday women opted for a shorter,
shoulder-length version of the wavy style.

3. The Cary Grant

With the Cary Grant, the movies struck again, this time influenc-
ing men's hairstyles of the mid-20th century. This was a precise
cut with a severe side part and a whole lot of styling wax to make it
shine. The look was suave and debonair, just like Grant himself.

4. The Bouffant

When the salon-size hair dryer was unveiled to the beauty industry,
the possibilities seemed endless. Starting in the 1950s, updos and
blow-dried styles were literally taken to new heights as the bouffant
and the beehive created big, round silhouettes on the head.

5. The Pompadour

The '50s were the era when T-shirts and jeans became the uniform
of young men everywhere. And the pompadour, popularized by

James Dean and Elvis Presley, was the haircut that went with it. Closely cut in the back, the top and sides were kept a little longer and combed up and back with hair gel for added shine. The look was masculine and instantly iconic.

6. The Flip

This spunky, youthful style was mega-popular among hordes of modern women throughout the 1960s. Shoulder-length hair was back-combed or teased slightly at the top, then the ends were curled up in a "flip" with rollers or a curling iron. Mary Tyler Moore sported the classic flip on *The Dick Van Dyke Show*, and Jackie Kennedy had her own more conservative version. Later, the style became so ubiquitous it was nicknamed "beauty pageant hair" or "Miss America hair," because for years nearly every contestant sported flip after perfect flip.

7. The Pixie

The pin-up figure went out of style when long, lean supermodel Twiggy came on the scene in the 1960s. Women everywhere tried to emulate her silhouette—and her hair. It reportedly took eight hours to create the style on Twiggy the first time, almost as long as it took to put on her fake eyelashes! The pixie was cut over the ears, with slightly longer hair on the top of the head. The defining feature was the close-cropped layers that framed the face.

8. The Mop Top

During the 1960s, the influence of The Beatles on popular culture was unlike anything the world had ever seen. Girls and boys alike mimicked the boyish charm of these Liverpool lads, especially when it came to hairstyles. Longer, over the ears, shaggy, and generally floppy on all sides, the mop top was also sported by another mega-band of the time, The Rolling Stones.

9. The No-Cut Haircut

If you were a guy in the 1970s who didn't like getting a haircut or shaving, you were in luck. As the decade marched on, men simply stopped cutting their hair, and mustaches and full beards were in.

Whether they were influenced by the free-loving culture of the hippies, growing antiwar sentiment, or just plain laziness, men's hair reached new lengths during this era.

10. The Farrah Fawcett

This iconic '70s hairstyle, made famous by *Charlie's Angels* star Farrah Fawcett, came to a soft point at the top of the head, creating a triangular silhouette with long, feathered flips cascading down the sides and the back. This hairdo was revived in the 2000s as part of a retro '70s and '80s fashion trend.

11. The Mohawk

The Mohawk has its roots in Native American culture but was popular with punk rockers in the '80s. Punk hairstyles in the UK and America reflected the attitude of these antiestablishment youngsters; hair was spiked, sprayed, shaved, and often multicolored and sent a clear message: We're not like you.

12. The Mullet

No one can be totally sure when this notorious hairstyle originated, but its popularity soared in the 1980s. The mullet was achieved by cutting hair short and spiky or feathered on the top and sides of the head and keeping it shoulder-length or longer in the back.

13. The Rat-Tail

Popular with young men (and some women) of the '80s, this style was characterized by hair cut short all over except for a long strip of hair (usually ½ to 1 inch wide) growing from the nape of the neck and dangling down the back. Rat-tails were typically 4 to 12 inches in length and were often braided.

14. Rock Hair

Many of the hairstyle changes and fashion trends in the 1980s had to do with the music of the era. "Hair bands" were so named because of their long, voluminous hair, which was often teased or permed. Heavy metal bands such as Mötley Crüe, Poison, and Bon Jovi helped popularize this look for both men and women.

15. The Meg Ryan

Immortalized by the 1989 romantic comedy *When Harry Met Sally,* Meg Ryan's tousled, permed locks were all the rage for women everywhere. Hairstylists reportedly did very little else for a period of several years, since women seemed to only want the spiral curls, highlights, and layered cut made famous by elite hairstylist Sally Hershberger.

16. The Fade

The early '90s brought hip-hop culture to the masses and the high-top fade haircut came with it. Popularized by rap duo Kid 'N Play, the fade was cut like a flattop but with the sides and back gradually fading from thickness at the top all the way to bare skin. Largely sported by African American males, men of all ethnic backgrounds gave it a try, often with mixed results.

17. The Rachel

Unless you lived under a rock in the mid-1990s, you knew about the group of *Friends* that hung out on the NBC sitcom for ten seasons. Jennifer Aniston's character Rachel spawned legions of hair clones. This long to medium length style was cut with many different layers in order to frame the face and give a woman's hair a full, healthy look.

18. The Faux-Hawk

Want the edgy look of a Mohawk but don't want to go all the way? Welcome the faux-hawk! By slicking back (or close-shaving) the sides of the hair, a fake or "faux" Mohawk can be achieved. Scores of fashionistas, both male and female, got a lot of mileage out of this look in the early 21st century.

19. The Chelsea

With roots in punk rock culture, this haircut refers to the Chelsea district in London, a popular hangout for punks. But in the UK, this radical cut is called "the feather cut." This unisex style is achieved by shaving the entire head, except for the bangs and a little on the right and left sides of the head.

OMG, THIS LIST IS GR8! LOL!
Fads of the Cyber-Chic 2000s

✳ ✳ ✳ ✳

The fads of the 2000s can be described as technologically driven and convenience-based. Everyone seems to be looking for the fastest, easiest ways to communicate, advertise, entertain themselves, eat, and even fall in love. As the decade winds down, these fads will soon be a thing of the past, but let's not get ahead of ourselves!

1. YouTube and MySpace

Sharing videos, songs, e-mail messages, pictures, favorites lists, and profiles is becoming de rigueur in the 21st century. With online sites like YouTube, you can search for, watch, and share video clips of just about everything—no TV required. If you find a really great video clip on YouTube, you can post a link to it on your MySpace page. MySpace is one of the most popular Web sites in existence, operating as a networking tool for anyone who can type their name and think of a password. Members have profiles, links to other people's profiles, primary and extended networks, and can use their MySpace pages for fun, personal use, or to promote themselves in business and artistic endeavors.

2. Reality TV

The craze that continues to keep us glued to the TV started in the 1990s with a little MTV show called *The Real World,* where seven strangers were picked to live together in a cool apartment in Manhattan. The show was a huge hit—people everywhere tuned in to see real people interacting in real life. But it wasn't until 2000 that reality television really exploded, spawning shows like *Survivor, Amazing Race,* and *American Idol.* By the mid-2000s, the industry was saturated with reality TV shows for every imaginable subject.

3. Text Messaging

These usually abbreviated, often truncated, and sometimes cryptic messages are sent via cell phones. The United States was actually behind the times when this trend initially hit in the late '90s. Asia and Europe had been using the Short Message System (or SMS) for several years, but we only got hip to "txt msgs" in the mid-2000s. Apparently, we're making up for lost time: In February 2008, cellular provider Verizon reported 20 billion text messages sent or received in that month alone, doubling the number from only eight months before in June 2007.

4. Sudoku

In Japanese, *su do ku* means "one number." A sudoku puzzle is a grid to fill with numbers so that the numerals one through nine occur only once in each row, column, and box. Each puzzle has some numbers filled in—you just need to work out the rest using your powers of deduction. It may not sound like it, but it's really fun. In 2005, British newspaper *The Times* published a sudoku puzzle by Wayne Gould and the game's popularity boomed. Soon, U.S. newspapers were printing the puzzles and everyone had their heads down, crunching the numbers.

5. Speed Dating

With so many MySpace profiles to update, text messages to type, and sudoku puzzles to solve, who has time to meet that special someone? Thanks to speed-dating services, busy people of the new millennium can meet dozens of singles—while a timer keeps the whole thing moving along at a steady pace. A couple chats for three to eight minutes or so, figuring out if there's any point in continuing their discussion later. A bell rings or a glass clinks and it's bye-bye to person number one and on to person number two. Fans of speed dating say it's a great way to meet a lot of people and, since first impressions are telling, you won't waste your time on someone who doesn't tickle your fancy right away. Critics say it's not fair to judge someone on a three-minute conversation, but with the pace we've set in the new millennium, three minutes may be all the time anyone can spare!

Chapter 5
MUSIC

* * * *

I WANNA HOLD YOUR WORLD RECORD
24 Beatles Hits

The story of The Beatles is truly epic. Not only did they create some of the most popular music in the history of rock 'n' roll, when Rolling Stone *magazine compiled its 500 Greatest Songs of All Time, The Beatles beat out everyone else with a whopping 23 songs on the list. For one week in 1964, John, Paul, George, and Ringo had 12 songs on* Billboard's Hot 100, *including the number one, two, three, four, and five songs. Nobody before or since has accomplished that feat. Here's a sampling of the Fab Four's music arsenal with 24 of their biggest hits.*

1. "I Want to Hold Your Hand" (1963)
This song, which started the "British Invasion," became the Fab Four's first number one tune in the States. It did pretty well elsewhere, too—it's their all-time best-selling single worldwide.

2. "She Loves You" (1963)
This peppy song made its debut in America in September 1963, but it didn't get much attention until it was rereleased in January 1964 after the success of "I Want to Hold Your Hand." That time it spent 15 weeks on U.S. charts, hitting number one on March 21.

3. "From Me to You" (1963)
The first number one for The Beatles in the UK, this song didn't make much of a splash in the States, reaching only number 41 upon its second release in 1964. However, across the pond it would mark the first of 11 number one singles, so they didn't have time to sulk about this tune, which was written by John and Paul while on their tour bus.

4. "Twist and Shout" (1964)

If you've ever rocked out to The Beatles' version of this Isley Brothers tune, you know that John's vocals are scratchy, growly, and decidedly different from other Beatles songs. While recording their album *Please, Please Me,* John started to lose his voice. Producer Brian Epstein saved the recording for "Twist and Shout" till the very end, and by then, John's voice was nearly shot and sounded strained—in fact, he shouted most of the song. The classic tune was recorded in one take not just because that was all John had left, but because it was pretty much perfect from the start.

5. "Can't Buy Me Love" (1964)

Pressure to create another huge hit after "I Want to Hold Your Hand" didn't phase The Beatles. This tune is one of the first songs ever to start with the chorus. The formula worked like a charm, creating another UK and U.S. number one.

6. "A Hard Day's Night" (1964)

This malapropism was uttered by Ringo, who often got American slang and phrases mixed up. He was stating that the band had had a hard day, but then realized it was already evening. "A Hard Day's Night" became another number one for the band and served as the title for their documentary released the same year.

7. "I Feel Fine" (1964)

This song came out of some downtime between John and Ringo, who were playing with a riff John had come up with while working on "Eight Days a Week." "I Feel Fine" eventually went to number one in every major market. The song featured reverb—Jimi Hendrix and The Who were using feedback in their concerts at the time, but The Beatles were the first to put the sound on vinyl.

8. "Eight Days a Week" (1965)

The title of this song was again based on a Ringo-ism; the drummer said that he'd worked so hard, it felt like he'd added another day to the week. Even though the song reached number one in the States, it wasn't a band favorite, and they seldom performed it live.

9. "Ticket to Ride" (1965)

The meaning behind this song is unclear—it could be about a prostitute, John getting his driver's license, or a girl walking out the door. Whatever the subject, it's a catchy tune that reached number one in both the UK and the United States.

10. "Help!" (1965)

John would later claim that he penned the lyrics to "Help!" after dealing with the pressures of being part of a group that was, as he so notoriously put it, "bigger than Jesus." He said that he wished the song had been recorded at a slower tempo, but fans liked it just fine, making it another chart-topper for the band.

11. "Yesterday" (1965)

When this melancholy tune about lost love came to Paul in a dream, he worried that he'd unintentionally plagiarized another artist's work. He hadn't. McCartney recorded the song without the other three Beatles, who were initially against its release in the UK. The song reached number one in the United States.

12. "We Can Work It Out" (1965)

One of the Fab Four's fastest-selling singles, this moody Lennon-McCartney collaboration touched a nerve with struggling lovers everywhere. When the group disbanded, this song took on an ironic overtone for the band that ultimately couldn't work things out.

13. "Nowhere Man" (1966)

This rather disturbing song was written by John about a man whose life is pointless and lonely. Lennon reportedly needed another song for *Rubber Soul,* but after several hours of writing nothing, he gave up. As soon as he did, this song simply came to him. "Nowhere Man" only reached the number three spot in America.

14. "Paperback Writer" (1966)

This number one was penned by Paul after an aunt reportedly told him to write a song that wasn't about a girl. The song clips along at a fast pace and tells the story of an aspiring writer, possibly based on a book Ringo was reading at the time.

15. "Yellow Submarine" (1966)

Though Paul vehemently denied it, "Yellow Submarine" (the song that later inspired an animated movie of the same name) got a reputation for being about hallucinogenic drug use. Ringo sings lead vocals on this goofy-but-catchy song that hit number one in the UK and number two in the States.

16. "Eleanor Rigby" (1966)

Paul wrote the lyrics to this song about "all the lonely people" and producer George Martin added a lush string score. It all meshed together to describe the loneliness of old age. It hit the top of the charts in the UK, but only made it to number 11 in the States.

17. "Hello, Goodbye" (1967)

Spending several weeks at number one on both the UK and U.S. charts, "Hello, Goodbye" was released around Christmastime 1967 and later on the *Magical Mystery Tour* album.

18. "With a Little Help from My Friends" (1967)

The cheers and applause that accompany this Ringo-led tune came from earlier recordings of The Beatles' live shows, since they were no longer touring when the song was recorded. The single wasn't a chart-topper, but it has a sweet message and a catchy melody that make it a classic Beatles fan favorite.

19. "Lady Madonna" (1968)

Before The Beatles left for India in 1969 (and changed directions musically) they recorded one last song for Parlophone/Capitol before releasing on their own label, Apple Records. "Lady Madonna" was that song, and it hit the top spot in the UK and reached number four in the States.

20. "Hey Jude" (1968)

Even though the lyrics don't exactly make sense, even though the song in its original version is over seven minutes long, even though it's technically a song about divorce, the song is beloved by many people. Written by Paul for John's son Julian during his parents' divorce, "Hey Jude" stayed at number one on U.S. charts for nine weeks, a record for any Beatles song. Across the pond, the full-length version of the song peaked at number one for two weeks.

21. "Come Together" (1969)

Originally written for Timothy Leary's short-lived gubernatorial campaign, "Come Together" was released on the *Abbey Road* album in 1969. The song was also the subject of a lawsuit by Chuck Berry's music publisher, who claimed that a line from one of Berry's songs had been stolen for use in The Beatles' tune. The suit was settled out of court. The song reached number one in the States and number four in the UK.

22. "Get Back" (1969)

The last song on the *Let It Be* album, this hard-driving rock tune tells the listener to "get back to where you once belonged." Since The Beatles did not release any more records together after *Let It Be,* this song was the end of the line, period. The single reached number one around the world and was the first Beatles tune to credit a fifth musician, Billy Preston on keyboards.

23. "Let It Be" (1970)

The *Let It Be* album, released in 1970 shortly after the band officially broke up, was the Fab Four's swan song. This single was a huge hit around the world, reaching number one in America and number two in the UK. Paul was inspired to write it following a dream he had of his mother (Mary), who died when he was 14. The song's theme of surrendering and letting go touched a chord with millions of fans. "Let It Be" is often played at funerals, due to its hopeful, farewell message.

24. "The Long and Winding Road" (1970)

This sad song about unrequited love, also released after The Beatles disbanded, would prove to be the group's last number one song in the United States. Paul reportedly wrote the song during a time when tensions were mounting among the band members.

IF YOU REMEMBER BEING AT WOODSTOCK, YOU PROBABLY WEREN'T THERE
All 32 Performers at Woodstock

✳ ✳ ✳ ✳

The Woodstock Music and Art Festival was held August 15–18, 1969, not in Woodstock but in Bethel, New York, 40 miles away. Woodstock was supposed to host the festival, but when rumors spread that attendance could reach a million people, the city backed out. Farmer Max Yasgur saved the concert by hosting the 500,000-plus attendees in his alfalfa field. With the huge crowd, there were shortages of food, water, and restrooms, but most revelers still enjoyed some of the best musical acts of the era. Here's the lineup from that fateful weekend.

1. Richie Havens

Richie Havens, a Greenwich Village folksinger, got the concert started around 5:00 P.M. on Friday, August 15. He played eight songs, including the memorable "Motherless Child," which he ended with the word *freedom* sung over and over. After Woodstock, Havens continued to tour and release albums, and in 1993, he performed at the inauguration ceremonies for President Bill Clinton.

2. Country Joe McDonald

Country Joe McDonald made an unscheduled appearance at Woodstock on Friday evening without his band, The Fish. McDonald's solo set included "I Find Myself Missing You," "I-Feel-Like-I'm-Fixin'-to-Die Rag," and the "Fish Cheer," a song where he usually spelled out the word *fish* with the audience, but at Woodstock he spelled another four-letter f-word instead.

3. John Sebastian

John Sebastian is best known as a founder of The Lovin' Spoonful, members of the Rock and Roll Hall of Fame. Sebastian wasn't scheduled to appear at the festival, but he played five songs, including "I Had a Dream" and "Rainbows Over Your Blues." In 1976, he had a number one single with the theme song from TV's *Welcome Back, Kotter.* Sebastian promoted a collection of the '60s greatest hits via infomercial and continues to record and tour.

4. Sweetwater

After three solo artists, Sweetwater—who pioneered the psychedelic rock/classical fusion style later picked up by Jefferson Airplane—was the first band to perform at the festival. They played eight songs, including "What's Wrong," "My Crystal Spider," and "Why Oh Why." After Woodstock, Sweetwater disbanded when lead singer Nansi Nevins was badly injured in a car accident.

5. The Incredible String Band

The Incredible String Band was a Scottish acoustic band that formed in the early '60s and later switched to psychedelic folk music. Their set of four songs included "The Letter" and "This Moment."

6. Bert Sommer

Bert Sommer was a folksinger and former member of the baroque-pop group The Left Banke. Sommer played ten songs at the festival, including "Jennifer," "Jeanette," and "America." He continued to record and perform until his death in 1990.

7. Tim Hardin

Tim Hardin was also a Greenwich Village folk musician and composer. During his hour-long set, Hardin performed only two songs—"Misty Roses" and "If I Were a Carpenter," which was a top ten hit for Bobby Darin. Hardin continued to record until 1973 and died of a heroin and morphine overdose in 1980.

8. Ravi Shankar

Bengali-Indian musician and composer Ravi Shankar is best known for teaching George Harrison to play the sitar. His work with Harrison and other rock stars landed him a gig at Woodstock, where he played five songs in the rain, including "Tabla Solo in Jhaptal." Today, his daughters Anoushka Shankar and Norah Jones are both successful musicians.

9. Melanie

Melanie, born Melanie Anne Safka-Schekeryk, made her first recording at age five and was successful in Europe with "Beautiful People," one of the two songs she performed at Woodstock. She later recorded "Lay Down (Candles in the Rain)" after being inspired by the Woodstock audience lighting candles during her set.

10. Arlo Guthrie

Prior to Woodstock, Arlo Guthrie—the son of folksinger and composer Woody Guthrie—was best known for his 18-minute-long song (and subsequent film) "Alice's Restaurant," which describes how he avoided the draft. Arlo played three songs at Woodstock, "Coming into Los Angeles," "Walking Down the Line," and "Amazing Grace." He continues to record and performed his song "City of New Orleans" at fund-raisers for victims of Hurricane Katrina.

11. Joan Báez

Day one at Woodstock closed with Joan Báez, probably the most famous folk and protest singer to perform at the festival. Báez performed 12 songs at Woodstock, including her hits "Joe Hill" and "Sweet Sir Galahad" and classics such as "Swing Low Sweet Chariot" and "We Shall Overcome." After more than 50 years in the music biz, Báez continues to record and perform songs about non-violence, civil and human rights, and the environment.

12. Quill

Day two at Woodstock kicked off around noon with the Boston band Quill. They had opened for several notable artists, including The Who, Sly & the Family Stone, The Grateful Dead, and Janis Joplin. At Woodstock, Quill played four songs, including "They Live the Life" and "Waitin' for You." After Woodstock, Quill released its first album, which fizzled, and the band broke up in 1970.

13. The Keef Hartley Band

The Keef Hartley Band, which mixed elements of jazz, blues, and rock, was one of the few British bands to play at Woodstock. Keef Hartley's career took off when he replaced Ringo Starr as the drummer for Rory Storm and The Hurricanes when Ringo joined The Beatles. At Woodstock, the band played eight songs, including "Spanish Fly" and "Rock Me Baby."

14. Santana

The career of Latin rock guitarist Carlos Santana got a major boost when concert producer Bill Graham got his band a gig at Woodstock, even though they hadn't yet released an album. They played seven songs, including "Waiting," "Jingo," and the 11-minute instrumental "Soul Sacrifice," which was considered a highlight of the festival. The 1970 album *Abraxas* reached number one on the album charts and sold more than four million copies, but Carlos Santana wouldn't duplicate this success until the 1999 release of *Supernatural,* a collaboration with Eric Clapton and other artists. The album won nine Grammy Awards, including Album of the Year and Record of the Year for the song "Smooth" with Rob Thomas.

15. Canned Heat

Blues-rock/boogie band Canned Heat performed four songs at Woodstock, including "Goin' Up the Country" and "Let's Work Together." In 1970, they brought in blues singer and guitarist John Lee Hooker to record the double album, "Hooker 'n' Heat." While many of the original members have died, Canned Heat has replaced them and continues to perform and record.

16. Mountain

The rock band Mountain was playing only its fourth live gig when it performed 13 songs at Woodstock, including "Stormy Monday," "Waiting to Take You Away," and "Theme for an Imaginary Western." Mountain broke up and re-formed a number of times after Woodstock and is currently back together and performing, but without founding member Felix Pappalardi, who was shot and killed by his wife on April 17, 1983.

17. Janis Joplin

Before her death from a heroin overdose in 1970, Janis Joplin made a huge impact on rock music with four albums and memorable performances. At Woodstock, she gave a spirited execution of ten songs including "To Love Somebody," "Try (Just a Little Bit Harder)," and "Piece of My Heart." Her biggest-selling album *Pearl,* released posthumously in 1971, featured her hit single "Me and Bobby McGee" and the a cappella song "Mercedes Benz."

18. Sly & the Family Stone

One of the first racially integrated bands, San Francisco's Sly & the Family Stone combined soul, funk, and psychedelia in its music. They played eight songs at Woodstock, including "Dance to the Music," "Stand!," "Everyday People," and "I Want to Take You Higher." Woodstock made the band popular, but Sly Stone's drug use brought them down. When the band was inducted into the Rock and Roll Hall of Fame in 1993, many of the founding members performed, but Sly, in a surprise appearance, accepted his award and disappeared. Then, during a Sly & the Family Stone tribute at the 2006 Grammy Awards, Sly joined the band in the middle of "I Want to Take You Higher," but left the stage before the song ended.

19. The Grateful Dead

The Grateful Dead were known for performing long jams of their combination of rock, folk, bluegrass, blues, country, jazz, gospel, and psychedelia. Formed in San Francisco in 1965 by guitarist Jerry Garcia, The Grateful Dead performed four songs at Woodstock: "St. Stephen," "Mama Tried," "Dark Star/High Time," and "Turn on Your Love Light." The Grateful Dead continued to tour regularly for its "Deadhead" followers until Jerry Garcia died in August 1995. The remaining members disbanded, but later reunited to form The Other Ones and in 2003 renamed themselves The Dead.

20. Creedence Clearwater Revival

Heavily influenced by the swamp blues music that came out of Louisiana in the late '50s and early '60s, Creedence Clearwater Revival formed in the San Francisco Bay area in 1959. They hit their peak in early 1969, just in time for Woodstock, where they performed an 11-song set that included "Bad Moon Rising" and

"Proud Mary." Their performance was not included in the Woodstock film or album, apparently because lead singer John Fogerty didn't like their performance. CCR broke up in 1972, but Fogerty emerged as a solo artist in the mid-1980s.

21. The Who

Woodstock was The Who's biggest performance since the release of their groundbreaking rock opera *Tommy*. Their 24-song set began around 3:00 A.M. and included many songs from *Tommy* as well as "I Can't Explain," "Shakin' All Over," and "My Generation." At the conclusion of their set, Pete Townshend slammed his guitar into the stage and threw it into the crowd. Drummer Keith Moon died in 1978 from a prescription drug overdose, and the group officially disbanded in 1983 but have reunited for various events and tours over the years. In 1990, The Who were inducted into the Rock and Roll Hall of Fame, and in 2006, founding members Townshend and Roger Daltrey released *Endless Wire* and returned to touring.

22. Jefferson Airplane

Jefferson Airplane's eight-song set took off at 8:00 A.M. on Sunday morning. This psychedelic rock band from San Francisco performed such hits as "Volunteers," "Somebody to Love," and "White Rabbit." After Woodstock, Jefferson Airplane continued to perform and record hits under different names, including Starship and Jefferson Starship The Next Generation. Jefferson Airplane was inducted into the Rock and Roll Hall of Fame in 1996.

23. Joe Cocker

After an all-night music marathon, Joe Cocker took the stage around 2:00 P.M. The English rock and blues musician performed five songs, including his version of The Beatles' song "With a Little Help from My Friends," as well as "Delta Lady." Cocker continues to tour occasionally.

24. Country Joe and The Fish

After a rain delay lasting several hours, Country Joe returned, this time with his band The Fish, taking the stage around 6:00 P.M. They played four songs, including "Rock and Soul Music" and "Love Machine." In 2004, Country Joe formed the Country Joe Band with some of the original band members and went on tour.

25. Ten Years After

English blues-rock band Ten Years After performed five songs at Woodstock, including "Good Morning Little Schoolgirl," "Hear Me Calling," and "I'm Going Home." Between 1967 and 1974, Ten Years After recorded and released ten multimillion-selling albums, before breaking up in 1975. After their entire catalog was digitally remastered and rereleased in 2001, three of the founding members got back together and are again recording and touring.

26. The Band

Originally known as The Hawks, the careers of Canadian-American musicians The Band took flight when Bob Dylan recruited them as his backing band for his 1965–1966 world tour. They subsequently recorded four albums with Dylan. At Woodstock, their 11-song set included the songs "Tears of Rage," "Long Black Veil," and "Loving You Is Sweeter Than Ever." The Band broke up in 1976, then reformed in 1983 without founding guitarist and main songwriter Robbie Robertson. They are members of both the Canadian Music Hall of Fame and the Rock and Roll Hall of Fame.

27. Blood, Sweat & Tears

When they performed at Woodstock, jazz-rock band Blood, Sweat & Tears were still riding high from their 1969 Grammy win for Album of the Year for their self-titled sophomore album. The band's five-song set at Woodstock included "Spinning Wheel" and "Something Coming On." Blood, Sweat & Tears broke up and re-formed a number of times and continue to tour.

28. Johnny Winter

Albino blues singer and guitarist Johnny Winter released his first album in 1968. He performed nine songs at Woodstock, including two with his brother Edgar Winter, also an albino blues singer. The set included "Johnny B. Goode," "I Can't Stand It," and "Tobacco

Road." In 1977, Johnny produced Muddy Waters' Grammy Award-winning comeback album, *Hard Again*. In 1988, Johnny was inducted into the Blues Foundation Hall of Fame, and he continues to record and tour.

29. Crosby, Stills, Nash & Young

Folk rock supergroup Crosby, Stills, Nash & Young began their 16-song set around 3:00 A.M. Made up of former members of The Byrds, The Hollies, and Buffalo Springfield, Woodstock was only their second gig. Their nine-song acoustic set included "Suite: Judy Blue Eyes" and "Marrakesh Express." The electric set that followed included "Long Time Gone" and "Find the Cost of Freedom." They later recorded the song "Woodstock" to commemorate the festival, and for a while they rivaled The Beatles in terms of popularity. But their superegos caused this supergroup to disband in mid-1970. They've all enjoyed success as solo artists and have reunited in various configurations to record and tour over the years.

30. Paul Butterfield Blues Band

Paul Butterfield was a harmonica player and singer who brought the Chicago electric blues style to rock. The Paul Butterfield Blues Band's five-song set at Woodstock included "Everything's Gonna Be Alright," "Driftin'," and "Born Under a Bad Sign." Butterfield broke up the Blues Band in 1970 and formed a new group called Better Days. He performed solo in the late '70s and early '80s and died in 1987 from a drug and alcohol overdose.

31. Sha Na Na

By far the funniest band to perform at Woodstock was Sha Na Na, a group that covered doo-wop songs from the 1950s while clowning around in period outfits. At Woodstock—only the seventh gig of their career—they performed nine songs, including "Yakety Yak," "Wipe Out," and "At the Hop." At the time, Sha Na Na did not have a record deal, but they received one immediately afterward and went on to release more than 25 albums. From 1977 to 1982, the group even had its own hit TV show, and they continue to tour with some of the original members.

32. Jimi Hendrix

Perhaps the most influential guitarist in rock music history, Jimi Hendrix insisted on closing the show. He was scheduled to perform at midnight, but his set was delayed until around 8:00 A.M. Monday morning. By that time, the crowd, which had once numbered more than 500,000, had dwindled to an estimated 80,000. Still, Hendrix played a 16-song set that featured hits such as "Foxy Lady," "Purple Haze," and "Hey Joe." He also played a striking and memorable rendition of "The Star-Spangled Banner." On September 18, 1970, Jimi Hendrix was found dead in London. It is believed that he asphyxiated on his own vomit following an overdose of sleeping pills. Hendrix was inducted into the Rock and Roll Hall of Fame in 1992 and the UK Music Hall of Fame in 2005.

12 Unusual Band Names

✳ ✳ ✳ ✳

1. Aardvark Spleen
2. Barenaked Ladies
3. Dexy's Midnight Runners
4. Lavay Smith and Her Red Hot Skillet Lickers
5. Moby Grape
6. Ned's Atomic Dustbin
7. Nine Inch Nails
8. Squirrel Nut Zippers
9. Strawberry Alarm Clock
10. The Flying Burrito Brothers
11. Ugly Kid Joe
12. Vanilla Fudge

WE LOVE YOU, TOO, U2
The Messages Behind 28 Favorite U2 Songs

✳ ✳ ✳ ✳

September 1976: A 14-year-old drummer posts a notice at school that he's looking to start a band. Rehearsals are held in his parents' kitchen in Dublin, and The Larry Mullen Band is born. The name didn't last, but more than 30 years and 22 Grammys later, the band, which would eventually be called U2, has proven that it has what it takes to stay on top. The keys to U2's longevity include respect for each other and their fans; the ability to continuously reinvent themselves and their musical style; and powerful music with a message. Bono is a genius at writing ambiguous lyrics, allowing listeners to decide what each song means to them. Read on to take a musical journey with the band that Time *magazine once named "Rock's Hottest Ticket."*

1. "I Will Follow" (1980)

This peppy '80s tune, released on the *Boy* album, is still as fresh today as when it debuted nearly three decades ago. The song is charged with Edge's gritty guitar riffs and Larry Mullen, Jr.'s pounding drum beat, still played with the intensity of an 18-year-old. According to Bono, the lyrics are about the unconditional love between mother (or God) and child.

2. "Out of Control" (1980)

Another toe-tapper from *Boy*, "Out of Control" was the first of their songs the guys heard played on the radio. Bono wrote the lyrics in the wee hours of the morning following his eighteenth birthday. "It was one dull morning/I woke the world with bawling/I was so sad/They were so glad. . . . " The song is about being born—or rather objecting to it—and feeling that you have no control over your life.

3. "Gloria" (1981)

No, it's not a cover of fellow Irishman Van Morrison's '60s hit. This one comes from U2's sophomore album, *October*, which was heavily laden with references to religion and spirituality. Bono has said he had a difficult time writing the lyrics, so he turned it into a psalm, complete with verses in Latin. The music is quite edgy, considering the subject matter, which is what makes it classic U2.

4. "Tomorrow" (1981)

Most U2 lyrics are pretty heavy. But with "Tomorrow," from *October*, Bono was truly speaking from the heart. When he was 14, his mother suffered a brain hemorrhage at her father's funeral and died a few days later. Bono would later state that the melancholy lyrics to "Tomorrow" were a description of her funeral.

5. "Sunday Bloody Sunday" (1983)

From the *War* album, "Sunday Bloody Sunday" is a powerhouse in the U2 canon, performed on every major tour since its debut. It's a classic U2 protest song about the Troubles in Northern Ireland. Larry's militaristic drumming and Edge's abrasive guitar drive the song, while Bono's powerful lyrics cry out "How long, how long must we sing this song?" The song has become a global plea to end the violence that threatens the world today.

6. "New Year's Day" (1983)

This song, inspired by the solidarity movement in Poland, reached number two on U.S. charts. It was also the first U2 video to get major airplay on MTV, giving the band the exposure that would get them named "Band of the Eighties" by *Rolling Stone* magazine just two years later. During live shows, Edge takes control on this song, playing guitar and keyboard and also singing backup vocals.

7. "40" (1983)

Also from *War*, Bono based the lyrics of this bass-driven song on Psalm 40. Although the song was only released in Germany, it is a fan favorite that has frequently been used to close shows. When a show ends with "40," guitarist Edge and bassist Adam Clayton switch instruments, and the band members leave the stage one by one—first Bono, Adam, then Edge, leaving Larry alone onstage to perform a brief (but kickin') drum solo, as fans chant the chorus.

8. "Pride (In the Name of Love)" (1984)

Released on *The Unforgettable Fire* album, this song about Jesus ("one man betrayed with a kiss") and Martin Luther King, Jr., reached number two in the States. Bono gave his all recording "Pride," shouting the lyrics from the depths of his soul. But don't rely on the Irishman for a lesson in U.S. history; the lyric referring to Dr. King ("Early morning, April four/Shot rings out in the Memphis sky...") is incorrect—King was actually killed around 6:00 P.M. Bono has since realized his mistake and now sings "Early evening, April four" in live shows.

9. "Bad" (1984)

From *The Unforgettable Fire* album, "Bad" was never released as a single, but it's a fan favorite that sometimes closes shows. As always, the lyrics are subject to much debate, but according to Bono, the song is about drug addiction, specifically heroin, which ran rampant in Dublin in the early '80s and had taken hold of one of his friends. Ever the perfectionist, Bono feels the song could've been better if he'd "finished" it. Most fans think it's a masterpiece as it stands.

10. "With or Without You" (1987)

This perpetual crowd-pleaser, released on the Grammy Award-winning album *The Joshua Tree,* was U2's first number one song in America. Some feel the song is about Jesus ("see the thorn twist in your side"); others think it's about romantic love and longing for someone you can't be with. The song is rife with symbolism, in both the lyrics and the music. Adam's bass is the pulse. Larry's drumming is the heartbeat. Edge's guitar chords represent the agony of a heart breaking. And Bono's voice and haunting lyrics are the personification of love and longing and the agony of unrequited love. When his voice cries out, you know he's feeling the pain of loving someone he can't be with... and you feel that pain with him.

11. "I Still Haven't Found What I'm Looking For" (1987)

No dual meaning here—U2's second song to top U.S. charts, "I Still Haven't Found What I'm Looking For" is a gospel song about searching for and understanding one's spiritual beliefs. U2 even took a gospel choir on the road with them to sing backup vocals during The Joshua Tree tour.

12. "Where the Streets Have No Name" (1987)

Although "Streets" didn't crack the top ten in the States, it's a fan favorite that was frequently used to open shows on The Joshua Tree tour. The lyrics were inspired by a trip Bono and his wife, Ali, took to Ethiopia in the mid-1980s, during which they volunteered at a refugee camp orphanage. With Edge's distinctive scratchy chords, Larry's enthusiastic drumming, and Adam's deep bass holding it all together, even the band admits that it's much better live.

13. "Desire" (1988)

With "Desire," released as the first single from the album *Rattle and Hum,* Bono parodies and criticizes evangelical preachers, politicians, and the greed ingrained in the landscape of 1980s America. But the lyrics can have a more carnal interpretation as well. Either way, the song was a hit, reaching number one in the States. The song also won a Grammy for Best Rock Performance.

14. "Angel of Harlem" (1988)

With "Angel of Harlem," U2 again hit number one on U.S. charts. Recorded at Sun Studios in Memphis, Elvis's legendary music engineer Cowboy Jack Clement pitched in, and it was all captured on film in the "rockumentary" *Rattle and Hum.* The song chronicles the band's arrival in America for their first tour in 1980 ("It was a cold and wet December day/When we touched the ground at JFK. . . . ") and pays tribute to Billie Holiday, the "Angel of Harlem."

15. "All I Want Is You" (1989)

Bono has said that "All I Want Is You," from *Rattle and Hum,* is dedicated to his wife, Ali. The poetic and symbolic lyrics describe his desire for true, unconditional love, and the promises his lover makes show the depth of her feelings. The song closed the *Rattle and Hum* movie, and much to the surprise of fans (because it seldom closes a live show), it was the last song played on the Vertigo tour, when it closed the show in Honolulu in December 2006.

16. "Mysterious Ways" (1991)

In the 1990s, U2 took a new musical direction, attempting to "chop down *The Joshua Tree*" by reinventing themselves with a funkier, more experimental sound on the album *Achtung Baby*. Clearly it worked because "Mysterious Ways," powered by Edge's abrasive guitar riffs and Bono's enigmatic lyrics, scored U2 another number one in the States. Fans disagree over the song's meaning—some feel it's deeply spiritual, with references to John the Baptist, while others believe the lyrics are more sexual in nature, and others just think it's a funky dance groove.

17. "One" (1992)

Such a simple title, such a powerful lyric. Tensions were running high while recording *Achtung Baby,* and the band was reportedly on the brink of breaking up. "One" is the song that brought them back together, essentially saving the band. The lyrics can be interpreted in several ways: a gay son coming out to his father; a relationship in which a couple loves each other but have hurt each other too deeply to stay together; or Bono's rocky relationship with his own father. Whatever the meaning, the song reminds us that all humans are equal and that we need to help those less fortunate: "We're one, but we're not the same/We get to carry each other, carry each other." "One" topped U.S. charts and has been played at every U2 concert since its debut on the ZooTV tour in 1992.

18. "Numb" (1993)

U2 got even more experimental with the album *Zooropa*. "Numb," the first single from that album, reached number two on U.S. charts. Edge takes lead vocals on this song, speaking the lyrics in a monotone voice with backup vocals by Bono and Larry—a very rare occurrence for the drummer. Bono has said the lyrics symbolize information overload from the constant barrage of media coverage.

19. "Please" (1997)

"Please" appeared on *Pop*, the band's most experimental and dance-oriented album to date, which band members agree needed a few more weeks to really polish it. "Please" is a song about terrorism and the Troubles in Northern Ireland, but the song and its prophetic lyrics ("September, streets capsizing.../Shards of glass, splinters like rain...") took on new meaning following 9/11. In recordings from the Popmart tour, Bono pours out his heart and soul, crying out "please, please," almost desperate, begging. But then, just as your heart starts to break for him, you hear the ping of Larry's drumstick against the cymbal as "Streets" takes off. It's like a security blanket or the voice of an old friend, and with the reassuring sounds of an old favorite, fans know all will be okay.

20. "Beautiful Day" (2000)

With the release of *All That You Can't Leave Behind,* U2 once again reinvented themselves, ditching their dance-oriented experimental phase and returning to their roots, albeit with a harder, rock-based sound. "Beautiful Day," the first single from the multiplatinum, Grammy Award-winning album, is a reminder that no matter how bad life can get, we should always be thankful for what we have. The song went to number five in the States, and it secured three more Grammys for the Dublin lads—Song of the Year, Record of the Year, and Best Rock Performance.

21. "Stuck in a Moment You Can't Get Out Of" (2001)

"Stuck," the second single from *All That You Can't Leave Behind,* reached only number 35 on U.S. charts. Nevertheless, this in-your-face number earned the boys another Grammy for Best Pop Performance. Bono wrote the lyrics as a conversation he wishes he'd had with his friend Michael Hutchence to prevent the INXS singer from committing suicide in 1997.

22. "Elevation" (2001)

"Elevation," also from *All That You Can't Leave Behind,* climbed to number eight on U.S. charts and won the band a Grammy for Best Rock Performance. This crowd-pleaser is even better live, so it's not surprising that it appeared in every concert on the Elevation and Vertigo tours. With Adam's head-bobbing bass line, Edge's grinding chords, and Larry's powerful drumming, "Elevation" is a rockin' tune that makes fans (and Edge) jump up and down during live shows. Some feel the song is simply about passion and sexuality. Others feel there is a deeper meaning and that Bono is referring to his spirituality when he sings the tune.

23. "Walk On" (2001)

"Walk On" scored U2 another Grammy for Record of the Year. This song was supposedly inspired by Aung San Suu Kyi, a nonviolent Burmese political activist who has been under house arrest off and on since 1989. But many people feel the song is a tribute to someone nearing the end of his life (possibly Bono's father), who realizes that love is really the most important—and only—thing to take on this journey. ("You're packing a suitcase for a place none of us has been/A place that has to be believed to be seen. . . .") During the Elevation tour dates after 9/11, the band took NYC firefighters and police officers on tour with them and brought them onstage during this song, which adopted a special meaning after the terrorist attacks.

24. "Vertigo" (2004)

"Vertigo," was the first single from *How to Dismantle an Atomic Bomb,* which is harder and more upbeat than their previous efforts. No mixed messages with this U2 powerhouse—"Vertigo" is an adrenalized rocker about an evening at a nightclub. The song topped the charts in the States, garnered the band two more Grammys (Best Rock Performance and Best Rock Song), and was featured in a commercial for Apple's iPod. The fellas had so much fun performing the song that it was played at every concert of the Vertigo tour—sometimes twice!

25. "Sometimes You Can't Make It on Your Own" (2005)

U2 racked up two more Grammys for Song of the Year and Best Rock Performance with "Sometimes," which is a tribute to the somewhat distant relationship Bono had with his father, who passed away in 2001. The song reaches a climax when, from the depths of his soul, Bono cries out, "You're the reason I sing/You're the reason why the opera is in me . . . ," and fans are often moved to tears by his raw display of emotion.

26. "City of Blinding Lights" (2005)

U2 cleaned up at the 2005 Grammys, taking home five awards including Best Rock Song for "City" and Album of the Year and Best Rock Album for *How to Dismantle an Atomic Bomb.* Inspired by Bono's love for New York City and the band's love for their fans ("I miss you when you're not around"), this peppy, upbeat song quickly found a home as the opener on the Vertigo tour with Adam playing the opening notes on the keyboard.

27. "The Saints Are Coming" (2006)

U2 teamed up with Green Day for this cover of a 1970s punk rock song by The Skids. "Saints," one of two new songs on the compilation album *U2 18 Singles,* was recorded in the legendary Abbey Road studios in London where The Beatles recorded many of their albums. The song, which mentions New Orleans, storms, and flooding, took on new meaning when the two bands played it live the first time the New Orleans Saints returned to the Superdome following the devastation of Hurricane Katrina in 2005. This energetic and mighty rocker reached number one in Australia, Canada, and all over Europe, but didn't fare as well in the States due to lack of major airplay.

28. "Window in the Skies" (2006)

Another new song from *U2 18 Singles,* this cheerful, snappy tune was also recorded at Abbey Road studios and has a slight "Beatles" sound to it. Although it didn't fare well on U.S. charts due to lack of major airplay, it reached the top ten in many other parts of the world and became an instant fan favorite. Some argue that the lyrics are about romantic love, but most die-hard fans agree that this one is all about God's love and the grace, redemption, and forgiveness we receive by accepting his gift.

17 Famous Bands and Their Former Names

✳ ✳ ✳ ✳

Most famous bands had other names before they made it big.
See if you can match the former names to these famous bands.

1. Cheap Trick	a. Angel and the Snake
2. U2	b. Atomic Mass
3. The Beatles	c. Tea Set
4. Styx	d. The Detours, The High Numbers
5. Queen	
6. Led Zeppelin	e. Tom and Jerry
7. The Beach Boys	f. Feedback, The Hype
8. Green Day	g. Golden Gate Rhythm Section
9. KISS	h. Smile
10. The Who	i. Unique Attraction
11. Def Leppard	j. Fuse
12. Pink Floyd	k. The Tradewinds
13. Boyz II Men	l. Sweet Children
14. Blondie	m. Mookie Blaylock
15. Simon and Garfunkel	n. The New Yardbirds
16. Journey	o. Wicked Lester
17. Pearl Jam	p. The Pendletones
	q. The Quarrymen, Johnny and the Moondogs

Answers: 1. j; 2. f; 3. q; 4. k; 5. h; 6. n; 7. p; 8. l; 9. o; 10. d; 11. b; 12. c; 13. i; 14. a; 15. e; 16. g; 17. m

9 Fictional Bands and Their Hits

✳ ✳ ✳ ✳

Reaching the top ten or even the top 40 on the music charts is something that most bands can only dream of achieving after years of hard work. But the bands on this list didn't have to agonize over that because they weren't real bands in the first place. Check out these fictional hit makers, but be prepared to get at least one song stuck in your head.

1. The Archies

Stars of the comic strip *Archie* and the Saturday morning cartoon *The Archie Show,* The Archies were a garage band founded in 1968. Band members included Archie, Reggie, Jughead, Betty, and Veronica. Producer Don Kirshner gathered a group of studio musicians to perform the group's songs, the most popular being "Sugar, Sugar," which topped the pop charts in 1969 and was named *Billboard* magazine's song of the year, the only time a fictional band has ever claimed that honor. The Archies also reached the top 40 with "Who's Your Baby?," "Bang-Shang-A-Lang," and "Jingle Jangle."

2. The Blues Brothers

In April 1978, *Saturday Night Live* cast members John Belushi and Dan Aykroyd appeared on the show as The Blues Brothers. Dressed in black suits, fedoras, and sunglasses, Belushi sang lead vocals as "Joliet" Jake Blues while Aykroyd portrayed Elwood Blues, singing backup and playing harmonica. Their first album, *Briefcase Full of Blues,* went double platinum and reached number one on *Billboard*'s album chart. The record produced two top 40 hits with covers of Sam and Dave's "Soul Man" and The Chips' "Rubber Biscuit." The Blues Brothers went on tour, even opening for The Grateful Dead in December 1978, and in 1980, Belushi and Aykroyd starred in *The Blues Brothers,* a feature film that chronicled the life of the fictional duo. John Belushi died in 1982, but The Blues Brothers live on with Jim Belushi (John's brother), John Goodman, and other guests stepping in to fill his shoes.

3. The Chipmunks

The Chipmunks, a fictitious music group created by Ross Bagdasarian in 1958, consisted of three singing chipmunks: Alvin, the troublemaking frontman; Simon, the intellectual; and Theodore, the sweetheart. The trio was managed by their human "father," Dave Seville. In reality, Dave Seville was the stage name of Bagdasarian, who electronically sped up his own voice to create the higher-pitched squeaky voices of the chipmunks. This process was so new and innovative that it earned a Grammy for engineering in 1959. The Chipmunks released a number of albums and singles, with "The Chipmunk Song (Christmas Don't Be Late)" spending four weeks atop the charts in the late 1950s. They have also starred in their own cartoon series and feature films over the years.

4. Gorillaz

Guinness World Records named Gorillaz the most successful virtual band after its 2001 self-titled debut album sold more than six million copies. Created in 1999 by Damon Albarn and Jamie Hewlett, this alternative rock band is made up of four animated characters: 2D, Murdoc, Noodle, and Russel. The band's second album, *Demon Days,* received five Grammy nominations in 2006, including a victory for Best Pop Collaboration with Vocals.

5. The Heights

The Heights, a TV show about a rock 'n' roll band of the same name, aired for only one season in 1992. By day, the characters worked blue-collar jobs, but at night they were The Heights. The series depicted the struggles of the band, as well as the romances among the characters, and a new song was performed each week. The show's theme song, "How Do You Talk to an Angel," which featured actor Jamie Walters on lead vocals, topped the charts in mid-November. Ironically, the show was canceled a week later.

6. The Kids from The Brady Bunch

Marcia, Marcia, Marcia . . . is that you singing? The music group known as The Kids from The Brady Bunch was made up of—who else—the young cast members from the mega-popular sitcom that originally aired from 1969 to 1974. During the show's run, the cast recorded several albums, including *Christmas With the Brady Bunch* and *Meet the Brady Bunch.* None of the songs topped the charts, but some fan favorites include, "Sunshine Day," "Time to Change," and "Keep On." All of the kids sang on the albums, and Barry Williams (Greg) and Maureen McCormick (Marcia) both pursued careers in music after the show ended.

7. The Monkees

Hey, hey…were the Monkees a real band or a fake? In 1965, auditions were held for "folk & roll musicians" to play band members on a new TV show called *The Monkees.* Actors Davy Jones and Micky Dolenz, and musicians Mike Nesmith and Peter Tork were chosen as The Monkees. The show won two Emmy Awards in 1967, and the band was so successful that they went on tour—with the Jimi Hendrix Experience as their opening act! The Monkees reached the top of the charts three times with hits "I'm a Believer," "Last Train to Clarksville," and "Daydream Believer." Although the show was canceled in 1968, and the band officially broke up in 1970, they have continued to record and tour with some or all of the original members.

8. The Partridge Family

The Partridge Family, a popular television show that aired in the early 1970s, focused on Shirley Partridge (Shirley Jones) and her brood of five children, who suddenly find themselves with a hit song. The show chronicled the family's life on the road performing gigs, as well as their home life. To promote the show, producers released a series of albums by The Partridge Family. Although the music was originally created by studio musicians with Jones singing backup, David Cassidy, who played eldest son Keith, quickly convinced producers to let him sing lead vocals. The show and the band became overnight sensations, making Cassidy a teen idol. The group's most popular hits included the show's theme song "C'Mon, Get Happy," "I Woke Up in Love This Morning," and "I Think I Love You," which spent three weeks at number one in late 1970.

9. The Wonders

When your band's name is The Oneders (pronounced The Won-ders) and everybody calls you The Oh-nee-ders, it's time to change your name—even if you're just a fictional band. That's exactly what happened in the 1996 hit movie *That Thing You Do!*, written and directed by Tom Hanks. The film about a one-hit wonder band in the '60s starred Hanks, as well as Tom Everett Scott, Steve Zahn, and Liv Tyler. The band's hit song "That Thing You Do!" went as high as number 18 on *Billboard* charts and was nominated for an Oscar for Best Original Song. In addition, the sound track reached number 21 on *Billboard's* album chart.

The King's Top 30 Songs

✳ ✳ ✳ ✳

You don't become "The King of Rock 'n' Roll" without your share of number one songs. Here are 30 of Elvis Presley's chart-toppers.

1. "Heartbreak Hotel" (1956)

Released on January 27, 1956, this heart-wrenching tune was inspired by a suicide note printed in *The Miami Herald*. The tune didn't catch the public's attention until Elvis started appearing on television in the months following its release.

2. "Don't Be Cruel" (1956)

This was the first song that Elvis self-produced. And what a job he did! Not only did he rack up his second number one in three months, he also created a whole new style for himself—one charac-terized by a free, casual sound.

3. "Hound Dog" (1956)

This song was a blues classic long before anyone had heard of Elvis Presley. But it was the King's July 1956 TV appearances, in which he crooned to a real pup, that propelled it to the top of the pop charts. The machine-gun-like drumming of D. J. Fontana perfectly complemented Elvis's edgy vocals.

4. "Love Me Tender" (1956)

This song's tune came from a Civil War ballad called "Aura Lee." The lyrics were written for Elvis's first movie, also called *Love Me Tender*. The movie was forgettable—the song was anything but!

5. "Too Much" (1957)

Released on January 4, 1957, "Too Much" brought to the forefront the talents of Elvis's supporting players, especially guitarist Scotty Moore. And, of course, the King sounds great, too!

6. "All Shook Up" (1957)

You can't help but dance to this great tune. Released in March 1957, it epitomizes the rock 'n' roll sound that energized teens all over the world. Listen for the sound of Elvis slapping his guitar.

7. "(Let Me Be Your) Teddy Bear" (1957)

Teddy bear sales went through the roof with this June 1957 hit. The song's popularity also helped get people into theaters to see Elvis's second movie, *Loving You*.

8. "Jailhouse Rock" (1957)

Jailhouse Rock marked Elvis's third foray into film and gave him another number one song. Even if the song hadn't been a hit, the movie's dance sequence alone would have made it memorable.

9. "Don't" (1958)

This ballad brilliantly conveyed the teen angst felt by many Elvis fans. Elvis put his heart and soul into the lyrics, connecting on a personal level with listeners, and it was one of his personal faves.

10. "Hard Headed Woman" (1958)

Released on June 10, 1958, this hit came out of the movie *King Creole*, which would be the last movie for Elvis until 1960, after his discharge from the army.

11. "One Night" (1958)

"One Night" was a hit for New Orleans blues musician Smiley Lewis just two years before Elvis covered it. The lyrics and overall sound were softened to appeal to a white teen audience.

12. "(Now and Then There's) A Fool Such as I" (1959)

Elvis liked this Hank Snow song so much that he covered it, adding his own special flavor. In fact, many people consider it their favorite Elvis tune.

13. "A Big Hunk o' Love" (1959)

This song came from the only recording session that Elvis made while in the army. That session was also his first without his original backing band.

14. "Stuck on You" (1960)

Fans wondering if a post-army Elvis still had it could rest assured with the release of this easy-listening track. Yet, this Elvis was definitely different—more mature and sophisticated.

15. "It's Now or Never" (1960)

Elvis's musical maturity is fully showcased in this ballad. Elvis had worked on developing his vocal range while in the army, and the operatic notes in this song demonstrate this new ability.

16. "Are You Lonesome Tonight?" (1960)

This old Al Jolson hit from 1927 just happened to be a favorite of the wife of Elvis's manager, Colonel Tom Parker. In fact, it was the only song that Parker specifically asked Elvis to sing.

17. "Surrender" (1961)

This hit was an adaptation of the Italian-Neapolitan ballad "Torna a Surriento," a hit song for Dean Martin, one of Elvis's inspirations.

18. "(Marie's the Name) His Latest Flame" (1961)

Released on August 8, 1961, this fun tune came from the writing team of Doc Pomus and Mort Shuman. The single was paired with "Little Sister," its mirror opposite in terms of style and mood.

19. "Can't Help Falling in Love" (1961)

This much-loved tune, which appeared in the movie *Blue Hawaii*, was actually based on an 18th-century French ballad. In the 1970s, Elvis often used the song as the closing number for his shows, including his final concert in June 1977.

20. "Good Luck Charm" (1962)

A lightweight, feel-good song that struck a chord, this tune epitomized the sound popular with teens of the early 1960s.

21. "She's Not You" (1962)

A beautiful ballad that Elvis sang with deep conviction, this song has the power to move and inspire.

22. "Return to Sender" (1962)

Not intended for a movie sound track, "Return to Sender" was so well received following its October 2, 1962, release that it soon found its way into *Girls! Girls! Girls!* Elvis sings with great intensity and enthusiasm, making for a very catchy three minutes.

23. "(You're the) Devil in Disguise" (1963)

After venturing into lightweight pop tunes, Elvis returned to his rock 'n' roll roots with this one—giving an intense, emotional performance.

24. "Wooden Heart" (1964)

Directly inspired by Elvis's army stint in Germany, this tune was adapted from a German children's song and was featured in the king's first post-army movie, *G.I. Blues.*

25. "Crying in the Chapel" (1965)

Elvis was passionate about singing gospel, and in 1960, he got the chance to record an entire gospel album. "Crying in the Chapel" was recorded during that session but would not be released for another five years. A huge hit, it was definitely worth the wait.

26. "In the Ghetto" (1969)

After a four-year drought without a number one hit, Elvis was back with "In the Ghetto," his most socially responsible song. The haunting lyrics come together with Elvis's passionate expression to create an experience that will move the coldest of hearts.

27. "Suspicious Minds" (1969)

Released on August 26, 1969, this song has a similar feel to "In the Ghetto," which was recorded during the same session in Memphis. Both songs highlighted the now well-established maturity and emotional control that Elvis brought to his work.

28. "The Wonder of You" (1970)

By April 1970, Elvis was performing in Las Vegas, and "The Wonder of You" was the first hit to emerge from that phase of his career. After 14 years of number ones, he continued to push his vocal range, revealing new facets of his amazing gift.

29. "Burning Love" (1972)

"Burning Love" emerged during a very difficult period in Elvis's life. He lacked motivation, and his producer had to work hard to get him to record this song. When he did record, he put the full measure of his angst into his music.

30. "Way Down" (1977)

Just a few months before he died, Elvis dragged himself into the studio for what would prove to be his final recording session. When the King died, this song was climbing the charts. His tragic death undoubtedly gave it a boost.

11 Classic One-Hit Wonders

�֎ �֎ �֎ ✖

Who knows why an artist scores a hit once but never again. In some cases, the hit makers weren't even recording artists in the first place. Chances are you've heard these tunes, so sing along as we remember these 11 one-hit wonders. *

1. "99 Luft Ballons" by Nena (1984)

This protest song by German artist Nena came along toward the end of the Cold War. Although versions in both German and English ("99 Red Balloons") were released in the States, the German version proved more popular, floating all the way to number two. However, Nena could not duplicate the song's success and has not had a hit single outside of Europe since.

2. "Disco Duck" by Rick Dees (1976)

"Disco Duck," a satirical disco song by deejay Rick Dees, went all the way to number one in 1976. Dees may be a one-hit wonder as a recording artist, but other musical artists hope to gain his attention; he is known around the world for his Weekly Top 40 Countdown radio show. He was inducted into the Radio Hall of Fame in 1999 and even earned a star on Hollywood's Walk of Fame.

3. "Don't Give Up on Us Baby" by David Soul (1976)

In 1976, right in the middle of his hit TV show *Starsky & Hutch*, David Soul, aka "Hutch," traded his tough guy image for that of a sweet-voiced ballad singer and it paid off. "Don't Give Up on Us Baby" shot all the way to number one on U.S. charts. Afterward, Soul released several more albums that were much more popular in the UK than they were in the States. Today, Soul lives in England and works in theater.

4. "Don't Worry, Be Happy" by Bobby McFerrin (1988)

This upbeat song was featured in the Tom Cruise movie *Cocktail*. The song stayed at number one for two weeks, making it the first a cappella song to top the *Billboard* Hot 100 chart. McFerrin continues to enjoy a successful career as a jazz musician and "Don't Worry, Be Happy" lives on in television and movies.

5. "Funkytown" by Lipps, Inc. (1980)

In 1980, a Minneapolis band named to poke fun at the concept of lip-synching spent four weeks at number one with their hit tune "Funkytown." The group had disbanded by 1983, but a few of the group's members lent their experience to Minneapolis's next big thing—Prince's band, The Revolution.

6. "Harper Valley P.T.A." by Jeannie C. Riley (1968)

Better known as a country singer, Jeannie C. Riley became an overnight sensation with "Harper Valley P.T.A.," which topped both the pop and country charts. The song even spawned a variety show hosted by Riley in 1969, as well as a movie (1978) and television show (1981), both starring Barbara Eden.

7. "I'm Too Sexy" by Right Said Fred (1992)

British brothers Fred and Richard Fairbrass and their friend Rob Manzoli wrote this "corker" of a song over a pot of tea. Without the help of a record company, they got the song played on top radio stations, and it became a hit in 30 countries, going all the way to number one in the United States. The group may be off the radar in the States, but they are still releasing albums and touring in Europe.

8. "Macarena" by Los del Rio (1996)

In 1996, Spanish group Los del Rio occupied the top of the U.S. charts for 14 weeks with their catchy tune "Macarena," which had sold 11 million copies by 1997. The song even had its own dance, sparking a trend amongst the line-dancing set. VH1 ranks this song number one on their list of 100 Greatest One-Hit Wonders.

9. "Mickey" by Toni Basil (1982)

Singer/choreographer Toni Basil took this song all the way to number one on U.S. charts and number two in the UK. With its snappy beat, catchy tune, and peppy video, this '80s classic has become a favorite with cheerleaders.

10. "She's Like the Wind" by Patrick Swayze (1988)

Originally written for another movie, "She's Like the Wind" reached number three on *Billboard*'s Hot 100 after appearing in the blockbuster movie *Dirty Dancing* (starring Swayze and Jennifer Grey). The movie's sound track sold 11 million copies and remained on top of the charts for 18 weeks.

11. "Spirit in the Sky" by Norman Greenbaum (1969)

Former Boston University coffeehouse musician Norman Greenbaum hit the top of the charts with "Spirit in the Sky." The record, which sold two million copies, soared to number three in the States and all the way to number one in the UK.

°Artists deemed one-hit wonders in the United States based on song positions on Billboard *magazine's Hot 100 chart.*

25 All-Time Best-Selling Albums

✳ ✳ ✳ ✳

Title	Artist
1. *Eagles/Their Greatest Hits 1971–1975*	Eagles
2. *Thriller*	Michael Jackson
3. *Led Zeppelin IV*	Led Zeppelin
4. *The Wall*	Pink Floyd
5. *Back in Black*	AC/DC
6. *Greatest Hits Volume I & Volume II*	Billy Joel
7. *Double Live*	Garth Brooks
8. *Come on Over*	Shania Twain
9. *The Beatles*	The Beatles
10. *Rumours*	Fleetwood Mac
11. *Boston*	Boston
12. *The Bodyguard* (sound track)	Whitney Houston/ Various Artists
13. *The Beatles 1967–1970*	The Beatles
14. *No Fences*	Garth Brooks
15. *Hotel California*	Eagles
16. *Cracked Rear View*	Hootie & The Blowfish
17. *Greatest Hits*	Elton John
18. *Physical Graffiti*	Led Zeppelin
19. *Jagged Little Pill*	Alanis Morissette
20. *The Beatles 1962–1966*	The Beatles
21. *Saturday Night Fever* (sound track)	Bee Gees/Various Artists
22. *Appetite for Destruction*	Guns N' Roses
23. *Dark Side of the Moon*	Pink Floyd
24. *Supernatural*	Santana
25. *Born in the U.S.A.*	Bruce Springsteen

Source: Recording Industry Association of America

24 of Madonna's Most Popular Songs

❋ ❋ ❋ ❋

This fiery, petite Italian-American was born in 1958 in Bay City, Michigan. From the start, Madonna Louise Veronica Ciccone had big dreams, and at 19, she moved to New York City where she began to make a name for herself as a singer and dancer. In a career that has spanned more than two decades, "Madge" has sold more than 200 million albums and has stayed on top by constantly reinventing herself. Though many disagree with some of her artistic choices, the numbers don't lie: Madonna's 2006 Confessions tour was the most successful concert tour by a female artist in history. Here are 24 of the biggest hits that put her on top.

1. "Holiday" (1983)
From her self-titled debut album, "Holiday" was the first of Madonna's songs to make *Billboard*'s Hot 100, peaking at number 16. It is now one of her signature songs.

2. "Borderline" (1984)
Madge's second single broke the top ten on U.S. charts, which was impressive for a newcomer. In this video, look for a very young John Leguizamo, who plays a friend of Madonna's boyfriend.

3. "Like a Virgin" (1984)
This song was Madonna's first number one on U.S. charts, perhaps due to her legendary appearance at the first ever MTV Video Music Awards. Rolling around in a wedding dress, Madonna sang this song and cemented a mutually beneficial relationship with music videos.

4. "Material Girl" (1985)
This song, which earned Madonna the moniker "the Material Girl," painted the singer as a girl who would rather have a rich boyfriend than a love-struck one, although it was meant to parody the commercialism and greed of the '80s. "Material Girl," the second single from Madonna's *Like a Virgin* album, reached number two on U.S.

charts, with the video imitating Marilyn Monroe's famous musical number "Diamonds Are a Girl's Best Friend."

5. "Crazy for You" (1985)

From the sound track of the film *Vision Quest*, "Crazy for You" was Madonna's second number one song. Madonna makes a cameo in the movie, belting out this tune in a nightclub scene.

6. "Live to Tell" (1986)

Written and produced by Madonna and longtime collaborator Patrick Leonard, "Live to Tell" is the story of a woman facing a difficult decision. The song was written for the movie *At Close Range*, starring Sean Penn, Madonna's husband at the time. With this number one ballad, Madonna emerged as more mature, abandoning the street urchin look for that of a grown-up.

7. "Papa Don't Preach" (1986)

Another more serious ballad, the song tells the story of a pregnant teen who decides to keep her baby. You'd think such a heavy topic wouldn't fly as a pop song, but this was another number one for Madonna in the summer of '86. Groups that had once condemned Madge now commended her for the song's antiabortion theme, although some were concerned that it glorified teen pregnancy.

8. "Open Your Heart" (1986)

In classic Madonna style, "Open Your Heart" was buoyed by a risqué video. In it, Madonna plays an exotic dancer who performs for a room that includes an underage boy. Plenty of people were outraged, but the song was another number one hit.

9. "Who's That Girl" (1987)

Nominated for a Grammy, "Who's That Girl" sped to number one in the summer of '87 when it appeared in the movie of the same name, which starred Madonna. The movie didn't do so well, but the sound track went platinum. Other artists are included on the sound track, but this song and another Madonna hit, "Causing a Commotion," were the reasons most people picked it up.

10. "Like a Prayer" (1989)

"Like a Prayer," with its dramatic lyrics and gospel choir backup, is undoubtedly one of Madonna's biggest hits of all time. But with burning crosses and Madonna making out with a black saint, the video was just a tad controversial. Pepsi had signed a deal to use the song for a soda commercial, but they backed out when they saw the scandalous video. Still, the song topped the charts in every major music market in the world, and the video won an MTV Viewers Choice Award, sponsored by—you guessed it—Pepsi!

11. "Express Yourself" (1989)

A call to women everywhere to stick up for what they want, "Express Yourself" was a top-five hit around the world, peaking at number two in the States. The notorious conical bra made its debut in the video. Designed by Jean-Paul Gautier, the pink corset with the pointy cups was worn under a black suit in the video and throughout Madonna's Blonde Ambition Tour as well.

12. "Cherish" (1989)

The third hit single off the *Like a Prayer* juggernaut, "Cherish" is a song that finds Madonna in an innocent frame of mind, singing about the joys of true love. The song reached number two in the States, her seventeenth single to reach the top ten on U.S. charts.

13. "Vogue" (1990)

There have been a few megahit dance crazes in American pop music history: The Twist, The Macarena, and Vogue to name a few. This song, from the *Dick Tracy: I'm Breathless* sound track, featured instructions on "vogue" dancing, an expressive style of dance popular in the underground gay clubs of New York City. Leave it to Madonna to make it a number one song.

14. "Justify My Love" (1990)

Madonna teamed up with songwriters Ingrid Chavez and Lenny Kravitz to pen this steamy song, which became her ninth number one in the States. The video was so racy, MTV banned it! As a result, the "Justify My Love" video was the first video single ever released, and it immediately sold out in stores everywhere.

15. "This Used to Be My Playground" (1992)

Madonna's tenth single to reach number one, this ballad was featured in the movie *A League of Their Own*. Madonna's performance in the movie was also well received by critics. The song wasn't included on the sound track, but it appeared on Madonna's ballad compilation, *Something to Remember*, released in 1995.

16. "Take a Bow" (1994)

Following the release of her controversial, best-selling book *Sex* (1992), Madonna experienced sagging chart positions. But "Take a Bow" changed all that. This ballad was a record breaker for Madonna, spending seven weeks at number one on U.S. charts.

17. "Frozen" (1998)

This single, which featured dark themes, eastern instruments, and techno beats, was a huge hit for the recently reinvented Madonna. "Frozen" reached number one or two in most major music markets, foretelling the enormous success of *Ray of Light*, the album on which it was featured.

18. "Ray of Light" (1998)

This techo-infused dance hit broke a record for Madonna, selling 73,000 singles in the first week of its release. The second track from her Grammy Award-winning album of the same name, "Ray of Light" was a massive club hit that received major remix attention from the most in-demand deejays. The single reached the top ten on charts the world over, peaking at number five in the States.

19. "Beautiful Stranger" (1999)

Another song-from-a-movie hit for Madonna, this bouncy tune was penned by Madonna and *Ray of Light* album coproducer William Orbit for *Austin Powers: The Spy Who Shagged Me*. The song reached number 19 in the United States—even though it was never officially released—and it garnered the singer another Grammy.

20. "American Pie" (2000)

Don McLean's classic tune got the Madonna treatment for inclusion in the movie *The Next Best Thing*. The movie flopped, but the song did well—reaching number one in the UK, Canada, and Australia, among others. Oddly enough, although the song wasn't released in the States, it reached number 29 off airplay alone.

21. "Music" (2000)

"Music," Madonna's twelfth single to top U.S. charts was in the running for a Grammy for Record of the Year, but lost to "Beautiful Day" by U2. The video featured Madonna (five months pregnant at the time) and comedy star Sacha Baron Cohen.

22. "Don't Tell Me" (2000)

When "Don't Tell Me" went gold, Madonna tied The Beatles for second place for the most gold, platinum, or multiplatinum singles—a total of 24—trailing Elvis, who's way ahead of the pack with a whopping 52. "Don't Tell Me" made it to number four on U.S. charts, and the video shows Madge hanging out with cowboys and riding a mechanical bull. Yee-haw!

23. "American Life" (2003)

The first single off her highly criticized album of the same name, "American Life" lambasted the materialistic culture of America and the lack of satisfaction in the face of so much abundance. But Americans weren't ready for a political statement from the woman who used to sing about the joys of sex. This single reached the top ten (and often the number one spot) in much of Europe, as well as Canada and Japan, but only made it to number 37 on U.S. charts.

24. "Hung Up" (2006)

The first single off her album *Confessions on a Dance Floor,* "Hung Up" included an infectious sample from superstar dance group ABBA. A disco-fied Madonna emerged in this dance hit, signaling the return of the megastar after lukewarm album sales for *American Life.* "Hung Up" topped the charts in an unprecedented 41 countries but peaked at number seven in the States.

Chapter 6

AROUND THE WORLD

＊ ＊ ＊ ＊

THE WEIRD WIDE WORLD OF SPORTS
9 Silly Sporting Events

When it comes to sports, if it involves a ball or a club, men will play it, and if it's on TV, men will watch it. Here are some of the most unusual sports from around the world.

1. Cheese Rolling

If you're a whiz at cheese rolling, you may want to head to Brockworth in Gloucestershire, England, for the annual Cooper's Hill Cheese Roll held each May. The ancient festival dates back hundreds of years and involves pushing and shoving a large, mellow, seven- to eight-pound wheel of ripe Gloucestershire cheese downhill in a race to the bottom. With the wheels of cheese reaching up to 70 miles per hour, runners chase, tumble, and slide down the hill after their cheese but don't usually catch up until the end. Winners take home the cheese, while the runners-up get cash prizes.

2. Man Versus Horse Marathon

The Man Versus Horse Marathon is an annual race between humans and horse-and-rider teams held in early June in the Welsh town of Llanwrtyd Wells. The event started in 1980 when a pub keeper overheard two men debating which was faster in a long race—man or horse. Slightly shorter than a traditional marathon, the 22-mile course is filled with many natural obstacles, and horses win nearly every year. But in 2004, Huw Lobb made history as the first runner to win the race (in 2 hours, 5 minutes, and 19 seconds), taking the £25,000 (about $47,500) prize, which was the accumulation of 25 yearly £1,000 prizes that had not been claimed. Apparently, when the horse wins, it doesn't get to keep its winnings.

3. Tomato Tossing

Tomatoes aren't just for salads and sauce anymore. La Tomatina is a festival held in late August in the small town of Buñol, Spain, where approximately 30,000 people come from all over the world to pelt one another with nearly 140 tons of overripe tomatoes.
The fruit fight dates back to the mid-1940s but was banned under Francisco Franco, then returned in the 1970s after his death. After two hours of tomato-tossing at La Tomatina, there are no winners or losers, only stains and sauce, and the cleanup begins.

4. Tuna Throwing

Popular in Australia, tuna throwing requires contestants to whirl a frozen tuna around their heads with a rope and then fling it like an Olympic hammer thrower. Since 1998, the record holder has been former Olympic hammer thrower Sean Carlin, with a tuna toss of 122 feet. With $7,000 in prize money overall, the event is part of Tunarama, an annual festival held in late January in Port Lincoln, South Australia. Animal rights activists will be pleased to know that the tuna have now been replaced with eco-friendly plastic replicas.

5. Toe Wrestling

This little piggy went to the World Toe Wrestling Championship held annually in July in Derbyshire, England. Contestants sit facing each other at a "toedium"—a stadium for toes—and try to push each other's bare foot off a small stand called a "toesrack." Three-time champion Paul Beech calls himself the "Toeminator." Toe wrestling began in the town of Wetton in 1970, and the international sport is governed by the World Toe Wrestling Organization, which once applied for Olympic status but was rejected.

6. Human Tower Building

If you enjoy watching cheerleaders form human pyramids, you'll love the castellers, people who compete to form giant human towers at festivals around Catalonia, Spain. Castellers form a solid foundation of packed bodies, linking arms and hands together in an intricate way that holds several tons and softens the fall in case the tower collapses, which is not uncommon. Up to eight more levels of people are built, each layer standing on the shoulders of the people below. The top levels are made up of children and when complete, the castell resembles a human Leaning Tower of Pisa.

7. Wife Carrying Championship

Held annually in Sonkajärvi, Finland, the Wife Carrying Championship requires contestants to carry a woman—it needn't be their wife—over an 832-foot course with various obstacles en route. Dropping the woman incurs a 15-second penalty, and the first team to reach the finish line receives the grand prize— the weight of the "wife" in beer! This bizarre event traces its origins to the 19th century when a local gang of bandits commonly stole women from neighboring villages.

8. Bull Running

While bullfighting is popular in many countries, the sport of bull running—which should really be called bull outrunning—is pretty much owned by Pamplona, Spain. The event began in the 13th and 14th centuries as a combination of festivals honoring St. Fermin and bullfighting. Every morning for a week in July, the half-mile race is on between six bulls and hundreds of people. Most of the participants try to get as close to the bulls as possible, and many think it's good luck to touch one.

9. Pooh Sticks

Christopher Robin knows that pooh sticks is not a hygiene problem but a game played by Winnie the Pooh. To play, one must find a stick, drop it into a river, then see how long it takes to get to the finish line. There is even an annual World Pooh Sticks Championship held in mid-March in Oxfordshire, England. Individual event winners receive gold, silver, and bronze medals, and a team event has attracted competitors from Japan, Latvia, and the Czech Republic.

✳ ✳ ✳

"Not every age is fit for childish sports."

—Titus Maccius Plautus, Ancient Roman playwright

7 Natural Wonders of the World

✳ ✳ ✳ ✳

Each of the following sites captures the imagination with its natural power and beauty. And they have one thing in common: Nothing made by humans can approach their majestic dignity.

1. Aurora Borealis (Northern Lights)

The aurora borealis (also called the northern lights) consists of awe-inspiring twirls of light in the sky, caused by "solar wind"—electrically charged particles interacting with Earth's magnetic field. The aurora borealis can be up to 2,000 miles wide, but it fluctuates in size, shape, and color, with green being the most common color close to the horizon while purples and reds appear higher. Named after Aurora, Roman goddess of dawn, and Boreas, Greek god of the north wind, these ribbons of color are best viewed in northern climates like Alaska, but have been seen as far south as Arizona.

2. Giant Sequoia Trees

Ancient giant sequoia trees are nature's ever-growing wonders, thriving naturally on the western slopes of California's Sierra Nevada Mountains at elevations from 5,000 to 7,000 feet. Some are as tall as a 26-story building, with their trunks spanning up to 100 feet and the bark on the older specimens reaching two to four feet thick. California's Sequoia National Park is home to several noteworthy giants, including the General Sherman, which is the world's largest tree by volume, measuring 274.9 feet high, almost 103 feet around, and comprising 52,508 cubic feet of wood. Giant sequoia trees are estimated to be between 1,800 and 2,700 years old. Depending on the tree and where it is situated, giant sequoias can grow up to two feet in height every year, producing almost 40 cubic feet of additional wood each year.

3. Grand Canyon

The Grand Canyon in northwestern Arizona was formed by erosion and the Colorado River and its tributaries as they scoured away billion-year-old rocks. Although known to Native Americans for thousands of years, the vast gorge was not discovered by the first Spanish explorers until 1540. Grand Canyon National Park was established in 1919 to preserve the 1.2 million-plus acres of colorful cliffs and waterways that are home to 75 species of mammals, 50 species of reptiles and amphibians, 25 species of fish, and more than 300 species of birds. The canyon stretches 277 miles, with some sections reaching a mile deep and 18 miles across. More than five million visitors view the canyon annually, often hiking or riding mules down to the canyon floor, while the more adventurous opt for boating or rafting the Colorado River through the canyon.

4. Great Barrier Reef

The Great Barrier Reef blankets 137,600 square miles and extends a dramatic 1,242 miles along Australia's northeastern coast, making it the largest group of reefs in the world. The reef began forming more than 30 million years ago and is made up of the skeletons of marine polyps. Four hundred species of living polyps can also be found there, along with 1,500 species of fish, as well as crabs, clams, and other sea life. The area is an Australian national park and is visited by two million tourists a year.

5. Mount Everest

Mount Everest, part of the Himalayan Mountains located between Nepal and Tibet, was formed about 60 million years ago due to the shifting of Earth's rocky plates. Named after Sir George Everest, a British surveyor-general of India, Everest is the highest mountain on Earth, looming some 29,035 feet high and growing a few millimeters every year. Climbing Everest isn't easy, due to avalanches, strong winds, and thin air. Nevertheless, in 1953, Edmund Hillary and Sherpa Tenzing Norgay were the first climbers to reach the peak. More than 700 others have done so since, with at least 150 persons dying on their quest.

6. Paricutin

Paricutin provides one of nature's best lessons in how volatile Earth is. Exploding out of a Mexican cornfield in 1943, Paricutin was the first known volcano to have witnesses at its birth. Within a year, the cone had grown to more than 1,100 feet high. The flow eventually spread over 10 square miles, engulfing the nearby towns of Paricutin and San Juan Parangaricutiro. The eruptions ceased in 1952, and the cone now soars 1,345 feet high.

7. Victoria Falls

Victoria Falls, originally called Mosi-oa-Tunya ("smoke that thunders"), was named after Queen Victoria of England in 1855. The raging waters of the Zambezi River pour 142 trillion gallons of water per minute into a gorge that is 1.25 miles wide and 328 feet deep, making this the largest curtain of falling water in the world. Located between Zambia and Zimbabwe, Victoria Falls is flanked by national parks and is now one of the world's greatest tourist attractions, with resorts, hiking trails, and observation posts springing up around it. White-water rafting at the foot of the falls makes for a thrilling adventure.

6 Kooky American Museums

1. The World's Largest Collection of the World's Smallest Versions of the World's Largest Things, Various Locations

Artist Erika Nelson is the owner of this mobile attraction. She drives a van around the country visiting the world's largest roadside attractions—ball of twine, kachina doll, statues of Paul Bunyan and Babe—adding data to her archive of information. Then, she crafts and displays miniature renderings of the world's largest things.

2. Sing Sing Prison Museum, Ossining, New York

The 2,000-plus inmates that call Sing Sing Prison home may not think it's worth celebrating, but a museum down the street does just that. The Sing Sing Prison Museum houses a variety of artifacts from the town of Ossining and Sing Sing itself. A re-creation of two cell blocks and a replica electric chair are among the highlights, along with a display of confiscated makeshift prison weapons.

3. National Museum of Health and Medicine, Washington, D.C.

For those interested in the effects of injuries and disease on the human body, this is one you won't want to miss. The National Museum of Health and Medicine was established in 1862 to research and document the effects of war wounds and diseases on the human body. Exhibits include more than 5,000 skeletons, 10,000 preserved organs, and 12,000 historical objects, such as the bullet that killed Abraham Lincoln and bone fragments and hair from his skull. Visitors can compare a smoker's lung to a coal miner's lung, touch the inside of a stomach, and view kidney stones and a brain still attached to the spinal cord.

4. Lizzie Borden Museum, Fall River, Massachusetts

The Fall River Historical Society has a collection of all things related to Lizzie's infamous slaying of her parents—gruesome crime scene photos, bloodstained linen and clothing, and a hatchet purported to be the murder weapon itself. If that's not enough, tourists can spend the night at the scene of the crime when they stay at the Lizzie Borden Bed and Breakfast, which has been faithfully restored to its appearance at the time of the murders.

5. Liberace Museum and Foundation, Las Vegas, Nevada

The Liberace Museum houses Liberace's world-famous collection of 18 rare and antique pianos, including a mirror-encrusted concert grand and a rhinestone-covered Baldwin grand. Also on display are the showman's bejeweled, sequined, and rhinestone-studded costumes; jewelry; and cars, including a rhinestone-laden roadster and a mirror-tiled Rolls-Royce. In addition, Liberace's lavish bedroom from his Palms Springs estate is re-created in all its glittering splendor. The Liberace Foundation, located in the museum, offers scholarships to talented students pursuing careers in the arts.

6. Circus World Museum, Baraboo, Wisconsin

This national historic landmark is located on the banks of the Baraboo River where the Ringling Bros. Circus spent the winter months from 1884 to 1918. Circus World Museum is a not-for-profit educational facility that includes a museum, library, and research center to showcase the historic role of the circus in American life. Other exhibits include a miniature circus, a clown exhibit, and the world's largest collection of antique circus wagons. Live circus performances take place from May through September.

YOU'RE FROM *WHERE*?
23 Silly City Names in North America

✳ ✳ ✳ ✳

1. Bird-in-Hand, Pennsylvania
2. What Cheer, Iowa
3. Ding Dong, Texas
4. Elbow, Saskatchewan
5. Monkeys Eyebrow, Kentucky
6. Flin Flon, Manitoba
7. Goofy Ridge, Illinois
8. Hell, Michigan
9. Intercourse, Pennsylvania
10. Joe Batt's Arm, Newfoundland
11. Cut and Shoot, Texas
12. Jackass Flats, Nevada
13. Owl's Head, Maine
14. Peculiar, Missouri
15. Placentia, Newfoundland
16. Saint-Louis-du-Ha! Ha!, Quebec
17. Suck-Egg Hollow, Tennessee
18. Swastika, Ontario
19. Tightwad, Missouri
20. Toad Suck, Arkansas
21. Truth or Consequences, New Mexico
22. Wahoo, Nebraska
23. Paint Lick, Kentucky

Off-the-Beaten-Path Tourist Attractions

※ ※ ※ ※

*Jaunting around America and Canada can be a visual adventure.
But to truly experience the kitschy side, sometimes you need to
meander the back roads. That's where you'll find giant roadside
statues, fascinating collections, and these unusual attractions.*

1. Paul Bunyan Statues

There are enough Paul Bunyan statues around the continent to
delight any teller of tall tales. Representations of the big fella—
known for his ability to lay down more trees in a single swath of his
ax than any contemporary logging firm—can be found wherever
there have been logging camps. One of the most memorable statues
is located in Bangor, Maine, the lumberjack's alleged birthplace,
where a 31-foot-tall, 37,000-pound Paul shows off his ax and scythe.
Other statues, such as those in Klamath, California, and Demidji,
Minnesota, show Bunyan accompanied by his faithful companion,
Babe the blue ox.

2. Coral Castle

The Coral Castle was the brainchild of Edward Leedskalnin, who
was jilted by his fiancée the day before their wedding. Crushed by
the rejection, Leedskalnin moved from his home in Latvia and set
out to build a monument to his lost love. The result was the Coral
Castle in Homestead, Florida. Without any outside help or heavy
machinery, the distraught lover sculpted more than 1,100 tons of
coral into marvelous shapes. The entry gate alone is made of a single coral block weighing nine tons. The fact that Leedskalnin was
only five feet tall and weighed barely 100 pounds adds to the feat.

3. Jolly Green Giant Statue

Ho, ho, ho! The Jolly Green Giant remains the towering symbol of
the Green Giant food company, located in Blue Earth, Minnesota.
Since 1979, the 55-foot-tall statue, who sports a size 78 shoe, honors
one of the most recognized advertising icons of the 20th century.

4. Corn Palace

The city of Mitchell, South Dakota, proudly calls itself the "Corn Capital of the World," and it even has a palace in which to celebrate. The Mitchell Corn Palace, originally constructed in 1892, is now an auditorium with Russian-style turrets and towers and murals that local artists create each year out of corn and other South Dakota grains. After the annual fall harvest, pigeons and squirrels are allowed to devour the palace's murals until the next year when the process begins anew.

5. Albert, the World's Largest Bull

Located in Audubon, Iowa, Albert, the world's largest bull, stands 30 feet tall and weighs in at 45 tons... of concrete. Named after local banker Albert Kruse, the monster Hereford statue was built in the 1960s for Operation T-Bone Days, an event held each September to honor the days when local cattle would board trains to the Chicago stockyards. As an interesting side note, Albert's internal steel frame is made from dismantled Iowa windmills.

6. Lucy the Elephant

Looming 65 feet over the beach at Margate, New Jersey, Lucy the Elephant is the only example of "zoomorphic architecture" left in America. With staircases in her legs leading to rooms inside, the wide-eyed elephant was originally built in 1881 as a real-estate promotion. Over the years Lucy has served as a summer home, a tavern, and a hotel. Relocation in 1970 spared Lucy from demolition, and she received a loving face-lift and restoration in 2000.

7. Superman Statue

Metropolis, in far southern Illinois, has nothing to fear these days because Superman lives there. In 1972, the town decided to capitalize on its famous name and subsequently adopted the moniker, "Hometown of Superman." A seven-foot-tall statue was erected in 1986, only to be replaced in 1993 by a more impressive 15-foot-tall monument. In 2009, a statue of Lois Lane will be erected next to her hunky beau in Superman Square.

8. Crazy Horse Memorial

The Crazy Horse Memorial in Crazy Horse, South Dakota, is a labor of love that sculptor Korczak Ziolkowski began in 1948 to honor the great Native American leader. As Ziolkowski's life's work (until his passing in 1982), the sculpture is likely the most ambitious roadside project ever undertaken. Ziolkowski's family continues the project, but the statue remains very much a work in progress. The carving is a depiction of the legendary warrior on horseback and will measure 641 feet long by 563 feet high when completed.

9. World's Largest Ball of Twine

Determining the world's largest ball of twine can be difficult. But the hands-down winner in the solo winder category has to be the nearly 9-ton, 11-foot-tall hunk of string on display in Darwin, Minnesota. Francis Johnson spent four hours a day between 1950 and 1979 rolling the ball. To ensure uniform wrapping, he used a crane to hoist the ever-expanding ball as it grew.

Another ball in the running is the 1,300-mile-plus length of string originally rolled by Frank Stoeber of Cawker City, Kansas. From 1953 until his death in 1974, Stoeber diligently wound this twine ball. Every August, Cawker City hosts a festival during which anyone can add a bit of twine to the ball, so it now outweighs the one in Darwin, but it has had more than one person working on it.

10. House on the Rock

Resting atop Deer Shelter Rock, a 450-foot-tall stone formation near Spring Green, Wisconsin, the House on the Rock is one of the best-known architectural oddities in the United States. Built by eccentric artist Alex Jordan in the 1940s, the House on the Rock was his vacation home before being turned into a museum in 1961. Jordan sold the building in the early 1980s, but it continues to grow as a tourist attraction. With 14 unique and lavishly decorated rooms—including the Infinity Room, with 3,264 windows—and a surrounding complex that houses a miniature circus and the world's largest carousel, the House on the Rock is at once wacky, tacky, innovative, and elegant.

Chapter 7

RELIGION, FOLKLORE, AND THE PARANORMAL

* * * *

HEY THERE... WHAT'S YOUR SIGN?
Insight into the Signs of the Zodiac

The ancient Greek term zodiac *means "circle of little animals." The stargazing Greeks used the zodiac symbols to make sense of the connection between time, space, and humans. Astrologers swear we can all find insight into our personalities by studying the zodiac sign that corresponds to our birthday.*

1. Aries: The Ram (March 21–April 19)

Aries personalities are Minotaur-like, meaning that they are headstrong folks who seek excitement. They are often innovative, assertive, quick-tempered, and self-assured. Aries people, such as Russell Crowe, are also notoriously bad at finishing what they start.

2. Taurus: The Bull (April 20–May 20)

These folks are stubborn, cautious, conservative, dependable, materialistic, and persistent. But Tauruses are most noted for their determination. Case in point: Cher, who is on comeback number 4,628.

3. Gemini: The Twins (May 21–June 21)

Named after the twin brothers of Helen of Troy, Geminis can like something and its opposite at the same time. They are often flexible, lively, quick-witted conversationalists that embody the yin and the yang. Watch out for duplicity in a Gemini (a trait some would say business tycoon Donald Trump possesses), and enjoy the fruits of a Gemini's boundless curiosity (as with award-winning journalist Bill Moyers).

4. Cancer: The Crab (June 22–July 22)

 Cancers are emotional, sensitive, security-conscious, moody, maternal, and can be quite traditional. The word *cancer* literally means "the crab," and modern slang has produced the misconception that Cancers are grouchy. Famous Cancer the Dalai Lama proves that simply isn't true.

5. Leo: The Lion (July 23–August 22)

 The lion symbol has origins in Hebrew culture, but is also connected to the Greek god Apollo, who represented order and intellectual pursuits while serving as the leader of the Muses—the spirits that bring inspiration to artists. Leos are notoriously egocentric and love the limelight. They are also optimistic, honorable, dignified, confident, flamboyant, charismatic, competitive, and have strong leadership skills. All this *and* a desperate need for approval? Just ask Leos Madonna and Martha Stewart.

6. Virgo: The Virgin (August 23–September 22)

 Modesty is one of the main traits of a Virgo, as exhibited in Virgo Mother Teresa. That doesn't mean Virgos are prudish, however—considering that Pee Wee Herman was also born under this sign. Other traits Virgos possess include practicality, responsibility, discriminating taste, and a critical eye. Virgos are as loyal as Leos but can become obsessed with perfection.

7. Libra: The Scale (September 23–October 23)

 The judicial system adopted the Libra image of the scales to represent the balance of justice. This makes sense, considering Libras are idealistic peacemakers, diplomatic, poised, kind, courteous, and fair-minded. Unfortunately for the judicial system, the scales represent people who can be painfully indecisive. Famous level-headed Libras include Barbara Walters, Sting, and Jimmy Carter.

8. Scorpio: The Scorpion (October 24–November 21)

 These stingers are intense and powerful, courageous, resourceful, mysterious, and self-reliant. Aside from the scorpion, the phoenix is another symbol for this sign. Some believe that within one year before or after the death of a Scorpio, there will be a birth within the same family. Wonder if that was true when Scorpios Grace Kelly or Robert F. Kennedy died?

9. Sagittarius: The Centaur (November 22–December 21)

 The centaur is a character from Greek mythology that was half man, half horse. People born under this sign follow their big hearts but can become bulls in china shops if they're not careful. Famous Sag Jon Stewart is a good example of someone using their strong Sagittarius opinions to their advantage. These generally friendly people are often idealistic, optimistic, freedom-loving, casual, gregarious, enthusiastic, and philosophical. Woody Allen and Britney Spears are well-known Sagittarians.

10. Capricorn: The Goat (December 22–January 19)

 According to Greek mythology, Zeus was weaned on goat's milk and that was enough to include the animal in the pantheon of astrological signs. Capricorns are ambitious, self-disciplined, conservative, practical, persistent, and methodical. Famous Capricorn Mel Gibson has lost his footing a few times, but he's good at dusting himself off and starting again, a classic Capricorn maneuver.

11. Aquarius: The Water Bearer (January 20–February 18)

Symbolized by the water bearer—a young man or woman with water barrels hoisted over the shoulder, who brings together the community of humankind—these folks hold on to the concept of friendship stronger than anyone. Always individualistic, progressive, independent, and altruistic, they can sink into detachment. They seem to "march to the beat of a different drummer." Think of Oprah Winfrey, a textbook Aquarius, who is famous for her generous and independent nature.

12. Pisces: The Fish (February 19–March 20)

The symbol of two fish pointing in different directions tends to throw people off, making them think Pisces people can't make up their minds. On the contrary, this group is focused and choosy, going for the big time or the quiet time with little in between. Think Liza Minnelli blazing her public career path or Bobby Fischer (no pun intended) checkmating cloistered monks in Madagascar. These fishy folks are compassionate, artistic, dedicated, and can be more than a little reclusive.

14 Deities and Their Duties

�֍ �֍ �֍ �֍

Greek	Job Title	Roman
1. Zeus	Supreme god (King of the gods)	Jupiter
2. Hera	Goddess of marriage (Queen of the gods)	Juno
3. Apollo	God of beauty, poetry, music	Apollo
4. Hermes	Messenger of the gods	Mercury
5. Ares	God of war	Mars
6. Poseidon	God of the sea, earthquakes, and horses	Neptune
7. Aphrodite	Goddess of love and beauty	Venus
8. Dionysus	God of wine	Bacchus
9. Athena	Goddess of war and wisdom	Minerva
10. Artemis	Goddess of the hunt and moon	Diana
11. Demeter	Goddess of agriculture	Ceres
12. Hades	God of the dead and the underworld	Pluto
13. Hephaestus	God of fire and crafts	Vulcan
14. Hestia	Goddess of the hearth	Vesta

Legendary American Folk Heroes

❊ ❊ ❊ ❊

The American pioneers who crossed the country to settle the West and slogged through the muggy South all had to face formidable obstacles including famine, predators, and what must have been extended periods of sheer boredom. Without television and movies, entertainment in late 18th- and early 19th-century America was limited to stories and tales told around the fireside. You can't blame storytellers for embellishing to raise interest levels and inspire weary listeners. The following folk legends helped pioneers cope with uncertainty during hard times and inspired the blind ambition needed to explore the American frontier.

1. Pecos Bill

One of the most popular American folk heroes, Pecos Bill was lost while crossing the Pecos River with his parents. He was found by a pack of coyotes and lived among them until he met a cowboy and realized his true calling. No one was better at ranching than Pecos Bill because he had an uncanny ability to convince animals to work for him. Bill married a nice girl named Slue Foot Sue and lived a long life of ranching, herding, and singing by the campfire.

2. Davy Crockett

Born in 1796, Davy Crockett was nearly a legend without fictitious additions to his story, but they came nonetheless. By Crockett's own account, he killed a bear when he was only three years old. True? Maybe not, but Crockett swore it happened. More stories emerged of Crockett's rough and tough childhood with lots of bear, bully, and snake encounters that all ended with him as the victor—whether or not these stories are true is unclear. What is true is that Crockett represented Tennessee in Congress, but when he was defeated for reelection, he went off to explore Texas. His travels led him into battle at the Alamo, where he was shot and killed. Tales of Davy Crockett show him wearing a coonskin cap and carrying his rifle, which he lovingly called "Old Betsy."

3. Johnny Appleseed

If you dig too deep into the roots of American folk heroes, you might be disappointed—the man known as Johnny Appleseed wasn't a magical scatterer of apple seeds from sea to shining sea, he was just a regular guy named John Chapman who worked as a nurseryman in the late 1700s. While that's not as exciting as the legend, Chapman's real life was interesting enough—he owned land from Ohio to Indiana, worked as a Christian missionary, and helped make peace between Native Americans and white settlers.

4. Geronimo

Geronimo, an Apache leader from the Arizona area, was captured and forced onto a reservation by the U.S. Army in 1876. The persecuted Apache leader fled to Mexico, but after that, things get murky and exaggerated. The story goes that Geronimo's wrath toward the white man was so strong that he killed thousands over the years, using magical powers and ESP to seek them out. It's said that it took several thousand soldiers and scouts to track down the warrior. By the time Geronimo finally surrendered in 1886, his group consisted of only 16 warriors, 12 women, and 6 children. Geronimo and his people were shipped to Florida, then relocated to Alabama and Oklahoma where they were placed in prisons and reservations. Geronimo died a prisoner of war in 1909.

5. Old Stormalong

Though stories about Stormalong vary, most place him in Cape Cod as a big baby—a baby more than 18 feet tall! Stormalong, a gifted sailor, joined the crew of a ship. When the ship had an encounter with a kraken—a beast from Norse mythology—Stormalong fought back but didn't kill the sea giant. Eventually, he wound up back on the high seas in search of the kraken that had escaped him. The ship he used was said to have slammed into the coast of Panama, forming the Panama Canal. According to legend, the same boat supposedly got stuck in the English Channel, requiring the crew to slick it up with soap in order to get it out. The soap and the scraping action turned the White Cliffs of Dover white.

6. John Henry

Unlike most tall tales, the story of John Henry is somewhat based in fact. There probably really was a John Henry who was born a slave in the South in the mid-1800s. Legend has it that he was around six feet tall and weighed more than 200 pounds. In those days, that was big enough to guarantee you'd be given exceptionally tough work—like building railroads or tunnels. If Henry did exist, he likely worked on the Big Bend Tunnel that went through the mountains of West Virginia. Some stories say Henry challenged the tunnel-making machinery to a duel to see who could drive stakes and blast rock faster. Most stories claim that he won, but that he died from exhaustion after the contest. Others say he won and went on swingin' his hammer from coast to coast.

7. Mike Fink

Tales of Mike Fink originated in the 19th century and were based on a real man born near Pittsburgh around 1780. The real Fink sailed keelboats on the Ohio and Mississippi rivers and fought against various tribes of Native Americans. Fink was an exceptional marksman but was reportedly a rather hard-drinking and hard-living character. By many accounts it was Fink who started spreading tall tales about himself, including that he was "half-man, half-alligator" and totally impervious to pain, which may explain his low standing among more noble legends like Paul Bunyan and John Henry.

8. Paul Bunyan

America just wouldn't be as interesting geographically if it weren't for Paul Bunyan, whose story was adapted from French-Canadian lumber camp legends. Bunyan was reportedly delivered to Earth by five giant storks, since he was already dozens of feet tall as a baby. Wherever he went as he got older, he created major landmarks. His footprints created Minnesota's 10,000 lakes; his shovel created the Grand Canyon as it dragged behind him; his use of rocks to extinguish a campfire created Mount Hood. Statues of Bunyan and his blue ox, Babe, have been erected all across the country as a testament to America's love of a tall tale.

13 Mythical Creatures

✳ ✳ ✳ ✳

1. Basilisk .... a serpent, lizard, or dragon said to kill by breathing on or looking at its victims
2. Centaur .... half human, half horse
3. Cerberus .... a dog with many heads that guards the entrance to the underworld
4. Chimera .... part serpent, lion, and goat
5. Faun .... half man, half goat
6. Gorgons .... winged and snake-haired sisters
7. Griffin .... half eagle, half lion
8. Harpy .... a creature with the head of a woman and the body, wings, and claws of a bird
9. Hippocampus .... a creature with the tail of a dolphin and the head and forequarters of a horse
10. Pegasus .... a winged horse with the ability to fly
11. Siren .... half bird, half woman
12. Unicorn .... a horse with a horn
13. Wyvern .... a winged dragon with a serpent's tail

WHO YOU GONNA CALL?
5 Ghost-Busting Methods

✳ ✳ ✳ ✳

Something strange in your neighborhood? Something weird and it don't look good? Here's a do-it-yourself guide to ghost-busting. But please note: In the world of ghost-busting, there are no guarantees, so proceed at your own risk.

1. **Give it a good talking-to.** The first tactic is simply to ask your ghost, politely but firmly, to leave. If you think the ghost is hanging around the physical world because of fear of punishment in the spirit world, tell it that it will be treated with love and forgiveness. Try not to show anger (which may give a negative spirit more

power) or fear (since it's unlikely that a spirit will be able to harm you, especially in your own home).

2. **Clean and serene.** If tough talking doesn't work, the next step is a spiritual cleansing or "smudging." Open a window in each room of your home, then light a bundle of dry sage and walk around with it (have something handy to catch the ashes), allowing the smoke to circulate while you intone the words: "This sage is cleansing out all negative energies and spirits. All negative energies and spirits must leave now and not return." Do this until you sense that the negative energy has left the building (and before you set fire to the house), and then say, "In the name of God, this room is now cleansed."

3. **Bless this house.** If smudging doesn't do the trick, it may be time to call in the professionals. Ask a local priest or minister to come to your home and bless it. There is usually no charge for this service, but you might be expected to make a small donation to the church.

4. **The Exorcist.** Exorcism is usually carried out by clergy using prayers and religious items to invoke a supernatural power that will cast out the spirit. Roman Catholic exorcism involves a priest reciting prayers and invocations, often in Latin. The priest displays a crucifix and sprinkles holy water over the place, person, or object believed to be possessed. Exorcism has been sensationally depicted in movies but it's no laughing matter—in the past, people who would now be diagnosed as physically or mentally ill have undergone exorcism, sometimes dying in the process.

5. **What not to do.** Don't be tempted to use Ouija boards, tarot cards, or séances, as these may "open the door" to let in other unwanted spirits. Also be very leary of commercial ghost-busting services that offer to rid your home of a spirit in return for payment. They're likely to be charlatans, and you're unlikely to get your money back if their services don't work.

The 7 Deadly Sins

✳ ✳ ✳ ✳

1. Lust .... Excessive thoughts and actions of a carnal nature
2. Gluttony .... Wanting to consume more than one needs
3. Greed .... Excessive desire for material wealth or gain
4. Sloth .... Avoidance of physical and spiritual work
5. Wrath .... Uncontrolled feelings of hatred and rage
6. Envy .... Excessive desire for another's possessions or abilities
7. Pride .... Excessive belief in one's own abilities

Mysterious Disappearances in the Bermuda Triangle

✳ ✳ ✳ ✳

The Bermuda (or Devil's) Triangle, an infamous stretch of the Atlantic bordered by Florida, Bermuda, and Puerto Rico, has been the location of strange disappearances throughout history. The Coast Guard does not recognize the Bermuda Triangle or the supernatural explanations for the mysterious disappearances in its midst. There are some logical explanations for the missing vessels—hurricanes, undersea earthquakes, and magnetic fields that interfere with compasses and other positioning devices. But it's much more interesting to think they got sucked into another dimension, abducted by aliens, or simply vanished into thin air.

1. The *Spray*

Joshua Slocum, the first man to sail solo around the world, never should have been lost at sea. But in 1909, he and his vessel, the *Spray*, left Martha's Vineyard for Venezuela via the Caribbean Sea and were never heard from or seen again. His ship was solid, and Slocum was a pro, so perhaps the *Spray* was felled by a larger ship or taken down by pirates. No one knows for sure that Slocum disappeared within Triangle waters, but Bermuda buffs claim Slocum's story as part of the legacy of the Devil's Triangle.

2. USS *Cyclops*

As America battled during World War I, the *Cyclops,* commanded by Lt. G. W. Worley, stayed mostly on the East Coast of the United States until 1918 when it was sent to Brazil to refuel Allied ships. With 309 people onboard, the ship left Rio de Janeiro in February and reached Barbados in March, but was never heard from again. The Navy says in its official statement, "The disappearance of this ship has been one of the most baffling mysteries in the annals of the Navy, all attempts to locate her having proved unsuccessful. There were no enemy submarines in the western Atlantic at that time, and in December 1918 every effort was made to obtain from German sources information regarding the disappearance of the vessel."

3. Flight 19

On the afternoon of December 5, 1945, five Avenger torpedo bombers left Fort Lauderdale, Florida, with Lt. Charles Taylor in command of a crew of 13 student pilots. About 90 minutes into the flight, Taylor radioed the base to say that his compasses weren't working, but he figured he was somewhere over the Florida Keys. The lieutenant who received the signal told Taylor to fly north toward Miami, as long as he was sure he was actually over the Keys. Although he was an experienced pilot, Taylor got horribly turned around, and he and his crew ended up further and further out to sea. As night fell, radio signals worsened, until, finally, there was nothing at all from Flight 19. A U.S. Navy investigation ruled that Taylor's confusion caused the disaster, but his mother convinced them to change the official report to read that the planes went down for "causes unknown." The planes have never been recovered.

4. *Star Tiger*

The *Star Tiger,* commanded by Capt. B. W. McMillan, was flying from England to Bermuda in January 1948. On January 30, McMillan said he expected to arrive in Bermuda at 5:00 A.M., but neither he nor any of the 31 people onboard the *Star Tiger* were ever heard from again. When the Civil Air Ministry launched an investigation, they learned that the S.S. *Troubadour* had reported seeing a low-flying aircraft halfway between Bermuda and the entrance to Delaware Bay. If that aircraft was the *Star Tiger*, it was drastically off course. According to the Civil Air Ministry, the fate of the *Star Tiger* remains an unsolved mystery.

5. *Star Ariel*

A Tudor IV aircraft like the *Star Tiger* left Bermuda on January 17, 1949, with 7 crew members and 13 passengers en route to Jamaica. That morning, Capt. J. C. McPhee reported that the flight was going smoothly. Shortly afterward, he sent another more cryptic message stating that he was changing his frequency, and then nothing more was heard ever again. More than 60 aircraft and 13,000 men were deployed to look for the *Star Ariel,* but not even a hint of debris or wreckage was ever found. After the *Ariel* disappeared, Tudor IVs were no longer produced.

6. *Teignmouth Electron*

In addition to swallowing ships and planes, can the Bermuda Triangle make a man go mad, too? The *Sunday Times* Golden Globe Race of 1968, which required each contestant to sail his ship solo, left England on October 31. Donald Crowhurst was one of the entrants, but he never made it to the finish line. The *Teignmouth Electron* was found abandoned in the middle of the Bermuda Triangle in July 1969. Logbooks recovered from the ship reveal that Crowhurst was deceiving organizers about his position in the race and going a little nutty out in the big blue ocean. The last entry of his log was dated June 29—it is believed that Crowhurst jumped overboard and drowned himself in the Triangle.

7. Flight 201

This Cessna left Fort Lauderdale on March 31, 1984, en route for Bimini Island in the Bahamas, but it never made it. Not quite midway to its destination, the plane slowed its airspeed significantly but did not send a distress signal. Suddenly, the plane dropped from the air into the water, completely vanishing from the radar. A woman on Bimini Island swore she saw a plane plunge into the sea about a mile offshore, but no wreckage has ever been found.

Chapter 8
DEATH

✳ ✳ ✳ ✳

Strange and Unusual Ways to Die

Most of us strive to lead an interesting life, but some stake a place in history by dying in an unusual way. Some of the people on this list were just in the wrong place at the wrong time, while others met their ends at the hands of enemies who were particularly vindictive in their creativity. Either way, the cause of death on some of these death certificates could be listed as cruel irony.

1. **The tortoise in the air.** Those flying monkeys in *The Wizard of Oz* were scary enough to frighten even the toughest kid on the block, but did you ever think you'd have to worry about flying tortoises? Greek playwright Aeschylus probably didn't, but according to the story, he was killed when an eagle or a bearded vulture dropped a tortoise on his bald head after mistaking his noggin for a stone in an attempt to crack open the tortoise's shell.

2. **A terrible taste.** War is hell, but ancient wars were particularly brutal. After the Persians captured the Roman emperor Valerian during battle around A.D. 260, Persia's King Shapur I is said to have humiliated Valerian by using him as a footstool. But it only got worse for the Roman. After Valerian offered a king's ransom for his release, Shapur responded by forcing molten gold down his prisoner's throat, stuffing him with straw, and then putting him on display, where he stayed for a few hundred years.

3. **Too long in the tooth.** Sigurd I of Orkney was a successful soldier who conquered most of northern Scotland in the 9th century. Following a fever-pitched victory in A.D. 892 against Maelbrigte of Moray and his army, Sigurd decapitated Maelbrigte and stuck his opponent's head on his saddle as a trophy. As Sigurd rode with his

trophy head, his leg kept rubbing against his foe's choppers. The teeth opened a cut on Sigurd's leg that became infected and led to blood poisoning. Sigurd died shortly thereafter.

4. Deadly twist. Isadora Duncan was one of the most famous dancers of her time. Her fans marveled at her artistic spirit and expressive dance moves, and she is credited with creating modern dance. But it was another modern creation that prematurely ended her life. She was leaving an appearance on September 14, 1927, when her trademark long scarf got caught in the wheel axle of her new convertible. She died of strangulation and a broken neck at age 50.

5. So funny it hurts. The fatal guffaw struck Alex Mitchell, a 50-year-old English bricklayer on March 24, 1975, while he and his wife watched his favorite TV sitcom, *The Goodies*. Mitchell found a sketch called "Kung Fu Kapers" so hilarious that he laughed for 25 minutes straight, until his heart gave out and he died. Mitchell's wife sent the show a letter thanking the producers and performers for making her husband's last moments so enjoyable.

6. An unfair way to go. Mark Twain once said, "Golf is a good walk spoiled," and although many a duffer has spent a frustrating couple of hours on the links, few actually die as a result. In 1997, Irishman David Bailey was not so lucky. Bailey was retrieving an errant shot from a ditch when a frightened rat ran up his pant leg and urinated on him. The rat didn't bite or scratch the golfer, so even though his friends kept telling him to shower, Bailey didn't think much of the encounter and kept playing. His kidneys failed two weeks later, and he died. The cause was leptospirosis, a bacterial infection spread by rodents, dogs, or livestock that is usually mild but can cause meningitis, pneumonia, liver disease, or kidney disease.

7. Fantasy meets harsh reality. Many people who like playing video games or online computer games do so to escape the pressures of the real world for a bit. But when that escapism is taken too far, gamers can leave the real world altogether. That's what happened to South Korean Lee Seung Seop in August 2005. Lee had quit his job to spend more time playing Internet games. He set himself up at a local Internet café and played a game for nearly 50 hours straight, taking only brief breaks to go to the bathroom or nap. Exhaustion, dehydration, and heart failure caused Lee to collapse, and he died shortly thereafter at age 28.

CARVED IN STONE
11 Unforgettable Epitaphs

✳ ✳ ✳ ✳

They might be six feet under, but a good epitaph ensures they won't be forgotten. Here are some clever gravestone inscriptions.

1. **John Yeast:** "Here lies Johnny Yeast. Pardon me for not rising." History hasn't recorded the date or cause of John Yeast's death, or even his profession. We can only imagine that he was a baker.

2. **Hank Williams:** "I'll never get out of this world alive." The gravestone of the legendary country singer, who died of a heart attack in 1953 at age 29, is inscribed with several of his song titles, of which this is the most apt.

3. **Ludolph van Ceulen:** "3.14159265358979323846264338327950 288..." The life's work of van Ceúlen, who died from unknown causes in 1610 at age 70, was to calculate the value of the mathematical constant pi to 35 digits. He was so proud of this achievement that he asked that the number be engraved on his tombstone.

4. **Dee Dee Ramone:** "OK...I gotta go now." The bassist from the punk rock band The Ramones died of a drug overdose in 2002 at age 49. His epitaph is a reference to one of the group's hits, "Let's Go."

5. **Lester Moore:** "Here lies Lester Moore. Four slugs from a 44, no Les, no more." The date of birth of this Wells Fargo agent is not recorded, but the cause of his death, in 1880, couldn't be clearer.

6. Spike Milligan: "Dúirt mé leat go raibh mé breoite."
The Gaelic epitaph for this Irish comedian translates as, "I told you I was ill." Milligan, who died of liver failure in 2002 at age 83, was famous for his irreverent humor showcased on TV and in films such as *Monty Python's Life of Brian*.

7. Jack Lemmon: "Jack Lemmon in…"
The star of *Some Like It Hot, The Odd Couple,* and *Grumpy Old Men* died of bladder cancer in 2001 at age 76.

8. George Johnson: "Here lies George Johnson, hanged by mistake 1882. He was right, we was wrong, but we strung him up and now he's gone."
Johnson bought a stolen horse in good faith but the court didn't buy his story and sentenced him to hang. His final resting place is Boot Hill Cemetery, which is also "home" to many notorious characters of the Wild West, including Billy Clanton and the McLaury brothers, who died in the infamous gunfight at the O.K. Corral.

9. Joan Hackett: "Go away—I'm asleep."
The actress, who was a regular on TV throughout the 1960s and 1970s, appearing on shows such as *The Twilight Zone* and *Bonanza,* died in 1983 of ovarian cancer at age 49. Her epitaph was copied from the note she hung on her dressing room door when she didn't want to be disturbed.

10. Rodney Dangerfield: "There goes the neighborhood."
This comedian and actor died in 2004 from complications following heart surgery at age 82. His epitaph is fitting for this master of self-deprecating one-liners, best known for his catchphrase, "I don't get no respect."

11. Mel Blanc: "That's all folks!"
Arguably the world's most famous voice actor, Mel Blanc's characters included Bugs Bunny, Porky Pig, Yosemite Sam, and Sylvester the Cat. When he died of heart disease and emphysema in 1989 at age 81, his epitaph was his best-known line.

8 Stars Who Died Before Completing Their Last Movie

✳ ✳ ✳ ✳

Long after their time is up, movie stars live on through DVDs and cable reruns. But the stars on this list died before completing their last project, leaving directors in an emotional and logistical bind, and forever attaching a dark footnote to the film's history. In some cases the movie was canceled, in others the star was recast, while in others production moved forward with some creative editing.

1. Marilyn Monroe

Blonde bombshell Marilyn Monroe, famous for her film roles, multiple marriages, and memorable serenading of President Kennedy, died on August 5, 1962, before she could finish filming *Something's Got to Give.* The comedy, directed by George Cukor and also starring Cyd Charisse and Dean Martin, had been plagued with conflict from the start. At one point, Monroe was even fired. But Martin refused to work with any actress other than Monroe, so the famous beauty was rehired. However, before Monroe could resume her role, she was found dead in her Brentwood, California, home from an overdose of barbiturates. *Something's Got to Give* was scrapped, but parts of the unfinished film were included in a 2001 documentary titled *Marilyn: The Final Days.*

2. Oliver Reed

Oliver Reed, as famous for drinking and partying as he was for acting, died in a pub on May 2, 1999, before he could finish filming Ridley Scott's epic *Gladiator.* Reed, who was 61, collapsed on the floor of a bar in Malta and died of a heart attack. Most of his scenes in *Gladiator* had already been shot when he died, but Scott had to digitally re-create Reed's face for a few remaining segments. The Internet Movie Database estimated the cost of the digital touch-ups at $3 million. When *Gladiator* was released in 2000, it grossed more than $187 million in the United States alone and snared five Oscars, including Best Picture.

3. Vic Morrow

Vic Morrow, a tough-talking actor known for his role in the TV series *Combat!* as well as a string of B-movies, was killed in July 1982, in a tragic accident on the set of *Twilight Zone: The Movie.* The script called for the use of both a helicopter and pyrotechnics—a combination that would prove lethal. When the pyrotechnics exploded, the helicopter's tail was severed, causing it to crash. The blades decapitated Morrow and a child actor, and another child actor was crushed to death. Although the filmmakers faced legal action from the accident, the project was completed and the movie was released in June 1983. It performed poorly at the box office, based partially on the controversy surrounding the accident.

4. Brandon Lee

Brandon Lee, an aspiring actor and the son of martial arts star Bruce Lee, was killed in a freak accident on the set of *The Crow* on March 31, 1993. Lee, who was 28 at the time, was playing a character who gets shot by thugs upon entering his apartment. Tragically, the handgun used in the scene had a real bullet lodged in its barrel, which was propelled out by the force of the blank being shot. Lee was hit in the abdomen and died later that day. The movie was nearly complete at the time of the shooting, but a stunt double was needed to complete a few remaining scenes, and Lee's face was digitally superimposed onto the stunt double's body.

5. Steve Irwin

Steve Irwin, aka "The Crocodile Hunter," was in the Great Barrier Reef to film a documentary titled *The Ocean's Deadliest* when he was struck by a stingray and killed on September 4, 2006. Irwin, a 44-year-old Australian wildlife expert, was known for his daredevil stunts involving animals and could frequently be seen handling poisonous snakes and wrestling crocodiles on his Animal Planet TV show. Because of bad weather, Irwin was actually taking a break from filming his documentary at the time of the stingray attack; instead, he was taping some snorkeling segments for a children's show. *The Ocean's Deadliest* aired in January 2007.

6. River Phoenix

River Phoenix, a young actor who shot to stardom after appearing in Rob Reiner's *Stand by Me,* was near the end of filming *Dark Blood* when he died of a drug overdose on Halloween 1993 at age 23. The movie, a dark tale about a widower (Phoenix) living on a nuclear testing site, was subsequently canceled because Phoenix's presence was crucial to several yet-to-be-shot scenes. Phoenix was also slated to film *Interview with the Vampire* with Tom Cruise. His role was taken over by Christian Slater, who donated his salary from the film to a charity in Phoenix's honor.

7. John Candy

Funnyman John Candy, known for portraying portly, lovable losers in movies such as *Stripes, Uncle Buck,* and *Planes, Trains & Automobiles,* died of a massive heart attack on March 4, 1994, during the filming of *Wagons East.* A body double was used to replace Candy, and the film—a comedy set in the Wild West—was released later that summer. The movie was widely panned by critics as an unworthy farewell to Candy, who was just 43 when he died.

8. Heath Ledger

Fans and celebrities from America to Australia were in a state of shock when they heard of the tragic death of Heath Ledger at age 28. On January 22, 2008, the Aussie-born actor was found dead in his Manhattan apartment of an accidental overdose of prescription medications. Ledger's star was on the rise following his Oscar-nominated performance in *Brokeback Mountain* (2005), and he had just completed his role as the Joker in *The Dark Knight,* an intense and critically acclaimed performance that many predicted would win him a posthumous Oscar. But what some don't realize is that Ledger was midway through filming *The Imaginarium of Doctor Parnassus,* which will forever be remembered as his final flick. Ledger had just wrapped up shooting the realistic scenes of the film, which switches between fantasy and reality. Because of the film's nature, director Terry Gilliam was able to take a creative approach to filling Ledger's role. Instead of digitally re-creating or completely recasting Ledger, Gilliam kept his scenes intact and chose three actors—Johnny Depp, Colin Farrell, and Jude Law—to portray a "physically transformed" version of the character as he magically crosses into other worlds.

TOO YOUNG TO DIE
59 Celebs Who Died Before They Turned 40

❋ ❋ ❋ ❋

1. Heather O'Rourke (12)—Child actor—Bowel obstruction—1988
2. Anne Frank (15)—Dutch-Jewish author—Typhus in concentration camp—1945
3. Ritchie Valens (17)—Rock 'n' roll singer—Plane crash—1959
4. Eddie Cochran (21)—Rockabilly musician—Auto accident—1960
5. Aaliyah (22)—R&B singer—Plane crash—2001
6. Buddy Holly (22)—Rock 'n' roll singer—Plane crash—1959
7. Freddie Prinze (22)—Comedian/actor—Suicide—1977
8. River Phoenix (23)—Actor—Drug overdose—1993
9. Selena (23)—Mexican-American singer—Homicide—1995
10. James Dean (24)—Actor—Auto accident—1955
11. Otis Redding (26)—Soul singer—Plane crash—1967
12. Brian Jones (27)—British rock guitarist—Drug-related drowning, possibly homicide—1969
13. Janis Joplin (27)—Rock/soul singer—Heroin overdose—1970
14. Jimi Hendrix (27)—Rock guitarist/singer—Asphyxiation from sleeping pill overdose—1970
15. Jim Morrison (27)—Rock singer—Heart attack, possibly due to drug overdose—1971
16. Kurt Cobain (27)—Grunge rock singer/guitarist—Gunshot and lethal dose of heroin, presumed suicide—1994
17. Reggie Lewis (27)—Basketball player—Heart attack—1993
18. Brandon Lee (28)—Actor—Accidental shooting on the set of *The Crow*—1993

19. Heath Ledger (28)—Actor—Accidental overdose of prescription drugs—2008
20. Shannon Hoon (28)—Rock singer—Drug overdose—1995
21. Hank Williams (29)—Country musician—Heart attack, possibly due to an accidental overdose of morphine and alcohol—1953
22. Andy Gibb (30)—Singer—Heart failure due to cocaine abuse—1988
23. Jim Croce (30)—Singer/songwriter—Plane crash—1973
24. Patsy Cline (30)—Country music singer—Plane crash—1963
25. Sylvia Plath (30)—Poet and author—Suicide—1963
26. Brian Epstein (32)—Beatles manager—Drug overdose—1967
27. Bruce Lee (32)—Martial arts actor—Possible allergic reaction—1973
28. Cass Elliot (32)—Singer—Heart attack brought on by obesity—1974
29. Karen Carpenter (32)—Singer and musician—Cardiac arrest from anorexia nervosa—1983
30. Keith Moon (32)—Rock drummer—Overdose of medication—1978
31. Carole Lombard (33)—Actor—Plane crash—1942
32. Chris Farley (33)—Comedian/actor—Overdose of cocaine and heroin—1997
33. Darryl Kile (33)—Major League Baseball pitcher—Coronary heart disease—2002
34. Jesus Christ (33)—Founder of Christianity—Crucifixion—A.D. 30
35. John Belushi (33)—Comedian/actor—Overdose of cocaine and heroin—1982
36. Sam Cooke (33)—Soul musician—Homicide—1964
37. Charlie Parker (34)—Jazz saxophonist—Pneumonia and ulcer, brought on by drug abuse—1955
38. Dana Plato (34)—Actor—Prescription drug overdose—1999
39. Jayne Mansfield (34)—Actor—Auto accident—1967
40. Andy Kaufman (35)—Comedian/actor—Lung cancer—1984
41. Josh Gibson (35)—Negro League baseball player—Stroke—1947
42. Stevie Ray Vaughan (35)—Blues guitarist—Helicopter crash—1990
43. Bob Marley (36)—Reggae musician—Melanoma that metastasized into lung and brain cancer—1981
44. Diana, Princess of Wales (36)—British royal—Auto accident—1997
45. Marilyn Monroe (36)—Actor—Barbiturate overdose—1962

46. Bobby Darin (37)—Singer/actor—Complications during heart surgery—1973
47. Lou Gehrig (37)—Major League Baseball player—Amyotrophic lateral sclerosis (ALS)—1941
48. Michael Hutchence (37)—Rock singer—Hanged, possibly suicide—1997
49. Sal Mineo (37)—Actor—Homicide—1976
50. Florence Griffith Joyner (38)—Olympian/sprinter—Possible asphyxiation during epileptic seizure—1998
51. George Gershwin (38)—Composer—Brain tumor—1937
52. Harry Chapin (38)—Singer/songwriter—Auto accident—1981
53. John F. Kennedy, Jr. (38)—Journalist/publisher—Plane crash—1999
54. Roberto Clemente (38)—Major League Baseball player—Plane crash—1972
55. Sam Kinison (38)—Comedian—Auto accident caused by drunk driver—1992
56. Anna Nicole Smith (39)—Model/actor—Accidental prescription drug overdose—2007
57. Dennis Wilson (39)—Rock 'n' roll drummer—Drowning due to intoxication—1983
58. Malcolm X (39)—Civil rights leader—Assassination—1965
59. Martin Luther King, Jr. (39)—Civil rights activist/minister—Assassination—1968

I WOULDN'T GO IN THERE IF I WERE YOU!
7 Celebrities Who Died in the Bathroom

When these people said they had to go, they weren't kidding! All of these people ended their time on Earth in the bathroom—some accidentally, others intentionally. One thing is for certain—none of them got a chance to wash their hands before leaving!

1. Orville Redenbacher

Orville Redenbacher, founder of the popcorn company that bears his name, was born in 1907, in Brazil, Indiana. Millions came to know him through his folksy television commercials for the specialty popcorn he invented. He sold the company to Hunt-Wesson Foods in 1976 but remained as a spokesperson until September 20, 1995, when he was found dead in a whirlpool bathtub in his condominium, having drowned after suffering a heart attack.

2. Lenny Bruce

Controversial comedian Lenny Bruce was born Leonard Alfred Schneider in October 1925. Bruce was famous in the 1950s and 1960s for his satirical routines about social themes of the day, including politics, religion, race, abortion, and drugs. His use of profanity—rarely done at that time—got him arrested numerous times. He was eventually convicted on obscenity charges but was freed on bail. On August 3, 1966, Bruce, a known drug addict, was found dead in the bathroom of his Hollywood Hills home with a syringe, a burned bottle cap, and other drug paraphernalia. The official cause of death was an accidental overdose of morphine.

3. Robert Pastorelli

Born in 1954, actor and former boxer Robert Pastorelli was best known as Candace Bergen's housepainter on the late '80s sitcom *Murphy Brown*. He had numerous minor roles on television and also appeared in *Dances with Wolves, Sister Act 2,* and *Michael*, as well as a number of made-for-TV movies. Pastorelli struggled with drug use and, in 2004, was found dead on the floor of his bathroom of a suspected heroin overdose.

4. Albert Dekker

Actor Albert Dekker, who appeared in *Kiss Me Deadly, The Killers,* and *Suddenly, Last Summer,* was blacklisted in Hollywood for several years for criticizing anticommunist Senator Joe McCarthy. Dekker later made a comeback, but in May 1968, he was found strangled to death in the bathroom of his Hollywood home. He was naked, bound hand and foot, with a hypodermic needle sticking out of each arm and obscenities written all over his body. The official cause of death was eventually ruled to be accidental asphyxiation.

5. Claude François

Claude François was a French pop singer in the 1960s who had a hit with an adaptation of Trini Lopez's folk song "If I Had a Hammer." On March 11, 1978, François' obsession with cleanliness did him in when he was electrocuted in his Paris apartment as he tried to fix a broken lightbulb while standing in a water-filled bathtub.

6. Jim Morrison

Born on December 8, 1943, Jim Morrison was best known as the lead singer for The Doors, a top rock band in the late 1960s. His sultry looks, suggestive lyrics, and onstage antics brought him fame, but drug and alcohol abuse ended his brief life. On July 3, 1971, Morrison was found dead in his bathtub in Paris. He reportedly had dried blood around his mouth and nose and bruising on his chest, suggesting a massive hemorrhage brought on by tuberculosis. The official report listed the cause of death as heart failure, but no autopsy was performed because there was no sign of foul play.

7. Elvis Presley

On January 8, 1935, Elvis Presley, the King of Rock 'n' Roll, was born in Tupelo, Mississippi. He was discovered in Memphis by Sun Records founder Sam Phillips, who was looking for a white singer with an African American sound and style. Elvis catapulted to fame following three appearances on *The Ed Sullivan Show* in 1956 and 1957. Although he was pushed off the charts by The Beatles and the rest of the British Invasion in the early 1960s, he still sold more than a billion records in his lifetime, more than any other recording artist in history. His movie career kept him in the public eye until his comeback album in 1968, and in the 1970s, he sold out shows in Las Vegas as an overweight caricature of his former self. Elvis's addiction to prescription drugs was well known, and on August 16, 1977, he was found dead on the bathroom floor in his Graceland mansion. A vomit stain on the carpet showed that he had become sick while seated on the toilet and had stumbled to the spot where he died. A medical examiner listed the cause of death as cardiac arrhythmia caused by ingesting a large amount of drugs.

Chapter 9
HEALTH, FITNESS, AND THE HUMAN BODY

* * * *

13 People Born with Extra Body Parts

Doctors call them supernumerary body parts, but here are a few people who always had a spare hand (or finger, or head...).

1. Hermaphroditism—the condition of being born with both male and female reproductive organs—is more common than you might think, existing in some degree in around 1 percent of the population. In 1843, when Levi Suydam, a 23-year-old resident of Salisbury, Connecticut, wanted to vote for the Whig candidate in a local election, the opposition party objected, saying Suydam was really a woman and therefore did not have the right to vote. A doctor examined Suydam and declared that he had a penis and was therefore a man. He voted, and the Whig candidate won by a single vote.

2. It might seem unusual for a woman to have two uteruses, but the condition known as uterine didelphys occurs in about one in 1,000 women. In fact, Hannah Kersey, her mother, and her sister all have two wombs. But Hannah made history in 2006 when she gave birth to triplets—a set of identical twin girls from one womb and a third, fraternal sister from the other womb. There have been about 70 known pregnancies in separate wombs in the past 100 years, but the case of triplets is the first of its kind and doctors estimate the likelihood is about one in 25 million.

3. Craniopagus parasiticus is a medical condition in which a baby is born with two heads. The extra head does not have a functioning brain, which is what differentiates this condition from that of conjoined twins. In effect, the baby is born with the head of its dead twin attached to its body. There have only ever been eight known cases, and, of these, only three have survived birth. One of these was Rebeca Martínez, born in the Dominican Republic in December 2003, the first baby to undergo an operation to remove the second head. She died on February 7, 2004, after an 11-hour operation.

4. A similar condition is polycephaly, the condition of having more than one functioning head. There are many documented occurrences of this in the animal kingdom, although in most human cases we refer to the condition as conjoined twins. One recent case was that of Syafitri, born in Indonesia in 2006. These conjoined twins were given just one name by their parents who insisted that they were, in fact, one baby girl since they had only one heart and shared a body. It would have been impossible for doctors to separate the conjoined twins, and Syafitri died of unknown causes just two weeks after she was born.

5. In 2006, a 24 year-old man from India checked himself into a New Delhi hospital and asked doctors to remove his extra penis so that he could marry and lead a normal sex life. To protect his privacy, doctors would not disclose his identity or that of the hospital but did confirm that the operation took place. The condition, known as diphallia or penile duplication, is extremely rare, with only around 100 cases ever documented.

6. Anne Boleyn, second wife to Henry VIII of England, is commonly believed to have had 11 fingers and possibly a third breast. Historians believe that she did have an extra finger or at least some sort of growth on her hand that resembled an extra finger, but it is unlikely that she had an extra breast. This rumor may have been started by her enemies because in Tudor times an extra breast was believed to be the sign of a witch.

7. In 2006, a boy named Jie-Jie was born in China with two left arms. All three of his arms looked normal, but neither left arm was fully functional. When he was two months old, doctors in Shanghai removed the arm closest to his chest, which was less developed.

8. While advances in medical technology mean that Jie-Jie will go on to lead a relatively normal life, Francesco Lentini, who was born in Sicily in 1889, had a life that was anything but. He was born with three legs, two sets of genitals, and an extra foot growing from the knee of his third leg—the remains of a conjoined twin that had died in the womb. Rejected by his parents, he was raised by an aunt, then in a home for disabled children before moving to America when he was eight. He became "The Great Lentini" and toured with major circus and sideshow acts, including the Ringling Brothers' Circus and Barnum and Bailey. Part of his act included using his third leg to kick a soccer ball across the stage. He married, raised four children, and lived longer than any other three-legged person, dying in Florida in 1966 at age 78.

9. Josephene Myrtle Corbin, born in 1868, could see Lentini his three legs and raise him one. She was a dipygus, meaning that she had two separate pelvises and four legs. As with Lentini, these were the residual parts of a conjoined twin. She could move all of the legs, but they were too weak to walk on. Like Lentini, she was a great success in sideshows with the stage name "The Four-Legged Girl from Texas." She married a doctor with whom she had five children. Legend has it that three of her children were born from one pelvis, and two from the other.

10. Another sideshow star of the early 20th century was Jean Libbera, "The Man with Two Bodies," who was born in Rome in 1884. Libbera was born with a parasitic conjoined twin attached to his front. Photos of Libbera show a shrunken body, about 18 inches long, emerging from his abdomen with its head apparently embedded inside. He died in 1934 at age 50.

11. Major league baseball pitcher Antonio Alfonseca has six fingers on each hand, but he claims the extra fingers do not affect his pitching, as they do not usually touch the ball. In most cases of polydactylism (extra fingers or toes), the extra digit has only limited mobility, or cannot be moved at all, and is often surgically removed shortly after birth. The condition is reported in about one child in every 500.

12. Actor Mark Wahlberg has a third nipple on the left side of his chest. Early in his career, he considered having it removed, but he later came to accept it. Around 2 percent of women and slightly fewer men have a supernumerary nipple, although they are often mistaken for moles. They can be found anywhere between the armpit and groin, and range from a tiny lump (like Wahlberg's) to a small extra breast, sometimes even capable of lactation.

13. Born in 1932 to a poor farming family in Georgia, Betty Lou Williams was the youngest of 12 children. Doctors claimed she was a healthy child . . . except for the two extra arms and legs emerging from the side of her body. From the age of two, Williams worked for Ripley's Believe It or Not! and earned quite a living on the sideshow circuit—she put her siblings through college and bought her parents a large farm. She grew up to be a lovely and generous young lady, but when she was jilted by her fiancé at age 23, she died from an asthma attack exacerbated by the head of the parasitic twin lodged in her abdomen.

WHAT ARE YOU AFRAID OF?
28 Phobias Defined

❋ ❋ ❋ ❋

1. Ablutophobia .... Fear of washing or bathing
2. Acrophobia .... Fear of heights
3. Agoraphobia .... Fear of open spaces or crowds
4. Ailurophobia .... Fear of cats
5. Alektorophobia .... Fear of chickens
6. Anthropophobia .... Fear of people
7. Anuptaphobia .... Fear of staying single
8. Arachnophobia .... Fear of spiders
9. Atychiphobia .... Fear of failure
10. Autophobia .... Fear of oneself or of being alone
11. Aviophobia .... Fear of flying
12. Caligynephobia .... Fear of beautiful women

13. Coulrophobia..................................Fear of clowns
14. Cynophobia...................................Fear of dogs
15. Gamophobia..................................Fear of marriage
16. Ichthyophobia ....Fear of fish
17. Melanophobia...............................Fear of the color black
18. Mysophobia ....Fear of germs or dirt
19. Nyctophobia ....Fear of the dark or of night
20. Ophidiophobia/Herpetophobia ......Fear of snakes
21. Ornithophobia ....Fear of birds
22. Phasmophobia/Spectrophobia ....Fear of ghosts
23. Philophobia...................................Fear of being in love
24. Photophobia..................................Fear of light
25. Pupaphobia...................................Fear of puppets
26. Pyrophobia....................................Fear of fire
27. Thanatophobia or Thantophobia ....Fear of death or dying
28. Xanthophobia................................Fear of the color yellow

BODY ODDITIES
Freaky Facts About the Human Body

✳ ✳ ✳ ✳

1. You may not want to swim in your spit, but if you saved it all up, you could. In a lifetime, the average person produces about 25,000 quarts of saliva—enough to fill two swimming pools!

2. The source of smelly feet, like smelly armpits, is sweat. And people sweat buckets from their feet. A pair of feet have 500,000 sweat glands and can produce more than a pint of sweat per day.

3. Your pet isn't the only one in the house with a shedding problem. Humans shed about 600,000 particles of skin every hour. That works out to about 1.5 pounds each year, so the average person will lose around 105 pounds of skin by age 70.

4. Don't stick out your tongue if you want to hide your identity. Similar to fingerprints, everyone also has a unique tongue print!

5. This will really make your skin crawl: Every square inch of skin on the human body has about 32 million bacteria on it, but fortunately, the vast majority of them are harmless.

6. No wonder babies have such a hard time holding up their heads: The human head is one-quarter of our total length at birth but only one-eighth of our total length by the time we reach adulthood.

7. Adults have fewer bones than babies. We're born with 350 bones, which fuse together during growth, so we end up with 206 as adults.

8. Blondes may or may not have more fun, but they definitely have more hair. Hair color helps determine how dense the hair on your head is, and blondes (only natural ones, of course), top the list. The average human head has 100,000 hair follicles, each of which is capable of producing 20 individual hairs during a person's lifetime. Blondes average 146,000 follicles. People with black hair tend to have about 110,000 follicles, while those with brown hair are right on target with 100,000 follicles. Redheads have the least dense hair, averaging about 86,000 follicles.

9. Your nose is not as sensitive as a dog's, but it can remember 50,000 different scents.

10. If you're clipping your fingernails more often than your toenails, that's only natural. The nails that get the most exposure and are used most frequently grow the fastest. Fingernails grow fastest on the hand that you write with and on the longest fingers. On average, nails grow about one-tenth of an inch each month.

11. Blood has a long road to travel: Laid end to end, there are about 60,000 miles of blood vessels in the human body. And the hard-working heart pumps about 2,000 gallons of blood through those vessels every day.

12. By 60 years of age, 60 percent of men and 40 percent of women will snore. But the sound of a snore can seem deafening. While snores average around 60 decibels—the noise level of normal speech—they can reach more than 80 decibels, which is as loud as

the sound of a pneumatic drill breaking up concrete. Noise levels over 85 decibels are considered hazardous to the human ear.

13. Did you know that you get a new stomach lining every three to four days? If you didn't, the strong acids your stomach uses to digest food would also digest your stomach.

14. When you say you're dying to get a good night's sleep, consider this: The human body can go without food for weeks, but ten days is tops for sleep deprivation. After ten days, you'll be asleep—forever!

15. The small intestine is about four times as long as the average adult is tall—about 18 to 23 feet long. If it weren't looped back and forth upon itself, it wouldn't fit into the abdominal cavity, which would make life rather messy.

16. The air from a human sneeze can travel at speeds of 100 miles per hour or more—another good reason to cover your nose and mouth when you sneeze, or duck when you hear one coming your way.

BURN, BABY, BURN
The Number of Calories that 12 Sports and Recreational Activities Burn*

✳ ✳ ✳ ✳

Everybody wants to burn the most calories in the least amount of time. Here are 12 activities and the approximate number of calories they burn. Before launching into any activity, be sure to consult your doctor. And be sure to warm up and stretch properly.

1. Basketball

The nonstop action of b-ball will help you drop around 288 calories every half hour, while at the same time develop flexibility, endurance, and cardiorespiratory health. But warm up properly because the sudden twists and turns can be high risk for the unprepared.

2. Boxing

If you're game enough to step into the ring, you'll be rewarded with a 324-calorie deficit for every half hour of slugging it out. Plus, your cardiorespiratory fitness and muscular endurance will go through the roof. Make sure you're match fit, though, or it may be all over before you build up a sweat!

3. Cross-Country Skiing

The very fact that you're out in the snow has already fired up your metabolism. As soon as you start mushing through it, you'll be churning through those calories at the rate of 270 every half hour. The varied terrain will provide a great interval training workout, too!

4. Cycling

Cycling is an excellent non-weight-bearing (your weight is not being supported by your body) exercise, and depending on your speed, burns around 300 to 400 calories in a half hour. It provides a great cardio workout and builds up those thighs and calves. However, it doesn't provide much in the way of an upper body workout.

5. Ice Skating

Ice skating gives you all the benefits of running without the joint stress. A half hour on the ice consumes about 252 calories. Skating provides an excellent workout for your thighs, calves, hamstrings, and buttocks. The twists and turns also tighten and tone your abs. Holding out your arms helps you balance and also works the deltoids, biceps, and triceps.

6. Racquetball

Churning through about 300 calories in 30 minutes, racquetball gives you a fantastic cardiorespiratory workout, builds lower body strength and endurance, and with all that twisting and pivoting, develops great flexibility around the core (back and abs). Just warm up first to avoid twisting an ankle.

7. Rock Climbing

Rock climbing relies on quick bursts of energy to get from one rock to the next. It won't do a lot for your heart, but your strength, endurance, and flexibility will greatly benefit, and you'll burn about 371 calories every half hour.

8. Rowing

The key to rowing is technique—coordinate the legs, back, and arms to work as one, and once you get going, you'll burn about 280 calories per half hour. Rowing also builds up endurance, strength, and muscle in your shoulders, thighs, and biceps. Kayaking and canoeing each burn around 170 calories in a half hour.

9. Running

With about 450 calories burned every 30 minutes (based on an 8-minute mile), running gives a fantastic cardio workout. Leg strength and endurance are maximized, but few benefits accrue to the upper body. Warm up thoroughly, wear the proper shoes, and keep a moderate pace to avoid injury.

10. Swimming

Swimming provides an excellent overall body workout, burning up to 360 calories in a half hour depending on the stroke used. However, most people have difficulty maintaining proper form for that long. The best swim workout is based on interval training; swim two lengths, catch your breath, and then repeat.

11. Swing Dancing

Yes, you can dance your way to fitness! Swing dancing burns about 180 calories in a half hour and gives you a moderately intense aerobic workout. You'll be developing flexibility, core strength, and endurance—and you won't even feel like you're exercising. So, get out there and celebrate the joy of movement!

12. Tennis

Here's a fun game that demands speed, agility, strength, and quick reaction time. It consumes about 250–300 calories in a half hour, providing a great opportunity to burn excess calories while developing cardio fitness. Wear proper footwear to avoid ankle injuries.

°Calories based on a 150-pound person. (A heavier person will burn more calories.)

Medical Mythology

❉ ❉ ❉ ❉

If you trust the source, you're most likely going to trust the information. That's what makes the following medical myths so hard to discredit— you usually hear them first from Mom, Dad, or someone else you trust—but it is nice to know the truth.

1. **Cold weather can give you a cold.** "Put your jacket on or you'll catch a cold!" How many times have you heard that? You may not want to tell her this, but dear old Mom was wrong. Viruses (more than 200 different kinds) cause colds, not cold weather. In order for you to catch a cold, the virus must travel from a sick person's body to yours. This usually happens via airborne droplets you inhale when an infected person coughs or sneezes. You can also get a cold virus by shaking hands with an infected person or by using something where the virus has found a temporary home, such as a phone or door handle. Colds are more prevalent during the colder months because people tend to spend more time inside, making it much easier for viruses to jump from person to person.

2. **Coffee will sober you up.** If you've had too much to drink, no amount of coffee, soda, water, or anything else is going to sober you up. The only thing that will do the trick is time. The liver can metabolize only about one standard drink (12 ounces of beer, 6 ounces of wine, or 1.5 ounces of hard liquor) per hour, so if you're drinking more than that every 60 minutes, you'll have alcohol in your system for some time. The idea of coffee's sobering effect may have started because caffeine acts as a stimulant, counteracting the sedative effect of alcohol to a small degree. However, it has no effect on the amount of alcohol in the blood. So if you've been drinking, spend your money on a cab rather than a cappuccino.

3. **You can get the flu from a flu shot.** Vaccinations are misunderstood because they are created from the offending viruses themselves. But when you get a flu shot, you're not being injected with

a whole virus—just an inactivated, or dead, virus. The part of the virus that can infect you and make you sick is turned off, but the part that stimulates your body to create antibodies is still on. The body's antibodies will kill the flu virus should you come into contact with it later. Even pregnant women are advised to get flu vaccinations, so you know they're safe. The only people who should avoid them are those who have severe allergies to eggs, because eggs are used to create the vaccines. No vaccine is 100 percent effective, so there is still a chance you can get the flu after receiving the shot, but that doesn't mean the vaccination gave it to you.

4. **Cracking your knuckles causes arthritis.** The knuckles are the joints between the fingers and hand, and these joints contain a lubricant called synovial fluid. When you crack your knuckles, you are pulling apart two bones at the joint, which means the synovial fluid has to fill more space. This decreases the pressure of the fluid, and dissolved gases that are present, such as nitrogen, float out of the area in tiny bubbles. The bursting of these bubbles is the familiar sound we hear when someone "cracks" his or her knuckles. This bubble-bursting is not the same as arthritis, which is when the body's immune system attacks joints. However, constant knuckle-cracking can injure joints and weaken fingers.

5. **Feed a cold and starve a fever.** This age-old advice may have evolved from the idea that illnesses could be classified as either low temperature (those that give chills, such as a cold) or high temperature (those with fever). With chills, it sounds reasonable to feed a person's internal fireplace with food. The logic follows that when an illness raises the body's temperature, cutting back on the "fuel" should help. However, scientific evidence does not endorse this advice—many illnesses must simply run their course. Nevertheless, if you are stuck in bed with a cold and a loved one brings over your favorite healthful foods, it is still okay to chow down. Alternatively, you may lose your appetite while fighting a fever-based sickness. When you're sick, it's okay to miss a meal or two as long as you are keeping up with fluid intake.

6. Don't swallow gum—it takes seven years to digest. Some misconceptions are hard to swallow, but people have been chewing on this one for years. This myth has probably been around since chewing gum became popular in the late 19th century and most likely originated due to a single word: *indigestible*. Gum is made of flavor, sweeteners, softeners, and gum base. The body is able to break down the first three ingredients, but gum base is indigestible. That simply means that the body can't dissolve it and extract nutrients. In the end, gum base works its way through the digestive system and, in a few days, goes out in basically the same shape it went in.

7. Wait 30 minutes after eating before swimming. For a kid, nothing ruins the fun of a carefree summer day like a worried parent banning swimming right after the big cookout, fearing that the child will get cramps and drown. There is a slight chance of minor abdominal cramping, but for most people, this isn't dangerous. The body does divert blood flow from the muscles to the gastrointestinal system to spur digestion, but not in amounts that diminish muscle function. Listen to your body and swim when you're comfortable—just like you probably wouldn't run a marathon right after Thanksgiving dinner, you don't want to swim laps right after a seven-course picnic. It is perfectly safe, though, to eat a light meal and then get wet. After all, athletes commonly eat right before competing.

8. Too much sugar makes kids hyperactive. Many parents limit sugary foods, thinking they cause hyperactivity. It's right to restrict these high-calorie treats because they offer little nutrition and can lead to obesity and other problems. But no scientific evidence says sugar causes hyperactivity. It can provide a short-term energy boost, but that's not the same as hyperactivity. The children at a birthday party acting like little tornadoes probably has more to do with the excitement of being around other kids, rather than the cake. And that unruly child with candy clutched in each fist who's throwing a fit at the grocery store? His parents probably haven't set appropriate behavior limits, and they most likely give him what he wants—which is more candy.

9. Chocolate and fried foods give you acne. Some speculate that this myth dates back to the baby boomers, who had worse acne than their parents and also had more access to chocolate and fried foods. Wherever this idea came from, it's wrong. Pimples form when oil glands under the skin produce too much of a waxy oil called sebum, which the body uses to keep skin lubricated. But when excess sebum and dead skin cells block pores, a pimple forms. It is unknown why sebaceous glands produce excess sebum, but hormones are the prime suspects, which explains why teenagers are affected more than others. Stress and heredity may also be factors, but chocolate bars and french fries are off the hook.

The Heaviest States

�֍ ✳ ✳ ✳

Some speculate that there's a correlation between poverty level and obesity because high-calorie, less healthful foods are usually cheaper. As you can see, nine of the eleven states listed below rank among the top 15 states with the highest poverty levels.

State	Overweight/ Obese Adults (%)	Poverty Rank
1. Kentucky	69.1	5
2. Mississippi	68.1	2
3. Tennessee	67.4	15
4. Alabama	66.6	6
5. Texas	65.8	7
6. Arkansas	65.6	9
7. South Dakota	65.5	28
8. South Carolina	65.3	12
9. Louisiana	65.2	1
10. Alaska	65.1	40
Oklahoma	65.1	8

Sources: Centers for Disease Control and Prevention, Behavioral Risk Factor Surveillance System, 2007; U.S. Census Bureau, 2006

Hiccup Home Remedies

✳ ✳ ✳ ✳

Hiccups are involuntary contractions in the diaphragm often caused by swallowing air while eating. Irritating foods can cause hiccups, too. It's hard to tell why they strike and when, so next time you get them, see if the following suggestions help.

1. The Brown Bag Cure

It might be that breathing into a brown paper bag cures hiccups because the hiccupping person is taking in more carbon dioxide when inhaling. Or, it might be that the person is concentrating more on breathing, slowing it down and smoothing it out.

2. The Hold Your Breath Cure

This is one of the oldest hiccup remedies, and it usually works pretty well. How does it work? Probably the same way a paper bag does—it forces a little more control over your breathing.

3. The Drinking Cure

Swallowing water interrupts the hiccupping cycle, which can quiet the nerves. Gargling with water may also have the same effect, but swallowing is probably the fastest way to cure hiccups.

4. The Pineapple Juice Cure

Some say that the acid in pineapple juice obliterates hiccups, but it's probably just the swallowing action that comes from drinking.

5. The Gulp Cure

Whatever you want to gulp down, go for it. Just like drinking water, swallowing any food or drink is a good way to dispel the dreaded hiccups. If water or juice bores you, why not have a snack? Chips, crackers—okay, carrots and broccoli—will work, too.

6. The Drink Upside Down Cure

If gulping down water is good, drinking it upside down must be, too. As with many home remedies, this one is a bit unusual, but it's not totally illogical. In addition to swallowing the water, it's pretty hard to figure out how to drink upside down. The concentration needed might equalize the breathing and cure the hiccups.

7. The Little Brother Cure

If you stick out your tongue, you'll stimulate your glottis, the opening of the airway to your lungs. Since a closed glottis is what causes hiccups in the first place, this usually works pretty well.

8. The Cotton Swab Cure

This cure works just like the Little Brother Cure. Take a cotton swab and tickle the roof of your mouth. People will wonder what you're doing, but it's better than drinking upside down, isn't it?

9. The Headstand Cure

Not everyone can stand on their head, but if you can, you might have a good hiccup cure. By standing on your head, you're probably using a fair amount of concentration and messing with your breathing. This should lead to a cessation of the hiccups.

10. The Sugar Cure

Especially popular among the six-year-old set, a lump of sugar not only tickles the glottis, it gets the hiccupping person swallowing—a double threat to the hiccups.

11. The Earlobe Cure

Earlobes aren't just good for nibbling or wearing earrings. If you rub them, you can cure your hiccups! This silly cure has no basis in logic or fact, but try it, what do you have to lose?

12. The Squeeze Cure

Can't stop hiccupping? Squeeze those suckers outta there! Sit in a chair and compress your chest by pulling your knees up to your chin. Lean forward and feel those hiccups magically disappear.

13. The Sternum Cure

Some hiccup experts claim that by massaging the sternum, hiccups will melt away. There's not a lot of science to substantiate this claim, but we've never met a massage we didn't like.

14. The Sound of Music Cure

If you sing or yell as loudly as you can for at least two minutes or longer, you might notice your hiccups leave the building. But your friends might leave the building, too.

15. The Sleeper Cure

Give your glottis, throat, and diaphragm a break—lie down on your back. This is a gentler way to get rid of those obnoxious hiccups.

16. The Scaredy-Cat Cure

If you ask someone to scare you, you're not going to be really, truly surprised. But if you have a friend with ESP, he or she might be able to help. Losing your breath or gasping might just reset your glottis automatically. Boo!

17. The Hear No Evil Cure

This cure was reported in the medical journal *Lancet*, so it has to work, right? The article claims that if you plug your ears, you will, in effect, short-circuit your vagus nerve, which controls hiccups.

18. The Run for It Cure

Run. Fast. For ten minutes. See?

Calories Burned by 20 Everyday Activities*

✽ ✽ ✽ ✽

The simple truth of weight loss, no matter what the latest trendy diet says, is that you have to use more calories than you consume. The good news is that you don't have to spend all your waking hours at the gym attached to some complicated, beeping hunk of metal because everything you do burns calories. Check out the following activities and the number of calories they burn.

1. Open up. Most dentists recommend that you brush your teeth for at least two minutes. In that time, you'll burn a whopping 5.7 calories, but then again, not everything is about weight loss.

2. A lean sweep. Moving a broom back and forth for ten minutes will burn 28 calories and you'll have a prop that can be anything from a microphone stand to a dance partner.

3. Pucker power. It may not burn as many calories as vacuuming, but 30 minutes of kissing is a lot more fun. You'll burn 36 calories and probably miss a bad sitcom.

4. Suck it up. You know the rug needs it, but you may not know that 20 minutes of vacuuming will burn 56 calories.

5. Click to fit? Even watching TV is worth something. One hour spent in front of the tube burns 72 calories. Of course, if you dusted at the same time. . . .

6. Sock it to me. You can now look forward to laundry day because 30 minutes of folding clothes will burn 72 calories. Fold enough clothes and you may soon be putting away a smaller size.

7. Work up an appetite. You'll burn 74 calories during the 30 minutes you spend preparing dinner. Of course, that work will be voided by high-calorie, fat-filled meals. Instead, choose healthful meals that contain plenty of fruits and vegetables.

8. Wrinkle-free weight loss. Burn 76.5 calories with 30 minutes of ironing; just be careful that you don't burn the clothes.

9. Make it shine. Do your tables, shelves, and knickknacks fail the white-glove test? Burn 80 calories by dusting the surfaces in your home for 30 minutes and you'll be ready the next time a drill sergeant stops by for an inspection.

10. Suds it up. Break out the bucket and hose—a mere 20 minutes of washing the car will burn 102 calories.

11. Swab the deck. Don't cry over spilled milk or anything else, especially when 30 minutes of mopping the floor will burn 153 calories.

12. Flake out. If you live in a warm climate, you're missing out on a great workout. Shoveling snow for 30 minutes burns 202.5 calories.

13. **Shop 'til you drop.** Pushing a cart up and down the supermarket aisles for an hour will burn 243 calories and you'll get acquainted with all kinds of nutritious, healthful foods. Bag your own groceries, take them out to the car yourself, and return the cart to the corral, and you'll burn even more.

14. **Fire the lawn boy.** One hour of pushing the lawn mower around the yard burns 324 calories. Sorry, sitting on a riding mower doesn't count. Lose the bag attachment and spend another 30 minutes raking up the clippings and you'll burn another 171 calories.

15. **How about Texas Lose 'Em?** Three hours of playing cards burns 351 calories. Ante up and go all in, but don't load up on high-calorie chips and dip.

16. **Count calories instead of sheep.** Even when you're sleeping you're burning calories. Eight hours of good shut-eye will erase 360 calories

17. **Get moving.** Offer to help your pals move. What's in it for you? Every hour of moving furniture burns 504 calories.

18. **Dig the benefits.** Two hours of gardening will burn 648 calories, and you'll grow some nice, healthful veggies at the same time.

19. **Paint thinner.** You know you need to paint the house, but you're lacking the motivation. Does it help to know that three hours of house painting will burn 1,026 calories? And by putting on that second coat, you might drop a whole pants size.

20. **Pick up trash and drop pounds.** Pick up some waste and reduce your waist by spending an afternoon cleaning up the neighborhood. In four hard-worked hours, you'll burn 1,800 calories and improve your community.

*Calories based on a 150-pound person. (A heavier person will burn more calories.)

The Slimmest States

✳ ✳ ✳ ✳

The following list examines the ten slimmest states, based on the percentage of obese and overweight adults and poverty rank.

State	Overweight/ Obese Adults (%)	Poverty Rank
1. Colorado	55.7	39
2. Hawaii	56.8	30
3. Utah	58.0	34
4. Vermont	58.8	40
5. Massachusetts	58.9	43
6. California	59.0	18
7. Connecticut	59.2	48
8. New Mexico	60.8	3
9. Montana	61.8	11
New Hampshire	61.8	50
10. New York	61.9	17
Virginia	61.9	44

Sources: Centers for Disease Control and Prevention, Behavioral Risk Factor Surveillance System, 2007; U.S. Census Bureau, 2006

Understanding Doctor Speak

✳ ✳ ✳ ✳

Doctors, nurses, and other health-care professionals need to communicate with each other quickly and effectively. They also have a sense of humor, as you'll notice in the following list of slang terms used in hospitals.

1. Appy: a person's appendix or an appendectomy

2. Baby Catcher: an obstetrician

3. **Bagging:** manually helping a patient breathe using a squeeze bag attached to a mask that covers the face

4. **Banana:** a person with jaundice (yellowing of the skin and eyes)

5. **Blood Suckers/Leeches:** those who take blood samples, such as laboratory technicians

6. **Bounceback:** a patient who returns to the emergency department with the same complaints shortly after being released

7. **Bury the Hatchet:** accidentally leaving a surgical instrument inside a patient

8. **CBC:** complete blood count; an all-purpose blood test used to diagnose different illnesses and conditions

9. **Code Brown:** a patient who has lost control of his or her bowels

10. **Code Yellow:** a patient who has lost control of his or her bladder

11. **Crook-U:** similar to the ICU or PICU, but referring to a prison ward in the hospital

12. **DNR:** do not resuscitate; a written request made by terminally ill or elderly patients who do not want extraordinary efforts made if they go into cardiac arrest, a coma, etc.

13. **Doc in a Box:** a small health-care center with high staff turnover

14. **Foley:** a catheter used to drain the bladder of urine

15. **Freud Squad:** the psychiatry department

16. **Gas Passer:** an anesthesiologist

17. **GSW:** gunshot wound

18. **MI:** myocardial infarction; a heart attack

19. **MVA:** motor vehicle accident

20. **O Sign:** an unconscious patient whose mouth is open

21. **Q Sign:** an unconscious patient whose mouth is open and tongue is hanging out

22. **Rear Admiral:** a proctologist

23. **Shotgunning:** ordering a wide variety of tests in the hope that one will show what's wrong with a patient

24. **Stat:** from the Latin *statinum,* meaning immediately

25. **UBI:** unexplained beer injury; a patient who appears in the ER with an injury sustained while intoxicated that he or she can't explain

MODERN MALADIES
7 Modern Age Health Problems

※ ※ ※ ※

Modern life, with its emphasis on information, automation, computerization, and globalization, has made work easier and given us more leisure options, but we now have a whole host of new health problems. Only time will tell if these modern health problems disappear like 8-track tapes and rotary phones. Until then, here are some of the new maladies we have in store for us.

1. **Sick building syndrome.** Rising energy costs aren't just harmful to your wallet; if you work in an office building, they could be making you physically ill. Businesses have found that by packing buildings with insulation, then adding caulking and weather stripping, they can seal buildings tight, keep indoor temperatures constant, and cut energy costs in the process. Such measures require the heating, ventilating, and air conditioning (HVAC) systems to work harder to recycle air. After all, when the building is sealed, you can't open a window to let fresh air circulate. The result is sick building syndrome, which according to the Environmental Protection Agency (EPA), makes building occupants experience discomforting health effects even though no specific cause can be found. Symptoms include headache; eye, nose, or throat irritation; dry cough;

dry or itchy skin; dizziness; nausea; fatigue; and sensitivity to odors. The EPA estimates that 30 percent of all U.S. office buildings could be "sick," so they recommend routine maintenance of HVAC systems, including cleaning or replacing filters, water-stained ceiling tiles, and carpeting; restricting smoking in and around buildings; and ventilating areas where paints, adhesives, or solvents are used.

2. **Social anxiety disorder.** Despite all the ways to interact with others in our technologically savvy world, those with social anxiety disorder feel boxed in by the shrinking globe. According to the National Institutes of Health (NIH), people with social anxiety disorder have an "intense, persistent, and chronic fear of being watched and judged by others and of doing things that will embarrass them." That fear can be so intense that it interferes with work, school, and other ordinary activities and can make it hard to make and keep friends. But the condition has physical manifestations, too, including trembling, upset stomach, heart palpitations, confusion, and diarrhea. The cause hasn't been nailed down, but social anxiety disorder is probably due to a combination of environmental and hereditary factors. About 15 million people in the United States are affected by social anxiety disorder, which usually begins during childhood. Like other anxiety disorders, treatment often involves medication and psychotherapy.

3. **Computer vision syndrome.** If you spend all day staring at a computer screen, you may be at risk for computer vision syndrome (CVS), also called occupational asthenopia. CVS encompasses all eye or vision-related problems suffered by people who spend a lot of time on computers. According to the American Optometric Association, symptoms of CVS include headaches; dry, red, or burning eyes; blurred or double vision; trouble focusing; difficulty distinguishing colors; sensitivity to light; and even pain in the neck or back. As many as 75 percent of computer users have symptoms of CVS due to glare, poor lighting, and improper workstation setup. To overcome CVS, keep your monitor about two feet away from you and be sure it's

directly in front of you to minimize eye movement. Adjust lighting to remove any glare or reflections. You can also adjust the brightness on your monitor to ease eyestrain. Even simple steps can help, like looking away from your monitor every 20 or 30 minutes and focusing on something farther away. And you can always use eye-drops to perk up your peepers!

4. **Orthorexia nervosa.** It seems like every day there's a new report about something you shouldn't eat. The constant bombardment of information about food and health can confuse anyone, but for people who have the eating disorder orthorexia nervosa, it can be downright dangerous. People with this condition are obsessed with eating healthful food and have constructed strict diets that they follow religiously. Although many people who have orthorexia nervosa become underweight, thinness is not their goal—nutritional purity is. Among the signs of orthorexia nervosa are: spending more than three hours a day thinking about healthful food; planning meals days in advance; feeling virtuous from following a strict healthful diet, but not enjoying eating; feeling socially isolated (such strict diets make it hard to eat anywhere but at home); and feeling highly critical of those who do not follow a similar diet. Although the psychiatric community does not officially recognize orthorexia nervosa as a disorder, those with the condition benefit from psychological treatment and sessions with eating-disorder specialists.

5. **E-thrombosis.** This condition is related to deep vein thrombosis, where blood clots form in deep veins, such as those in the legs. These clots can be fatal if they migrate to the lungs and cause a pulmonary embolism. Clots can form when blood supply slows or stops, such as in a period of prolonged immobility. Similarly, e-thrombosis is the development of clots in the deep veins of someone who spends long amounts of time in front of a computer without moving. Although only a handful of e-thrombosis cases have been reported, millions of people who spend most of their time in front of a computer are at risk. Avoiding e-thrombosis is simple: stand up and move around every hour, tap your toes while

you work, put equipment and supplies in different parts of your work area so you have to move to get them, don't cross your legs while sitting at your desk, don't spend your lunch break at your desk (go for a quick walk instead), and don't get too comfortable—if your workspace is ultra-cozy, you won't want to get up.

6. **Generalized anxiety disorder.** We all have worries, uncertainties, and fears, but generalized anxiety disorder (GAD) is excessive or unrealistic unease or concern about life's problems. Although the disorder often manifests without any specific cause, large issues of modern life (such as terrorism, the economy, and crime) can bring it about, as can individual circumstances like dealing with an illness. GAD affects about 6.8 million people in the United States, and symptoms include restlessness, fatigue, irritability, impatience, difficulty concentrating, headaches, upset stomach, and shortness of breath. Anxiety disorders like GAD are treated with antianxiety drugs, antidepressants, psychotherapy, or a combination of these.

7. **Earbud-related hearing loss.** Earbuds are the headphones used with many digital music players. They fit inside the ear but don't cancel out background noise, requiring users to turn up the volume, often to 110 to 120 decibels—loud enough to cause hearing loss after only an hour and 15 minutes. And today, people spend much more time listening to their portable players, exposing themselves to damaging noise for longer periods of time. As a result, young people are developing the type of hearing loss normally seen in much older adults. Experts recommend turning down the volume and limiting the amount of time spent listening to music players to about an hour a day. Headphones that fit outside the ear canal also help, as can noise-canceling headphones that reduce background noise so listeners don't have to crank up the volume.

✳ ✳ ✳

"[The body is] a marvelous machine... a chemical laboratory, a power-house. Every movement, voluntary or involuntary, full of secrets and marvels!"
—Theodor Herzl

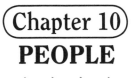

Chapter 10
PEOPLE

✳ ✳ ✳ ✳

Before They Were Stars

Most of us aren't born with a silver spoon in our mouths—even celebrities. Just like us, they've had to work their way up the job ladder. Here are ten examples that prove the old adage: It's not where you start, it's where you finish that counts.

1. Paula Abdul

As a freshman at Cal State University, Paula Abdul tried out for the Los Angeles Lakers cheerleading squad and was selected from more than 700 applicants. Her high-energy dance routines were an instant hit, and it took only three weeks for her to become head choreographer. In 1984, Abdul's career went into overdrive when she got the attention of the Jackson family, who immediately signed her to choreograph their *Torture* video. When Abdul embarked on a singing career in the late 1980s, her debut album, *Forever Your Girl*, went platinum and spawned four number one singles, including "Straight Up" and "Cold Hearted." She's now popular with a new audience as a judge on *American Idol*.

2. Clint Eastwood

Clint Eastwood has established himself as a Hollywood icon. From Westerns in the 1960s to no-nonsense, rebel cop Dirty Harry in the 1970s to a focus on directing since the 1980s, Eastwood has garnered respect, box office success, and numerous awards. But before that, he'd put in hard time working as a lumberjack, steel mill worker, aircraft factory worker, and gas station attendant. Eastwood also earned his daily bread digging swimming pools for the rich and famous of Beverly Hills, while at night he'd audition for bit parts. Now, he's the one lounging around the pool.

3. David Letterman

After graduating from Indiana's Ball State University in 1969, future late-night talk show host David Letterman landed a job at an Indianapolis television station as a local anchor and weatherman. But he was eventually let go for his unpredictable on-air behavior, which included erasing state borders from the weather map and predicting hail stones "the size of canned hams." Those canned hams eventually became popular door prizes on *The Late Show with David Letterman*.

4. Jason Lee

My Name is Earl star Jason Lee plays a character who never works, but in real life Lee once worked at Taco Bell. Then, in the late 1980s and early 1990s, Lee become a competitive skateboarder, performing tricks and other daring maneuvers. After appearing in a promotional skateboarding video shot by Spike Jonze, Lee began getting movie offers and left his skateboarding career in the dust.

5. Whoopi Goldberg

Academy Award-winning actor, comedian, and TV talk show host Whoopi Goldberg has firmly established herself as an outspoken and confident star. But Goldberg wasn't always living in the lap of luxury. Growing up in the tough Chelsea projects in New York City, her first job was as a bricklayer. When that position fizzled out, she took on the role of a garbage collector and then a funeral makeup artist—whatever job she could get to make ends meet.

6. Dennis Farina

Actor Dennis Farina often portrays cops, detectives, or mobsters and is best known for his roles in *Law & Order, Crime Story,* and *Get Shorty.* Some may think he's being typecast, but it's no wonder that Farina is so comfortable in his roles—from 1967 to 1985, he actually *was* a police officer in Chicago. Farina caught the acting bug after working with director Michael Mann as a police consultant. He started out in community theater and with bit parts on television before landing a starring role in *Crime Story* in 1986.

7. Matthew McConaughey

Matthew McConaughey's rugged good looks have won him many fans and seen him cast in a long list of romantic comedies and action films. But after graduating high school in 1988, he spent a year in Australia as an exchange student. During this time, he made some extra cash by shoveling chicken manure and washing dishes. Returning to the United States in 1990, McConaughey considered a career in law but chose acting instead.

8. Mick Jagger

Before he began strutting his stuff onstage, Rolling Stones' lead singer Mick Jagger worked as a porter at a mental hospital while he was a student at the London School of Economics. He earned just 4 pounds, 10 shillings per week (about $7.80 US). Perhaps Jagger's gig at the hospital inspired a couple of the Stones' early hits, such as "19th Nervous Breakdown" and "Mother's Little Helper."

9. Sean Connery

Sean Connery is probably best known for portraying James Bond seven times, setting the bar very high for those who would follow. He also showed his versatility with movies such as *Highlander* and *The Untouchables,* for which he won an Oscar. But Connery's first job was as a milkman in his native Scotland. After a stint in the Royal Navy, he had several jobs in the late 1940s and early 1950s, including lifeguard, ditchdigger, and artist's model. In 1953, he placed third in the tall man's division in the Mr. Universe contest.

10. Madonna

In the early 1980s, Madonna Louise Veronica Ciccone splashed onto the music scene with an attitude and some catchy pop tunes. Her *Like a Virgin* album and tour took the world by storm, and she's never looked back. But the early years in New York City were tough for Madonna, and she found herself working at a number of low-paying jobs, including a stint at a Dunkin' Donuts in Times Square. But, in true Madonna fashion, she was fired for squirting jelly filling all over customers!

18 Star-Crossed Lovers

✳ ✳ ✳ ✳

Behind every good man is a great woman. Or as Groucho Marx put it: "Behind every successful man is a woman, behind her is his wife." Can you match up the following couples who stayed together 'til death (or the end of TV syndication) did them part?

1. Robin Hood	a. Betty Bloomer
2. Clark Kent	b. Cleopatra
3. Kermit	c. Dale Evans
4. Romeo	d. Elizabeth Barrett
5. Marc Antony	e. Gracie Allen
6. JFK	f. Harriett Hilliard
7. Ricky Ricardo	g. Jacqueline Bouvier
8. Prince Albert	h. Juliet
9. Robert Browning	i. June Carter
10. Gerald Ford	j. Lauren Bacall
11. Fred Flintstone	k. Lois Lane
12. Ronald Reagan	l. Lucy McGillicuddy
13. Johnny Cash	m. Maid Marian
14. Ozzie Nelson	n. Miss Piggy
15. John Lennon	o. Nancy Davis
16. Humphrey Bogart	p. Queen Victoria
17. Roy Rogers	q. Wilma Slaghoople
18. George Burns	r. Yoko Ono

Answers: 1. m; 2. k; 3. n; 4. h; 5. b; 6. g; 7. l; 8. p; 9. d; 10. a; 11. q; 12. o; 13. i; 14. f; 15. r; 16. j; 17. c; 18. e

12 Dropouts Who Made It Big

✳ ✳ ✳ ✳

Everyone knows how important it is to stay in school, get a good education, and graduate with a diploma. But it may be hard to stay focused after reading about the success of these famous dropouts. Hard work, drive, natural talent, and sheer luck helped them overcome their lack of education, but many still returned to school later in life.

1. Bill Gates

Bill Gates is a cofounder of the software giant Microsoft and has been ranked the richest person in the world for a number of years. Gates dropped out of Harvard during his junior year after reading an article about the Altair microcomputer in *Popular Electronics* magazine. He and his friend Paul Allen formed Micro Soft (later changed to Microsoft) to write software for the Altair.

2. Walt Disney

In 1918, Disney dropped out of high school at age 16 to join the army, but because he was too young to enlist, he joined the Red Cross with a forged birth certificate instead. Disney was sent to France where he drove an ambulance that was covered from top to bottom with cartoons that eventually became his film characters. After becoming the multimillionaire founder of The Walt Disney Company and winning the Presidential Medal of Freedom, Disney received an honorary high school diploma at age 58.

3. Benjamin Franklin

Benjamin Franklin wore many hats: politician, diplomat, author, printer, publisher, scientist, inventor, founding father, and coauthor and cosigner of the Declaration of Independence. One thing he was not was a high school graduate. Franklin was the fifteenth child and youngest son in a family of 20. He spent two years at the Boston Latin School before dropping out at age ten and going to work for his father, and then his brother, as a printer.

4. Ray Kroc

Ray Kroc didn't found McDonald's, but he turned it into the world's largest fast-food chain after purchasing the original location from Dick and Mac McDonald. Kroc amassed a $500 million fortune during his lifetime, and in 2000, was included in *Time* magazine's list of the 100 most influential builders and titans of industry in the 20th century. During World War I, Kroc dropped out of high school at age 15 and lied about his age to become a Red Cross ambulance driver, but the war ended before he was sent overseas.

5. Elton John

Rock and Roll Hall of Famer Sir Elton John has sold more than 250 million records and has more than 50 Top 40 hits, making him one of the most successful musicians of all time. At age 11, Elton entered London's Royal Academy of Music on a piano scholarship. Bored with classical compositions, Elton preferred rock 'n' roll, and after five years, he quit school to become a weekend pianist at a local pub. At 17, he formed a band called Bluesology, and, by the mid-1960s, they were touring with soul and R&B musicians such as The Isley Brothers and Patti LaBelle. His album *Elton John* was released in the spring of 1970, and after the first single "Your Song" made the U.S. Top Ten, Elton was on his way to superstardom.

6. George Burns

George Burns was a successful vaudeville, TV, and movie comedian for nearly nine decades. When his father died, Burns left school in the fourth grade to go to work shining shoes, running errands, and selling newspapers. While employed at a local candy shop, Burns and his young coworkers decided to go into show business as the Peewee Quartet. After the group broke up, Burns continued to work with a partner, usually a girl, and was the funny one in the group until he met Gracie Allen in 1923. Burns and Allen got married, but didn't become stars until George flipped the act and made Gracie the funny one. They worked together in vaudeville, radio, TV, and movies until Gracie retired in 1958. Burns continued performing almost until the day he died in March 1996 at age 100.

7. Colonel Sanders

Colonel Harland Sanders overcame his lack of education to become the biggest drumstick in the fried chicken business. His father died when he was six years old, and because his mother worked, he did the cooking for his family. After dropping out of elementary school, Sanders worked many jobs, including firefighter, steamboat  driver, and insurance salesman, and he later earned a law degree from a correspondence school. But it was Sanders's cooking and business experience that helped him make millions as the founder of Kentucky Fried Chicken (now KFC).

8. Ringo Starr

Richard Starkey, better known as Beatles' drummer Ringo Starr, was born in Liverpool in 1940. At age six, Starkey's appendix ruptured, leaving him in a coma for ten weeks. After six months in recovery, he fell out of his hospital bed, necessitating an additional six-month hospital stay. After spending a total of three years in a hospital, he was considerably behind in school. He dropped out after his last visit to the hospital at age 15, barely able to read or write. While working at an engineering firm, 17-year-old Starkey taught himself to play the drums and eventually joined Rory Storm and The Hurricanes. He changed his name to Ringo Starr, joined The Beatles in 1962, and the rest is history.

9. Harry Houdini

The name Houdini is synonymous with magic. Before becoming a world-renowned magician and escape artist, Harry Houdini (born Ehrich Weiss) dropped out of school at age 12, working several jobs, including locksmith's apprentice. At 17, he teamed up with fellow magic enthusiast Jack Hayman to form the Houdini Brothers, named after Jean Eugène Robert Houdin, the most famous magician of the era. By age 24, Houdini had come up with the Challenge Act, offering to escape from any pair of handcuffs produced by the audience. With the success of the act came the development of the spectacular escapes that would make him a legend.

10. John D. Rockefeller

Two months before his high school graduation, history's first recorded billionaire, John D. Rockefeller, Sr., dropped out to take business courses at Folsom Commercial College. In 1870, at age 30, he created the Standard Oil Company. He made his billions before the company was broken up by the government for being a monopoly and spent his last 40 years giving away his riches, primarily to causes related to health and education. Ironically, this high school dropout helped millions get a good education.

11. Charles Dickens

Charles Dickens, author of numerous classics including *Oliver Twist, A Tale of Two Cities,* and *A Christmas Carol,* attended elementary school until his life took a twist of its own when his father was imprisoned for debt. At age 12, he left school and began working ten-hour days in a boot-blacking factory. Dickens later worked as a law clerk and a court stenographer. At age 22, he became a journalist, reporting parliamentary debate and covering election campaigns for a newspaper. His first collection of stories, *Sketches by Boz* (Boz was his nickname), was published in 1836 and led to his first novel, *The Pickwick Papers,* that same year.

12. Princess Diana

The late Diana Spencer, Princess of Wales, attended West Heath Girls' School where she was regarded as an academically below-average student, having failed all of her O-level examinations (exams given to 16-year-old students in the UK to determine their education level). At age 16, she left West Heath and briefly attended a finishing school in Switzerland before dropping out from there as well. Diana went to work as a part-time assistant at the Young England Kindergarten, a day care center and nursery school. Contrary to claims, she was not a kindergarten teacher since she had no educational qualifications to teach, and Young England was not a kindergarten, despite its name. In 1981, at age 19, Diana became engaged to Prince Charles and her working days were over.

18 Famous People with a Twin

✳ ✳ ✳ ✳

1. Mario Andretti.................twin brother, Aldo
2. Pier Angeli ....twin sister, Marisa Pavan
3. José Canseco...................twin brother, Ozzie
4. Aaron Carter...................twin sister, Angel
5. Montgomery Clift...........twin sister, Roberta
6. Vin Diesel ....twin brother, Paul
7. John Elway......................twin sister, Jana
8. Jerry Falwell ....twin brother, Gene
9. Maurice Gibb ....twin brother, Robin
10. Deidre Hall.....................twin sister, Andrea
11. Scarlett Johansson ....twin brother, Hunter
12. Ashton Kutcher ....twin brother, Michael
13. Ann Landers ....twin sister, Abigail Van Buren (Dear Abby)
14. Alanis Morissette............twin brother, Wade
15. Mary-Kate Olsen ....twin sister, Ashley
16. Isabella Rossellini...........twin sister, Isotta
17. Kiefer Sutherland...........twin sister, Rachel
18. Billy Dee Williams..........twin sister, Loretta

11 Celebs Who Were Orphaned or Adopted

✳ ✳ ✳ ✳

The image of the typical American family has changed over time. These days, families are "blended" and "progressive" and more than a little creative in terms of structure. Below are a few well-known celebrities that were ahead of the curve. Each famous figure listed below was orphaned, fostered, or adopted at a young age and clearly didn't let that set them back.

1. Marilyn Monroe

Born in 1926 to a single mother with a less than stable mental state, legendary screen siren Marilyn Monroe lived in many foster homes as a young girl and spent two years in an orphanage. When she was barely 16, she had the option of another orphanage or marriage. Monroe chose marriage to merchant marine James Dougherty, whom she remained married to for four years. In the years following her rocky beginnings, the blonde bombshell would nab a place in American culture unparalleled before or since.

2. Dave Thomas

Dave Thomas, founder of the fast-food chain Wendy's, was given up for adoption at birth. Sadly, his adoptive mother died when he was five. Thomas left high school in the tenth grade to work full-time at a restaurant. After a stint in the army, he moved to Columbus, Ohio, and opened his first Wendy's in 1969. He later founded the Dave Thomas Foundation for Adoption to promote adoption law simplification and reduce adoption costs in the United States.

3. Harry Caray

During his decades-long career, baseball announcer Harry Caray called the shots for the St. Louis Cardinals, Chicago White Sox, and Chicago Cubs. Harry Christopher Carabina was born in 1914 in one of the poorest sections of St. Louis and was still an infant when his father died. By the time he was ten, his mother had died, too, so an aunt raised him from that point. In 1989, Caray was inducted into the Baseball Hall of Fame as a broadcaster, and, in 1990, he joined the Radio Hall of Fame. A statue of him stands outside legendary Wrigley Field on Chicago's north side.

4. Scott Hamilton

Dorothy and Ernest Hamilton adopted Scott in 1958 when he was just six weeks old. In 1984, Hamilton won an Olympic gold medal in men's figure skating, making him the first American male to medal in the sport since 1960. These days, Hamilton produces Stars on Ice, a professional ice show that tours cities around the world.

5. Deborah Harry

Best known as the lead singer of Blondie, the '80s pop sensation who produced hits such as "Call Me" and "Heart of Glass," Deborah Harry was given up at three months and adopted by a couple from New Jersey. Harry led the typical rock-star lifestyle, but she has lived to tell the tale. Blondie was inducted into the Rock and Roll Hall of Fame in 2006, and Harry continues to tour and act.

6. Jamie Foxx

Actor and comedian Jamie Foxx was born Eric Bishop in 1967. His parents separated shortly thereafter, and his mother didn't feel capable of raising him on her own, so he was adopted at seven months by his maternal grandmother. Years later, during his Academy Award acceptance speech for his role in the critically acclaimed biopic *Ray,* Foxx thanked his grandmother for her hard work and unconditional love. He has also hosted holiday specials concerning adoption and often mentions the cause in interviews.

7. Faith Hill

Adopted when only a few days old, Audrey Faith Perry was raised in Star, Mississippi, by Ted and Edna Perry. The country music superstar was the only adopted kid in the family and formed a good relationship with her biological mother later in life. Faith always knew she was adopted and refers to her childhood as "amazing."

8. Malcolm X

"Black power" leader Malcolm X did not have a happy childhood. His father, Earl Little, was a Christian minister who was killed in 1931 when Malcolm was a small boy. Following his father's death, his mother had a nervous breakdown and was committed to a mental hospital. Malcolm and his siblings were put into an orphanage and later fostered by various families. Malcolm X would later convert to the Nation of Islam and emerge as one of the most influential civil rights activists of the modern era.

9. Melissa Gilbert

Best known for her portrayal of Laura Ingalls on *Little House on the Prairie,* Melissa Gilbert was adopted at birth by actors Ed Gilbert and Barbara Crane. Ed Gilbert died when Melissa was 11, and Michael Landon, who played her father on television, became her surrogate father. Melissa's siblings include adopted brother

Jonathan Gilbert, who portrayed Willie Oleson on *Little House,* and her sister Sara (who is not adopted) played Darlene on *Roseanne.* Melissa continues to act, mostly in made-for-TV movies, and she served as president of the Screen Actors Guild from 2001 to 2005.

10. Steve Jobs

The eventual cofounder of Apple Computers and the brain behind the iPod, Steven Paul was adopted as an infant by Paul and Clara Jobs in February 1955. Jobs held an internship with Hewlett-Packard and did a stint at Atari, Inc., before he and Stephen Wozniak developed the first Apple computer. These days, the white cord of the iPod is ubiquitous, and Macintosh computers are synonymous with style and technical savvy.

11. Babe Ruth

Born in Maryland in 1895, George Herman Ruth, Jr., lost six of his seven siblings in childhood due to disease and poverty. His parents placed him and his sister in orphanages, sending Babe to St. Mary's Industrial School for Boys. It was there that Babe met Brother Matthias, who taught him how to play baseball. The rest is history—Babe Ruth is one of the greatest and most beloved players to ever set foot on a baseball field.

11 Famous People and Their Beloved Pets

❊ ❊ ❊ ❊

"Make me the person my dog thinks I am," goes the old adage. And for those living in the spotlight—under the constant scrutiny of the public eye—that plea is likely invoked with an extra grain of truth. Dogs—and for that matter cats, pigs, and the occasional kinkajou—prove loyal companions to the famous and infamous in a sometimes less-than-friendly world.

1. Oprah Winfrey

Named World's Best Celebrity Dog Owner by the readers of *The New York Dog* and *The Hollywood Dog* magazines, Oprah Winfrey plays mommy to golden retrievers Luke and Layla. Oprah also gets props from pet lovers for introducing her audience to Cesar Millan, aka "The Dog Whisperer," and his revolutionary dog-training methods.

2. Britney Spears

Call her the anti-Oprah: Britney Spears was named World's Worst Celebrity Dog Owner in the same poll by the readers of *The New York Dog* and *The Hollywood Dog* magazines. In 2004, Brit was the proud owner of three Chihuahuas: Lacy, Lucky, and Bit-Bit. But one K-Fed and two kids later, and the pop diva appears to be dog-less. Apparently, she gave them away to friends.

3. George Clooney

George Clooney may be an eternal bachelor, but the two-time winner of *People* magazine's Sexiest Man Alive had no trouble committing to Max, the beloved potbellied pig he owned for 18 years. The Oscar-winning actor received Max in 1989 as a gift and often brought the 300-pound porker to movie sets with him. When Max died of natural causes in December 2006, Clooney told *USA Today* that he didn't plan to replace his porcine companion.

4. Martha Stewart

The woman who twice landed on *Forbes* magazine's list of the 50 Most Powerful Women may be a tough cookie in business, but she's a softie about her pets. Martha's menagerie includes several cats—Vivaldi, Verdi, Bartok, Electra, and Sirius, to name a few; two French bulldogs—Sharkey and Francesca; donkeys Clive and Rufus; canaries; horses; and a chinchilla named Snow White.

5. Adam Sandler

The best man at Adam Sandler's 2003 wedding was not a man at all, but an English bulldog named Meatball, dressed appropriately in a tux and yarmulke. Sandler, known for his goofball roles in films such as *Happy Gilmore* and *Billy Madison,* originally worked with Meatball's dad, Mr. Beefy, in the 2000 film *Little Nicky.* Sandler doted on Meatball, going so far as to film a comedy short with the pooch titled *A Day with the Meatball,* about a typical day in the dog's life. Meatball died of a heart attack at age four, but Sandler and his wife, Jackie, now enjoy the company of their newest bulldog, Babu.

6. Tori Spelling

A pregnant Tori Spelling caused a bit of a tabloid frenzy in December 2006 when she was photographed in Beverly Hills pushing her famous pug, Mimi La Rue, in a baby stroller. But kindness to animals comes naturally to the actor and daughter of late TV producer Aaron Spelling. Tori helps run Much Love, an animal rescue foundation that finds families for homeless pets. Although she purchased Mimi La Rue from a pet store, Tori adopted her other dog, Leah, a wire-haired terrier mix, from Much Love. She also has two cats, Madison and Laurel.

7. Bill Clinton

Famous for his foreign diplomacy, former president Bill Clinton was even able to persuade a cat and dog to peacefully coexist in the White House. Socks the cat came with Clinton when he moved into the executive mansion in 1993. Buddy, a chocolate Labrador retriever, arrived in 1997 as a gift. Socks and Buddy achieved national fame with the publishing of *Dear Socks, Dear Buddy: Kids' Letters to the First Pets,* by Hillary Rodham Clinton. Upon leaving office, Clinton gave Socks to secretary Betty Currie and took Buddy with him to New York. Sadly, Buddy was struck and killed by a car in 2002 near the Clintons' New York home.

8. Franklin Delano Roosevelt

Dogs in the White House are nothing out of the ordinary, but a dog at the signing of a war declaration? That would be Fala, Franklin Roosevelt's black Scottish terrier, who was a constant companion to the president—even in December 1941 when the nation entered World War II. In 1944, Fala traveled with the president to the Aleutian Islands, a trip that would live on in presidential infamy.

Rumors swirled that Fala was somehow left behind, and Roosevelt sent a destroyer back for him, costing taxpayers millions of dollars. FDR answered critics with the famous "Fala speech" on September 23, 1944, in which he vehemently denied the rumors.

9. John Lennon

John Lennon's mother, Julia, had a cat named Elvis (after The King), which fostered John's own fondness for felines. Growing up in Liverpool, the Beatle-to-be had three cats: Tich, Tim, and Sam. He and wife Cynthia had a tabby named Mimi. With May Pang, he had a white cat and a black cat—Major and Minor. John and Yoko Ono shared their New York home with another black-and-white pair—Salt and Pepper. You can see his sketches of his cats in the books *A Spaniard in the Works* and *Real Love: The Drawings for Sean.*

10. Jessica Simpson

What a difference a year makes. In 2004, when Jessica Simpson and Nick Lachey were happily married and starring in their reality show *The Newlyweds,* they acquired Daisy, a Maltipoo (Maltese-poodle). The dog's every scratch, sniff, and wag were recorded by the ever-present cameras: Daisy being toted around in Jessica's handbag, Daisy on the *Dukes of Hazzard* set, Daisy accompanying Jess to the tanning salon. In 2005, Nick and Jessica split up, but Daisy remains a loyal companion to the blonde bombshell.

11. Paris Hilton

Paris Hilton's best friends change about as frequently as the weather, but she's held on to her Chihuahua Tinkerbell since 2002. Tinkerbell achieved fame through her costarring role in all four seasons of *The Simple Life* and her memoir entitled *The Tinkerbell Hilton Diaries.* Tinkerbell went missing briefly in 2004 after Paris' apartment was burglarized, but the hotel heiress ponied up a $5,000 reward and the dog was soon returned. For a brief spell, Tinkerbell took a backseat to a pet kinkajou, Baby Luv, until the exotic animal bit Paris on the arm, sending the starlet to the emergency room in August 2006. The kinkajou hasn't been spotted publicly with Paris since.

Real Names of 19 Celebrities

✳ ✳ ✳ ✳

"A rose by any other name" is supposed to smell as sweet, but while that may be true in love, it isn't always so in show business. Below are the real names of some famous faces—see if you can match the real name to the alias.

1. Reginald Kenneth Dwight	a. John Wayne
2. Paul Hewson	b. Cary Grant
3. Mark Vincent	c. Woody Allen
4. David Robert Jones	d. Elton John
5. Caryn Elaine Johnson	e. Mark Twain
6. Nathan Birnbaum	f. Freddie Mercury
7. Archibald Leach	g. Bob Dylan
8. Eleanor Gow	h. George Michael
9. Samuel Langhorne Clemens	i. Whoopi Goldberg
10. Tara Patrick	j. Bono
11. McKinley Morganfield	k. Jason Alexander
12. Farrokh Bulsara	l. Demi Moore
13. Frances Gumm	m. Vin Diesel
14. Robert Allen Zimmerman	n. George Burns
15. Demetria Gene Guynes	o. David Bowie
16. Marion Morrison	p. Muddy Waters
17. Allen Konigsberg	q. Judy Garland
18. Georgios Panayiotou	r. Elle MacPherson
19. Jay Scott Greenspan	s. Carmen Electra

Answers: 1. d; 2. j; 3. m; 4. o; 5. i; 6. n; 7. b; 8. r; 9. e; 10. s; 11. p; 12. f; 13. q; 14. g; 15. l; 16. a; 17. c; 18. h; 19. k

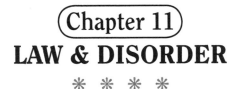

Chapter 11
LAW & DISORDER

* * * *

9 of the 20th Century's Grisliest Crimes

*Our TV screens are saturated with crime. Every night
we witness more bizarre slayings and mayhem than the night
before. Makes you wonder how far-fetched those scriptwriters
will get. After all, real people don't commit those types of crimes,
right? Wrong. In fact, the annals of history are crammed with
crimes even more gruesome than anything seen on television.
Here are some of the 20th century's wildest crimes.*

1. Ed Gein

Ed Gein had an overbearing mother who taught him that sex was
sinful. When she died in 1945, he was a 39-year-old bachelor living
alone in a rundown farmhouse in Plainfield, Wisconsin. After his
mother's death, he developed a morbid fascination with the medical atrocities performed by the Nazis during World War II. This led
him to dig up female corpses from cemeteries, take them home,
and perform his own experiments on them, such as removing the
skin from the body and draping it over a tailor's dummy. He was
also fascinated with female genitalia, which he would fondle and,
on occasion, stuff into women's panties and wear around the house.

He soon tired of decomposing corpses and set out in search of
fresher bodies. Most of his victims were women around his mother's age. He went a step too far, however, when he abducted the
mother of local sheriff's deputy Frank Worden. Learning that his
missing mother had been seen with Gein on the day of her disappearance, Worden went to the Gein house to question the recluse.
What he found there belied belief. Human heads sat as prize
trophies in the living room along with a belt made from human
nipples and a chair completely upholstered in human skin. But for

Worden, the worst sight was in the woodshed. Strung up by the feet was the headless body of his mother. Her front had been slit open and her heart was found on a plate in the dining room.

When Gein confessed, he told detectives that he liked to dress up in the carved out torsos of his victims and pretend to be his mother. He spent ten years in an insane asylum before he was judged fit to stand trial. He was found guilty, but criminally insane, and died of heart failure in 1984, at age 77.

2. John Wayne Gacy

In the mid-1960s, John Wayne Gacy was, by all outward appearances, a happily married Chicago-area businessman who doted on his two young children. But when Gacy was convicted of sodomy in 1968, he got ten years in jail, and his wife divorced him.

Eighteen months later, Gacy was out on parole. He started a construction company, and in his spare time, he volunteered as a clown to entertain sick children. He also began picking up homeless male prostitutes. After taking them home, Gacy would beat, rape, and slaughter his victims before depositing the bodies in the crawl space underneath his house.

In 1978, an investigation into the disappearance of a 15-year-old boy led police to Gacy, following reports that the two had been seen together on the night the boy disappeared. Suspicions were heightened when detectives uncovered Gacy's sodomy conviction, and a warrant was issued to search his home. When they returned to the house with excavating equipment, they made a gruesome discovery.

Gacy tried to escape the death penalty with a tale of multiple personalities, but it didn't impress the jury. It took them only two hours to convict him of 33 murders. On May 10, 1994, he was put to death by lethal injection.

3. Harold Shipman

The most prolific serial killer in modern history was British doctor Harold Shipman, who murdered as many as 400 of his patients between 1970 and 1998. Shipman was a respected member of the community, but in March 1998, a colleague became alarmed at the high death rate among his patients. She went to the local coroner, who in turn went to the police. However, investigators found nothing out of the ordinary. But when Kathleen Grundy died a few months later, it was revealed that she had cut her daughter Angela out of her will and, instead, bequeathed £386,000 to Shipman. Angela became suspicious, so she went to the police who began another investigation. Kathleen Grundy's body was exhumed and examined, and traces of diamorphine (heroin) were found in her system. Shipman was arrested and charged with murder. When police examined his patient files more closely, they realized that Shipman was overdosing patients with diamorphine, then forging their medical records to state that they were in poor health.

Shipman was found guilty and sentenced to 15 consecutive life sentences, but he hung himself in his cell in January 2004.

4. Fred and Rose West

In the early 1970s, a pattern developed in which young women were lured to the home of Fred and Rose West in Gloucester, England, subjected to sexual depravities, and then ritually slaughtered in the soundproof basement. The bodies were dismembered and disposed of under the cellar floor. As the number of victims increased, the garden became a secondary burial plot. This became the final resting place of their own daughter, 16-year-old Heather, who was butchered in June 1983.

Police became increasingly concerned about the whereabouts of Heather until one day they decided to take the family joke that she was "buried under the patio" seriously. When they began excavating the property in June 1994, the number of body parts uncovered shocked the world. With overwhelming evidence stacked against him, Fred West committed suicide while in custody in 1995. Rose received life imprisonment.

5. Ed Kemper

Ed Kemper had a genius IQ, but his appetite for murder took over at age 15, when he shot his grandparents because he wanted to see what it felt like. Nine years later, he was released from prison. Then, from 1972 to 1973, Kemper hit the California highways, picking up pretty women and killing them before taking the corpses back to his apartment, having sex with them, then dissecting them. He killed six women in that manner and then took an ax to his own mother, decapitating and raping her, then using her body as a dartboard. Still not satisfied, he killed one of his mother's friends as well.

Upset that his crimes didn't garner the media attention he felt they warranted, Kemper confessed to police. He gleefully went into detail about his penchant for necrophilia and decapitation. He asked to be executed, but because capital punishment was suspended at the time, he got life in prison and remains incarcerated in California.

6. Cameron Hooker

With the assistance of his wife Janice, Cameron Hooker snatched a 20-year-old woman who was hitchhiking in northern California in May 1977. He locked her in a wooden box that was kept under the bed he shared with Janice, who was well aware of what lay beneath. During the next seven years, the young woman was repeatedly tortured, beaten, and sexually assaulted. Eventually, she was allowed out of the box to do household chores, but she was forced to wear a slave collar. As time went by, Hooker allowed his prisoner more freedom, even letting her get a part-time job. Janice's conscience finally got the best of her, and she helped the young woman escape. After seven years of hell, she simply got on a bus and left. Hooker was convicted and sentenced to 104 years in a box of his own.

7. Andrei Chikatilo

Andrei Chikatilo was Russia's most notorious serial killer. Known as the Rostov Ripper, his rampage began in 1978 when he began abducting teenagers, subjecting them to unspeakable torture before raping and murdering them, and, often, cannibalizing their bodies. Authorities gave the crimes little attention, but as the body count grew, police were forced to face the facts—Russia had a serial killer.

Chikatilo was actually brought in for questioning when the police found a rope and butcher knife in his bag during a routine search, but he was released and allowed to continue his killing spree. In the end, he got careless and was arrested near the scene of his latest murder. Under interrogation, he confessed to 56 murders. During the trial, he was kept in a cage in the middle of the court, playing up the image of the deranged lunatic. It didn't help his cause, though. He was found guilty and executed with a shot to the back of the head on February 14, 1994.

8. Andras Pandy

Andras Pandy was a Belgian pastor who had eight children by two different wives. Between 1986 and 1989, his former wives and four of his children disappeared. Pandy tried to appease investigators by faking papers to show that they were living in Hungary. He even coerced other children into impersonating the missing ones. Then, under intense questioning, Pandy's daughter Agnes broke down. She told authorities that she had been held by her father as a teenage sex slave and then was forced to join him in killing her family members, including her mother, brothers, stepmother, and stepsister. The bodies were chopped up, dissolved in drain cleaner, and flushed down the drain. Pandy was sentenced to life in prison, while Agnes received 21 years as an accomplice. To this day, he still claims that all of the missing family members are living in Hungary.

9. Jeffrey Dahmer

Jeffrey Dahmer looked like an all-American boy, but as a child, he performed autopsies on small animals, including neighborhood dogs. At age 18, he graduated to humans, picking up a 19-year-old boy and taking him home to drink beer. Dahmer attacked him with a barbell, dismembered his body, and buried it in the backyard. More abductions and murders followed, and Dahmer also began to eat his victims.

In 1989, Dahmer was sentenced to eight years in jail for child molestation but only served ten months. After his release, he immediately resumed the slaughter. In May 1991, Dahmer picked up a 14-year-old boy, gave him money to pose for suggestive photos, and then plied him with alcohol and sleeping pills. While the boy slept,

Dahmer went to the store. Waking up alone, the boy fled but ran straight into Dahmer. When they were approached by police, Dahmer convinced the officers that the two were lovers. Upon returning to the apartment, Dahmer slaughtered the boy and then had sex with his corpse.

Two months later, this scenario was virtually reenacted when a 31-year-old man escaped from the apartment. With handcuffs dangling from one arm, he approached a nearby police officer. This time the officer decided to check out the apartment. What the officer and his partner saw horrified them. Dismembered bodies, skulls, and internal organs littered the place, and a skeleton hung in the shower. When they opened the refrigerator, they were confronted with a human head. Three more heads were wrapped up in the freezer, and a pan on the stove contained human brains.

During the ensuing trial, another gruesome fact emerged—Dahmer had drilled holes into the skulls of some of his victims and poured in acid in an attempt to keep them alive as zombielike sex slaves. He was given 15 life terms, but in November 1994, he was beaten to death in prison.

11 Silly Legal Warnings

✳ ✳ ✳ ✳

Our lawsuit-obsessed society has forced product manufacturers to cover their "you-know-whats" by writing warning labels to protect us from ourselves. Some are funny, some are absolutely ridiculous, but all are guaranteed to stand up in court.

1. A warning label on a nighttime sleep-aid reads: "Warning: May cause drowsiness."

2. The instructions for a medical thermometer advise: "Do not use orally after using rectally."

3. Both boys and girls should read the label on the Harry Potter toy broom: "This broom does not actually fly."

4. Cans of self-defense pepper spray caution: "May irritate eyes."

5. Cans of Easy Cheese contain this instruction: "For best results, remove cap."

6. A Power Puff Girls costume discourages: "You cannot save the world!"

7. The side of a Slush Puppy cup warns: "This ice may be cold." The only thing dumber than this would be a disclaimer stating: "No puppies were harmed in the making of this product."

8. A box of PMS relief tablets has this advice: "Warning: Do not use if you have prostate problems."

9. The box of a 500-piece puzzle reads: "Some assembly required."

10. A clothes iron comes with this caution: "Warning: Never iron clothes on the body." Ouch!

11. Child-size Superman and Batman costumes come with this warning label: "Wearing of this garment does not enable you to fly."

SO SUE ME!
8 Unbelievable Lawsuits

✳ ✳ ✳ ✳

One of the benefits of living in a democratic country with a well-established judicial system is the opportunity to use the courts to achieve justice and set wrongs right. But there is a drawback—some folks go to court about things that make most of us shake our heads. Take a look at these odd cases and judge for yourself.

1. Sue the Pants Off Them

In 2005, in one of the most outrageous lawsuits of recent times, Roy Pearson, a Washington, D.C. judge, sued a small mom-and-pop dry cleaner for $54 million for misplacing his pants. The shop's owners, Jin and Soo Chung, returned the pants a week later, but

Pearson refused them, saying they were not his $800 trousers but a cheap imitation. He also sued the Chungs and their son $1,500 each, per day, for more than a year, claiming that the store's signs, which read "Satisfaction Guaranteed" and "Same Day Service," were fraudulent. In 2007, a judge ruled in favor of the Chungs and ordered Pearson to pay the couple's court costs.

2. School Responsible for Bad Break-Up

In February 2004, a New York court ordered a school district to pay a former student $375,000 when his two-year affair with a school secretary ended. The young basketball star claimed that the break-up brought "emotional and psychological trauma," ruining any prospects for a professional hard-court career. The jury determined that the school was culpable for failing to supervise the secretary properly. It also ordered the secretary to pay the student another $375,000—even though she had not been named in the lawsuit

3. Trespass at the Owner's Risk

Let's say you're illegally sneaking onto a railroad's property so you can get a view from the top of a boxcar—and then an electrical wire above the car electrocutes you. What do you do? Obviously, you sue the railroad! In October 2006, a jury awarded more than $24 million to two young men who were severely burned while atop a parked railroad car in Lancaster, Pennsylvania, in 2002. The jury said that, although they were trespassing, the 17-year-old boys bore no responsibility. Instead the blame fell entirely on Amtrak and Norfolk Southern for failing to post signs warning of the danger from the electrified wires that power locomotives. For medical costs, pain and suffering, and "loss of life pleasures," one boy received $17.3 million and the other $6.8 million.

4. Bubbles Aren't Always Fun

Early on the morning of July 7, 2001, a prankster dumped detergent into a public park fountain in Duluth, Minnesota, creating a mountain of bubbles. A few hours later, passerby Kathy Kelly fell down and suffered several injuries. She sued the city because it had not cleaned up the suds (on Saturday morning) or posted warnings to citizens urging them not to walk through the slippery wall of bubbles. A jury in March 2004 found the city 70 percent responsible for Kelly's injuries—leaving her with only 30 percent of the blame—and thus awarded her $125,000.

5. No Good Deed Goes Unpunished

In July 2004, two teenage girls in Colorado baked cookies and delivered them to their neighbors. But the door-knocking apparently scared Wanita Young, who had an anxiety attack, went to the hospital, and sued the girls' families. A local judge awarded Young almost $900 for medical expenses but denied her half-baked demand for nearly $3,000 in itemized expenses, including lost wages and new motion-sensor lights for her porch.

6. Fingered as a Scam

In March 2005, Ann Ayala filed a claim against a Wendy's franchise owner, asserting that she had found a fingertip in a bowl of chili. But authorities found no evidence of missing fingers at the accused restaurant. Suspicion turned on Ayala, who dropped the suit when reporters discovered that she had previously accused several other companies of wrongdoing.

7. All Toys Are Not Equal

Jodee Berry, a Hooter's waitress in Florida, won the restaurant's sales contest and thought she'd just won the new Toyota that her bosses said the champion would get. The prize was actually a toy Yoda, not a Toyota, so she left her job and sued the franchisee for breach of contract and fraudulent misrepresentation. The force was with Berry—the out-of-court settlement in May 2002 allowed her to pick out any Toyota car she wanted.

8. Spilling the (Coffee) Beans

This list can only end with the most notorious of lawsuits: Stella Liebeck, of Albuquerque, sued McDonald's in 1992 after spilling a cup of the restaurant's coffee, which burned her lap severely and hospitalized her for a week. Two years later, a jury awarded her $160,000 in direct damages and $2.7 million in punitive damages, which a court later reduced to $480,000. Both parties appealed, and they eventually settled out of court for an undisclosed amount— surely enough for her to buy McDonald's coffee for the rest of her life. Liebeck inspired the creation of the Stella Awards, which highlight particularly "wild, outrageous, or ridiculous lawsuits."

9 of History's Unsolved Mysteries

✳ ✳ ✳ ✳

They were gruesome crimes that shocked us with their brutality. But as time passed, we heard less and less about them until we forgot about the crime, not even realizing that the perpetrator remained among us. Yet the files remain open, and the families of the victims live on in a state of semi-paralysis. Here are some of the world's most famous cold cases.

1. Jack the Ripper

In London in the late 1880s, a brutal killer known as Jack the Ripper preyed on local prostitutes. His first victim was 43-year-old Mary Ann Nichols, who was nearly decapitated during a savage knife attack. Days later, 47-year-old Annie Chapman had her organs removed from her abdomen before being left for dead. The press stirred up a wave of panic reporting that a serial killer was at large. Three weeks later, the killer was interrupted as he tore apart Swedish prostitute Elizabeth Stride. He managed to get away, only to strike again later that same night. This time the victim was Kate Eddowes. The killer, by now dubbed Jack the Ripper, removed a kidney in the process of hacking up Eddowes's body. His final kill was the most gruesome. On the night of November 9, 1888, Mary Kelly was methodically cut into pieces in an onslaught that must have lasted for several hours.

Dozens of potential Jacks have been implicated in the killings, including failed lawyer Montague John Druitt, whose body was fished out of the Thames River days after the last murder was committed. But the nature of the bodily dissections has led many to conclude that Jack was a skilled physician with an advanced knowledge of anatomy. Still, more than a century after the savage attacks, the identity of Jack the Ripper remains a mystery.

2. The Torso Killer

During the 1930s, more than a dozen limbless torsos were found in Cleveland, Ohio. Despite the efforts of famed crime fighter Eliot Ness, the torso killer was never found. The first two bodies, found in September 1935, were missing heads and had been horribly mutilated. Similar murders occurred during the next three years. Desperate to stop the killings, Ness ordered a raid on a run-down area known as Kingsbury's Run, where most of the victims were from. The place was torched, and hundreds of vagrants were taken into custody. After that, there were no more killings.

The key suspect in the murders was Frank Dolezal, a vagrant who lived in the area. He was a known bully with a fiery temper. Dolezal was arrested and subsequently confessed, but his confession was full of inaccuracies. He died shortly thereafter under suspicious circumstances.

3. The Black Dahlia

Elizabeth Short, also known as the Black Dahlia, was murdered in 1947. Like thousands of others, Elizabeth wanted to be a star. But unlike the bevy of blondes who trekked to Hollywood, this 22-year-old beauty from Massachusetts was dark and mysterious. She was last seen alive outside the Biltmore Hotel in Los Angeles on the evening of January 9, 1947.

Short's body was found on a vacant lot in Los Angeles. It had been cut in half at the waist, and both parts had been drained of blood and then cleaned. Her body parts appeared to be surgically dissected, and her remains were suggestively posed. Despite receiving a number of false confessions and taunting letters that admonished police to "catch me if you can," the crime remains unsolved.

4. The Zodiac Killer

The Zodiac Killer was responsible for several murders in the San Francisco area in the 1960s and 1970s. His victims were shot, stabbed, and bludgeoned to death. After the first few kills, he began sending letters to the local press in which he taunted police and made public threats, such as planning to blow up a school bus. In a letter sent to the *San Francisco Chronicle* two days after the murder of cabbie Paul Stine in October 1969, the killer, who called himself "The Zodiac," included in the package pieces of Stine's blood-soaked shirt. In the letters, which continued until 1978, he claimed a cumulative tally of 37 murders.

5. Jimmy Hoffa

In 1975, labor leader Jimmy Hoffa disappeared on his way to a Detroit-area restaurant. Hoffa was the president of the Teamsters Union during the 1950s and '60s. In 1964, he went to jail for bribing a grand juror investigating corruption in the union. In 1971, he was released on the condition that he not participate in any further union activity. Hoffa was preparing a legal challenge to that injunction when he disappeared on July 30, 1975. He was last seen in the parking lot of the Machus Red Fox Restaurant.

Hoffa had strong connections to the Mafia, and several mobsters have claimed that he met a grisly end on their say so. Although his body has never been found, authorities officially declared him dead on July 30, 1982. As recently as November 2006, the FBI dug up farmland in Michigan hoping to turn up a corpse. So far, no luck.

6. Bob Crane

In 1978, Bob Crane, star of TV's *Hogan's Heroes,* was clubbed to death in his apartment. Crane shared a close friendship with John Carpenter, a pioneer in the development of video technology. The two shared an affinity for debauchery and sexual excesses, which were recorded on videotape. But by late 1978, Crane was tiring of Carpenter's dependence on him and had let him know that the friendship was over.

The following day, June 29, 1978, Crane was bludgeoned to death with a camera tripod in his Scottsdale, Arizona, apartment. Suspicion immediately fell on Carpenter, and a small spattering of blood was found in Carpenter's rental car, but police were unable to connect it to the crime. Examiners also found a tiny piece of human tissue in the car. Sixteen years after the killing, Carpenter finally went to trial, but he was acquitted due to lack of evidence.

7. Swedish Prime Minister Olof Palme

In Stockholm, on February 28, 1986, Swedish Prime Minister Olof Palme was fatally shot in the back as he and his wife strolled home from the movies unprotected around midnight. His wife was seriously wounded but survived.

In 1988, a petty thief and drug addict named Christer Petterson was convicted of the murder because he was picked out of a lineup by Palme's widow. The conviction was later overturned on appeal when doubts were raised as to the reliability of Mrs. Palme's evidence. Despite many theories, the assassin remains at large.

8. Tupac Shakur

On September 7, 1996, successful rap artist Tupac Shakur was shot four times in a drive-by shooting in Las Vegas. He died six days later. Two years prior, Shakur had been shot five times in the lobby of a Manhattan recording studio the day before he was found guilty of sexual assault. He survived that attack, only to spend the next 11 months in jail. The 1994 shooting was a major catalyst for an East Coast–West Coast feud that would envelop the hip-hop industry and culminate in the deaths of both Shakur and Notorious B.I.G. (Christopher Wallace).

On the night of the fatal shooting, Shakur attended the Mike Tyson–Bruce Seldon fight at the MGM Grand in Las Vegas. After the fight, Shakur and his entourage got into a scuffle with a gang member. Shakur then headed for a nightclub, but he never made it. No one was ever arrested for the killing.

9. JonBenét Ramsey

In the early hours of December 26, 1996, Patsy Ramsey reported that her six-year-old daughter, JonBenét, had been abducted from her Boulder, Colorado, home. Police rushed to the Ramsey home where, hours later, John Ramsey found his little girl dead in the basement. She had been battered, sexually assaulted, and strangled.

Police found several tantalizing bits of evidence—a number of footprints, a rope that did not belong on the premises, DNA samples, and marks on the girl's body that suggested the use of a stun gun. The ransom note was also suspicious—it had been written with a pen and paper belonging to the Ramseys. The amount demanded—$118,000—was a small amount considering that John Ramsey was worth more than $6 million. Curiously, Mr. Ramsey had just received a year-end bonus of $118,117.50.

A number of suspects were considered, but one by one they were cleared. Finally, the police zeroed in on the parents. For years, the Ramseys were put under intense pressure by authorities and the public alike to confess to the murder. However, a grand jury investigation ended with no indictments. In 2003, a judge ruled that an intruder had killed JonBenét. Then, in August 2006, John Mark Karr confessed, claiming that he was with the girl when she died. However, Karr's DNA did not match that found on JonBenét. He was not charged, and the case remains unsolved.

Countries with the Most Prisoners

※ ※ ※ ※

Country	Prisoners per 100,000 People
1. United States	715
2. Russia	584
3. Belarus	554
4. Palau	523
5. Belize	459
6. Suriname	437
7. Dominica	420
8. Ukraine	416
9. Bahamas	410
10. South Africa	402

Source: *King's College of London: International Centre for Prison Studies*

Chapter 12
FOOD & DRINK

✳ ✳ ✳ ✳

A Taste of the World's Most Expensive Foods

Food is one of the basic needs that all living things have in common. But all foods are not created equal, especially in terms of price, as the following list illustrates.

1. Sandwich

Since the 19th century, the club sandwich has been a restaurant staple. But thanks to English chef James Parkinson, the von Essen Platinum club sandwich at the Cliveden House Hotel near London is also the world's most expensive sandwich at around $150. The sandwich, which weighs just over a pound, is made of the finest ingredients, including quail eggs, white truffles, Iberico ham that has been cured for 30 months, semi-dried Italian tomatoes, and 24-hour fermented sourdough bread.

2. Hamburger

At $200 a pop, Burger King's new burger completely redefines the term *whopper*. Known simply as The Burger, it contains Wagyu beef topped with Spanish-cured ham slices, white truffles, and onions fried in Cristal champagne, all served on a bun dusted with Iranian saffron. It's available once a week only at a BK restaurant in West London but may be available to special order soon. All proceeds from sales of The Burger go to charity.

3. Ice Cream Sundae

At $1,000, the Grand Opulence Sundae at New York's Serendipity 3 certainly lives up to its name. Made from Tahitian vanilla bean ice cream covered in 23-karat edible gold leaf and drizzled with Amedei Porcelana, the world's most expensive chocolate, this indulgence is studded with gold dragées and truffles and topped with dessert caviar.

4. Omelette

For $1,000, this gigantic concoction comes stacked with caviar and an entire lobster encased within its eggy folds. Still, one might expect a seafood fork made of platinum and a few precious stones within to justify the price of a few eggs (albeit with a few added trappings). Nicknamed "The Zillion Dollar Lobster Frittata," the world's most "egg-spensive" omelette is the objet d'art of chef Emilio Castillo of Norma's restaurant in New York's Le Parker Meridien Hotel. A smaller version is also available for $100.

5. Pizza

Americans love their pizza. And at $1,000 a pie (or $125 a slice), they better be able to put their money where their mouth is. The Luxury Pizza, a 12-inch thin crust, is the creation of Nino Selimaj, owner of Nino's Bellissima in Manhattan. To order this extravagant pizza, call 24 hours in advance because it is covered with six different types of caviar that need to be specially ordered. The pie is also topped with lobster, crème fraîche, and chives.

6. Spice

Saffron, the most expensive spice in the world, has sold in recent years for as much as $2,700 per pound! The price tag is so high because it must be harvested by hand and it takes more than 75,000 threads or filaments of the crocus flower to equal one pound of the spice! Most saffron comes from Iran, Turkey, India, Morocco, Spain, and Greece, and in the ancient world, the spice was used medicinally and for food and dye. Prices vary depending on the quality and the amount, but high quality saffron has been known to go for as much as $15 per gram (0.035 ounces).

7. Boxed Chocolates

In late 2008, Lebanese chocolatier Patchi unveiled the world's most expensive box of chocolates. Retailing for £5,000 (around $7,400 US), the decadent candies are sold in the famous London department store Harrods and are packaged inside a box encased in leather and silk. Each of the 49 chocolates is made from organic cocoa and is embellished with either a Swarovski crystal, a 24-carat gold flower, or a silk rose. The candy pieces are individually wrapped in suede and are separated by gold and platinum linings.

8. Pie

In 2006, a chef in northwestern England created the world's most expensive pie. Based on a traditional steak and mushroom pie, the dish includes $1,000 worth of Wagyu beef fillet, $3,330 in Chinese matsutake mushrooms (which are so rare that they are grown under the watchful eyes of armed guards), two bottles of 1982 Chateau Mouton Rothschild at a cost of about $4,200 each, as well as black truffles and gold leaf. The pie serves eight with a total cost around $15,900, or $1,990 per slice, which includes a glass of champagne.

9. Caviar

The world's most expensive caviar is a type of Iranian beluga called Almas. Pale amber in color, it comes from sturgeons in the Caspian Sea that are between 60 and 100 years old. A 2.2-pound container will set you back $27,355.

10. Bread

Forget Poilâne's famous French sourdough at $19.50 a loaf. In 1994, Diane Duyser of Florida noticed that the toasted sandwich she was eating appeared to contain an image of the Virgin Mary. She kept it for ten years (it never went moldy), before selling it to Canadian casino Goldenpalace.com for $28,000 in 2004.

11. Cake

And the award for the most expensive food goes to . . . a fruitcake? Encrusted with 223 small diamonds, this cake (which is edible without the gems, of course) was on the market for an unbelievable $1.6 million in December 2005. One of 17 diamond-themed displays in a Japanese exhibit called "Diamonds: Nature's Miracle," the masterpiece took a Tokyo pastry chef six months to design and one month to create.

14 Countries with the Most Chocolate Lovers

✵ ✵ ✵ ✵

Country	Pounds per Person per Year
1. Switzerland	22.36
2. Austria	20.13
3. Ireland	19.47
4. Germany	18.04
5. Norway	17.93
6. Denmark	17.66
7. United Kingdom	17.49
8. Belgium	13.16
9. Australia	12.99
10. Sweden	12.90
11. United States	11.64
12. France	11.38
13. Netherlands	10.56
14. Finland	10.45

POP STARS

19 Little-Known Facts About Popcorn

✵ ✵ ✵ ✵

*High in fiber, low in fat, and a tiny demon in every kernel—
here are 19 things you didn't know about popcorn.*

1. Popcorn is naturally high in fiber, low in calories, and sodium-, sugar-, and fat-free, although oil is often added during preparation, and butter, sugar, and salt are all popular toppings.

2. People have been enjoying popcorn for thousands of years. In 1948, 5,000-year-old popped kernels were found in caves in New Mexico.

3. Some Native American tribes believed that a spirit lived inside each kernel of popcorn. The spirits wouldn't usually bother humans, but if their home was heated, they would jump around, getting angrier and angrier, until eventually they would burst out with a pop.

4. Traditionally, Native American tribes flavored popcorn with dried herbs and spices, possibly even chili. They also made popcorn into soup and beer, and made popcorn headdresses and corsages.

5. It is believed that the Wampanoag Native American tribe brought popcorn to the colonists for the first Thanksgiving in Plymouth, Massachusetts.

6. Christopher Columbus allegedly introduced popcorn to the Europeans in the late 15th century.

7. Popcorn's scientific name is *zea mays everta,* and it is the only type of corn that will pop.

8. What makes popcorn pop? Each kernel contains a small amount of moisture. As the kernel is heated, this water turns to steam. Popcorn differs from other grains in that the kernel's shell is not water-permeable, so the steam cannot escape and pressure builds up until the kernel finally explodes, turning inside out.

9. Unpopped kernels are called "old maids" or "spinsters."

10. There are two possible explanations for old maids. The first is that they didn't contain sufficient moisture to create an explosion; the second is that their outer coating (the hull) was damaged, so that steam escaped gradually, rather than with a pop. Good popcorn should produce less than 2 percent old maids.

11. On average, a kernel will pop when it reaches a temperature of 347° F (175° C). Ideally, the moisture content of popcorn should be around 13.5 percent, as this results in the fewest old maids.

12. In 1885, Charles Cretors of Chicago invented the first commercial popcorn machine. The business he founded still manufactures popcorn machines and other specialty equipment.

13. American vendors began selling popcorn at carnivals in the late 1800s. When they began to sell outside movie theaters, theater owners were initially annoyed, fearing that popcorn would distract their patrons from the movies. It took a few years for owners to realize that popcorn could be a way to increase revenues, and since 1912, popcorn and the movies have gone hand in hand.

14. Nowadays, many movie theaters make a greater profit from popcorn than they do from ticket sales, since, for every dollar spent on popcorn, around 90 cents is pure profit. Popcorn also makes moviegoers thirsty and more likely to buy overpriced sodas.

15. When popped, popcorn comes in two basic shapes: snowflake and mushroom. Movie theaters prefer snowflake because it's bigger. Mushroom is used in confections, such as caramel corn, because it won't crumble.

16. Nebraska produces more popcorn than any other state in the country—around 250 million pounds per year. That's about a quarter of all the popcorn produced annually in the United States.

17. There are at least five contenders claiming to be the "Popcorn Capital of the World" due to the importance of popcorn to their local economies, and only one of them is in Nebraska. They are: Van Buren, Indiana; Marion, Ohio; Ridgway, Illinois; Schaller, Iowa; and North Loup, Nebraska.

18. Americans consume 17 billion quarts of popped popcorn each year. That's enough to fill the Empire State Building 18 times!

19. According to the *Guinness Book of World Records,* the world's largest popcorn ball measured 12 feet in diameter and required 2,000 pounds of corn, 40,000 pounds of sugar, 280 gallons of corn syrup, and 400 gallons of water to create.

A MOMENT ON THE LIPS...A LIFETIME ON THE HIPS
Number of Calories and Fat in 36 Fast Foods

✳ ✳ ✳ ✳

*Most health and fitness experts, as well as the USDA,
agree that the recommended daily caloric intake varies from
person to person, depending on an individual's age, gender,
and activity level. But on average, experts recommend a
2,000-calorie diet with about 60 to 65 grams of fat per day.
So, as you can see, some of the fast-food items on the following
list contain half or nearly all of the daily requirements.*

Food Item	Calories	Fat (grams)
1. Deluxe Breakfast Biscuit (McDonald's)	1,320	63
2. Double Whopper with cheese (Burger King)	990	64
3. Chocolate Shake (large, 22 ounces, Burger King)	950	29
4. Roast Turkey, Ranch & Bacon Sandwich (Arby's)	834	38
5. Baconator (Wendy's)	830	51
6. Onion Petals (large, Arby's)	828	57
7. TenderCrisp Chicken Sandwich (Burger King)	780	43
8. Nachos Bell Grande (Taco Bell)	770	44
9. Grilled Stuft Burrito (beef, Taco Bell)	680	30
10. Pepperoni Personal Pan Pizza (Pizza Hut)	640	29
11. Curly Fries (large, Arby's)	631	37
12. Chicken Club Sandwich (Wendy's)	610	31
13. French Fries (large, McDonald's)	570	30
14. Meatball Marinara (6-inch wheat sub, Subway)	560	24
15. Big Mac (McDonald's)	540	29
16. Tuna (6-inch wheat sub, Subway)	530	31

Food Item	Calories	Fat (grams)
17. Meat Lovers Hand-Tossed Pizza (1 slice, Pizza Hut)	490	27
18. Sausage, Egg, and Cheese Croissan'wich (Burger King)	470	32
19. Beef 'n' Cheddar Sandwich (Arby's)	445	21
20. Extra Crispy Chicken Breast (KFC)	440	27
21. Supreme Pan Pizza (1 slice, Pizza Hut)	440	23
22. Sweet & Spicy Wings (5, boneless, KFC)	440	19
23. Cheesy Tots (large, 12 pieces, Burger King)	430	24
24. Mozzarella Sticks (4 pieces, Arby's)	426	28
25. Burrito Supreme (beef, Taco Bell)	410	17
26. Cold Cut Combo (6-inch wheat sub, Subway)	410	17
27. Vanilla Frosty (medium, Wendy's)	410	10
28. Pepperoni Stuffed Crust Pizza (1 slice, Pizza Hut)	390	19
29. Asian Salad with Crispy Chicken (McDonald's)	380	17
30. Glazed Kreme Filled Doughnut (Krispy Kreme)	340	20
31. Original Recipe Thigh (KFC)	330	24
32. KFC Snacker (KFC)	320	16
33. Regular Roast Beef Sandwich (Arby's)	320	14
34. Hershey's Sundae Pie (Burger King)	310	19
35. Oven Roasted Chicken Breast (6-inch wheat sub, Subway)	310	5
36. Coca-Cola Classic (large, 32 ounces, McDonald's)	310	0

I WOULDN'T EAT THAT IF I WERE YOU
Foods that Have Been Banned

❋ ❋ ❋ ❋

The following foods and beverages have been banned either because the particular species is endangered or because, if ingested, they can seriously threaten the health, safety, and well-being of the consumer, and yet some people still choose to partake.

1. Foie Gras

Foie gras, which literally means "fatty liver," is what actor Roger Moore calls a "delicacy of despair." When Moore discovered how geese were tortured to create the hors d'oeuvre, he was so appalled that he teamed up with PETA (People for the Ethical Treatment of Animals) and APRL (Animal Protection and Rescue League) to educate the public. To create foie gras, ducks and geese are painfully force-fed up to four pounds of food per day by cramming it down their throats through metal pipes until, according to Moore, "they develop a disease that causes their livers to enlarge up to ten times their normal size!" Investigations into foie gras farms have revealed such horrible cruelty to animals that the dish has been banned in many countries and many parts of the United States.

2. Ortolan

In the same cruel fashion as foie gras, this tiny bird has little to sing about, as historically it was horribly tortured before being eaten as a gastronomic treat by the aristocracy of France. Its fate was often to be captured, have its eyes poked out, and be put in a small cage, then force-fed until it grew to four times its normal size. Next the poor bird would be drowned in brandy, roasted, and eaten whole. Now considered a protected species in France, the ortolan is also in decline in several other European countries. Nevertheless, hunters still kill about 50,000 birds every year, even though it is illegal to sell them.

3. Sassafras

Now recognized by the U.S. Department of Agriculture as a potential carcinogen, sassafras is the dried root bark of the sassafras tree native to eastern North America. Throughout history, sassafras has been used for making tea, as a fragrance for soap, a painkiller, an insect repellent, and a seasoning and thickener for many Creole soups and stews. But the best-known use of sassafras lies in the creation of root beer, which owes its characteristic flavor to sassafras extract. In 1960, the FDA banned the ingredient *saffrole*—found in sassafras oil—for use as an additive because in several experiments, massive doses of sassafras oil were found to induce liver cancer in rats. It should come as no surprise that chemicals and artificial flavors are used to flavor root beer today.

4. Blackened Redfish

In 1980, New Orleans chef Paul Prudhomme publicized his recipe for blackened redfish, which is still very popular today. The recipe was so popular that it spurred a blackened redfish craze in the 1980s, which so severely threatened the redfish stock that the Commerce Department had to step in and close down fisheries in July 1986. In Florida, strict conservation measures were enforced for two years, and, to this day, the state requires that anglers keep only one redfish per day and release any that do not fall into the 18- to 27-inch limit, handling their catch as little as possible to assure that the fish survives upon release.

5. Absinthe

The exact origin of absinthe is unknown, but this strong alcoholic liqueur was probably first commercially produced around 1797. It takes its name from one of its ingredients, *Artemisia absinthium,* which is the botanical name for the bitter herb known as wormwood. Green in color due to the presence of chlorophyll, it became an immensely popular drink in France by the 1850s. Said to induce creativity, produce hallucinations, and act as an aphrodisiac, the bohemian lifestyle quickly embraced it, and absinthe soon became known as *la fée verte* (the green fairy). But in July 1912, the

Department of Agriculture banned absinthe in America for its "harmful neurological effects," and France followed in 1915.

6. **Japanese Puffer Fish**
   Also known as blowfish, these creatures are so named for their ability to inflate themselves to several times their normal size by swallowing water or air when threatened. Although the eyes and internal organs of most puffer fish are highly toxic, the meat is considered a delicacy in Japan and Korea. Still, nearly 60 percent of humans who ingest this fish die from *tetrodotoxin,* a powerful neurotoxin that damages or destroys nerve tissue. Humans need only ingest a few milligrams of this toxin for a fatal reaction to occur. Symptoms include rapid numbness and tingling of lips and mouth, which are generally resolved within hours to days if treated promptly. Most puffer fish poisoning is the result of accidental consumption of other foods that are tainted with the puffer fish toxin rather than from the ingestion of puffer fish itself.

7. **Casu Marzu Maggot Cheese**
   Casu marzu, which means "rotting cheese" in Sardinian, is not just an aged and very smelly cheese, it is an illegal commodity in many places. Casu marzu is a runny white cheese made by injecting Pecorino Sardo cheese with cheese-eating larvae that measure about one-half inch long. Tradition calls for this cheese to be eaten with the maggots running through it. Sardinians claim these critters make the cheese creamier and that it's absolutely delicious. This cheese is widely, but not openly, eaten in Sardinia, even though the ban on it is only enforced sporadically.

Pizza Facts

1. The first known pizzeria, Antica Pizzeria, opened in Naples, Italy, in 1738. In the United States, the first pizzeria was opened in New York City by Gennaro Lombardi in 1895.

2. Pizzerias represent 17 percent of all U.S. restaurants.

3. Approximately three billion pizzas are sold in the United States every year, plus an additional one billion frozen pizzas, making pizza a $39.4 billion industry in the United States.

4. Ninety-three percent of Americans eat pizza at least once a month.

5. On average, each person in the United States eats around 23 pounds of pizza every year.

6. The record for the world's largest pizza depends on how you slice it. According to *Guinness World Records,* the record for the world's largest circular pizza was set at Norwood Hypermarket in South Africa in 1990. The gigantic pie measured 122 feet 8 inches across, weighed 26,883 pounds, and contained 9,920 pounds of flour, 3,968 pounds of cheese, and 1,984 pounds of sauce. In 2005, the record for the world's largest rectangular pizza was set in Iowa Falls, Iowa. Pizzeria owner Bill Bahr and a team of 900 helpers created the 110-foot by 98.6-foot pizza from 4,000 pounds of cheese, 700 pounds of sauce, and 9,500 sections of crust. The enormous pie was enough to feed each of the town's 5,200 residents ten slices of pizza.

7. More pizza is consumed during the week of the Super Bowl than any other time of the year.

8. Women are twice as likely as men to order vegetarian toppings on their pizza.

9. Pepperoni is the most popular topping in the United States; it's on about 36 percent of all pizzas.

10. October is National Pizza Month in the United States.

SUPERSIZE ME, MY LIEGE
A Typical Feast for Henry VIII

�֍ �֍ ✷ ✷

Henry VIII, who ruled England from 1509 until his death in 1547, was known for his voracious appetite. Portraits of him show a man almost as wide as he was tall. When he wasn't marrying, divorcing, or beheading his wives (he was on his sixth marriage when he died), this medieval ruler dined like a glutton. His kitchen at Hampton Court Palace filled 55 rooms. The 200 members of the kitchen staff provided meals of up to 14 courses for the 600 people in his court. Here are some dishes served at a typical feast.

1. Black Pudding
Black pudding was a popular dish in medieval times and is still served in parts of England today. This sausage is made by filling a length of pig's intestine with the animal's boiled, congealed blood.

2. Boar's Head
A boar's head, garnished with bay and rosemary, served as the centerpiece of Christmas feasts. It certainly outdoes a floral display.

3. Grilled Beavers' Tails
These tasty morsels were particularly popular on Fridays, when, according to Christian tradition, it was forbidden to eat meat. Rather conveniently, medieval people classified beavers as fish.

4. Internal Organs
If you're squeamish, stop reading now. Medieval cooks didn't believe in wasting any part of an animal, and, in fact, internal organs were often regarded as delicacies. Beef lungs, spleen, and even udders were considered fit for a king and were usually preserved in brine or vinegar.

5. Marzipan
A paste made from ground almonds, sugar, and egg whites and flavored with cinnamon and pepper, marzipan was occasionally served

at the end of a meal, although desserts weren't popular in England until the 18th century, when incredibly elaborate sugar sculptures became popular among the aristocracy.

6. Roasted Swan

Roasted swan was another treat reserved for special occasions, largely because swans were regarded as too noble and dignified for everyday consumption. The bird was often presented to the table with a gold crown upon its head. To this day, English law stipulates that all mute swans are owned by the Crown and may not be eaten without permission from the Queen.

7. Spiced Fruitcake

The exception to the no dessert rule was during the Twelfth Night banquet on January 6, when a special spiced fruitcake containing a dried pea (or bean) was served. Whoever found the pea would be king or queen of the pea (or bean) and was treated as a guest of honor for the remainder of the evening.

8. Spit-Roasted Meat

Spit-roasted meat—usually a pig or boar—was eaten at every meal. It was an expression of extreme wealth because only the rich could afford fresh meat year-round; only the very rich could afford to roast it, since this required much more fuel than boiling; and only the super wealthy could pay a "spit boy" to turn the spit all day. In a typical year, the royal kitchen served 1,240 oxen, 8,200 sheep, 2,330 deer, 760 calves, 1,870 pigs, and 53 wild boar. That's more than 14,000 large animals, meaning each member of the court was consuming about 24 animals every year.

9. Vegetables

Perhaps the only type of food Henry and his court didn't consume to excess was vegetables, which were viewed as the food of the poor and made up less than 20 percent of the royal diet.

10. Whale Meat

Another popular dish for Fridays, whale meat was fairly common and cheap, due to the plentiful supply of whales in the North Sea, each of which could feed hundreds of people. It was typically served boiled or very well roasted.

11. Whole Roasted Peacock
This delicacy was served dressed in its own iridescent blue feathers (which were plucked, then replaced after the bird had been cooked), with its beak gilded in gold leaf.

12. Wine and Ale
All this food was washed down with enormous quantities of wine and ale. Historians estimate that 600,000 gallons of ale (enough to fill an Olympic-size swimming pool) and around 75,000 gallons of wine (enough to fill 1,500 bathtubs) were drunk every year at Hampton Court Palace.

15 Countries with the Most Coffee Consumers
※ ※ ※ ※

Country	Pounds of Coffee per Person per Year
1. Norway	23.6
2. Finland	22.3
3. Denmark	21.4
4. Sweden	17.2
5. Netherlands	15.7
6. Switzerland	15.4
7. Germany	12.6
8. Austria	12.1
9. Belgium	11.0
10. France	8.6
11. Italy	7.1
12. United States	6.6
13. Canada	5.3
14. Australia	4.4
15. Japan	3.1

YOU ARE WHAT YOU EAT
41 Foods and Their Calories

✳ ✳ ✳ ✳

Despite what you hear from the purveyors of trendy fad diets,
specialty diet foods, and expensive weight-loss programs,
there is no secret to shedding pounds. You simply need to use
more calories than you consume. To put things into perspective,
here are the calorie counts for some typical foods—keep in
mind that the exact number of calories can vary.

Food	*Calories*
1. Apple, medium	72
2. Bagel	289
3. Banana, medium	105
4. Beer (regular, 12 ounces)	153
5. Bread (one slice, wheat or white)	66
6. Butter (salted, 1 tablespoon)	102
7. Carrots (raw, 1 cup)	52
8. Cheddar cheese (1 slice)	113
9. Chicken breast (boneless, skinless, roasted, 3 ounces)	142
10. Chocolate-chip cookie (from packaged dough)	59
11. Coffee (regular, brewed from grounds, black)	2
12. Corn (canned, sweet yellow whole kernel, drained, 1 cup)	180
13. Egg (large, scrambled)	102
14. Granola bar (chewy, with raisins, 1.5-ounce bar)	193
15. Green beans (canned, drained, 1 cup)	40
16. Ground beef patty (15 percent fat, 4 ounces, pan-broiled)	193
17. Hot dog (beef and pork)	137
18. Ice cream (vanilla, 4 ounces)	145
19. Jelly doughnut	289
20. Ketchup (1 tablespoon)	15
21. Milk (2 percent milk fat, 8 ounces)	122
22. Mixed nuts (dry roasted, with peanuts, salted, 1 ounce)	168

Food	Calories
23. Mustard, yellow (2 teaspoons)	6
24. Oatmeal (plain, cooked in water without salt, 1 cup)	147
25. Orange juice (frozen concentrate, made with water, 8 ounces)	112
26. Peanut butter (creamy, 2 tablespoons)	180
27. Pork chop (center rib, boneless, broiled, 3 ounces)	221
28. Potato, medium (baked, including skin)	161
29. Potato chips (plain, salted, 1 ounce)	155
30. Pretzels (hard, salted, 1 ounce)	108
31. Raisins (1.5 ounces)	130
32. Ranch salad dressing (2 tablespoons)	146
33. Red wine (cabernet sauvignon, 5 ounces)	123
34. Rice (white, long grain, cooked, 1 cup)	205
35. Salsa (4 ounces)	35
36. Shrimp (cooked under moist heat, 3 ounces)	84
37. Spaghetti (cooked, enriched, 1 cup)	221
38. Spaghetti sauce (marinara, ready to serve, 4 ounces)	92
39. Tuna (light, canned in water, drained, 3 ounces)	100
40. White wine (sauvignon blanc, 5 ounces)	121
41. Yellow cake with chocolate frosting (one piece)	243

Source: USDA National Nutrient Database for Standard Reference, Release 19 (2006)

6 Unexpected Surprises Found in Food Items

�֎ �֎ �֎ �֎

You've probably heard about the woman who claimed she found a human finger in a bowl of Wendy's chili. It turned out to be a hoax, but many such claims turn out to be true. The following is a sampling of some of the most disgusting items found in food products. Bon appétit!

1. In 2000, a two-year-old boy in the UK got the surprise of his life—and a stomachache—after munching on Burger King french fries that included a special treat—a fried lizard! The boy's family dutifully handed over the crispy lizard to the restaurant for further examination, and no lawsuit was filed.

2. In 2002, a woman was enjoying a bowl of clam chowder at McCormick & Schmick's Seafood in Irvine, California, when she bit down on something rubbery. Assuming it was calamari, she spit it into her napkin, only to find that it was actually a condom. The woman won an undisclosed amount in a lawsuit, and the restaurant unsuccessfully sued a supplier.

3. In Baltimore, Maryland, in 2003, a man was eating a three-piece combo meal at Popeyes Chicken & Biscuits when he bit down and found a little surprise wedged between the skin and the meat of his chicken—a deep-fried mouse! Sadly, the restaurant had other rodent infestation citations on its record.

4. During the summer of 2004, David Scheiding was enjoying an Arby's chicken sandwich, but it came with an unexpected topping—sliced human flesh. Turns out that the store manager sliced his thumb while shredding lettuce. Of course, he thoroughly sanitized the area, but the lettuce was still used! Scheiding refused to accept a settlement from Arby's and filed a lawsuit in 2005.

5. Imagine the surprise of five-year-old Jordan Willett of the UK when he poured a bowl of Golden Puffs breakfast cereal one morning in 2005, and out popped a snake! The two-foot long, nonvenomous corn snake was not inside the sealed cereal bag, so investigators are unsure how it got inside the cereal box.

6. In 2005, Clarence Stowers of North Carolina was savoring a pint of frozen custard. Thinking that a chunk at the bottom of the dessert was candy, he decided to save it for last. How disappointed he must have been to discover that it wasn't candy but was actually part of the index finger of a Kohl's Frozen Custard employee. What's more, Stowers kept the finger as evidence for his lawsuit, and by the time he decided to give it back, it was too late to reattach it.

Chapter 13
TELEVISION

* * * *

FROM LOVE IN THE AFTERNOON
TO DARLINGS OF THE ACADEMY
Celebs Whose Careers Started on Soap Operas

*If you ever catch some vintage soap opera footage, you may see
a few familiar faces. Here are some of today's hottest stars
who got their start on daytime dramas.*

1. David Hasselhoff

The man once listed in *Guinness World Records* as the "most
watched TV star in the world" got his start on daytime television.
Between 1975 and 1982, Hasselhoff could be seen on *The Young
and the Restless* as Dr. Snapper Foster, who was put through college by his poor mother and manicurist sister (Jill Abbott, who is
still on the show). After seven years, Hasselhoff left daytime TV
without knowing what would come next. But he didn't have to wonder for long—NBC President Brandon Tartikoff asked him to play
the lead (opposite a talking car) in a new show called *Knight Rider*.
By 1989, the phenomenon known as *Baywatch* hit the airwaves
with Hasselhoff at the helm as lead actor and executive producer.

2. James Earl Jones

Before he was the voice of Darth Vader in *Star Wars*, even before
he was nominated for an Oscar for his role in *The Great White
Hope*, James Earl Jones played doctor. Soap opera doctor, that is!
First he was Dr. Jerry Turner on *As the World Turns* and then
Dr. Jim Frazier on *The Guiding Light*, both in 1966. Most people
recognize his deep voice from his famous line in *Star Wars*, when
he said to Luke Skywalker, "I am your father." But in 1966, he
was probably warming up that voice with lines like "Where's my
stethoscope?"

3. Teri Hatcher

Voted by her 1982 high school class as "Girl Most Likely to Become a Solid Gold Dancer," Hatcher took a different direction and studied math in college. Her classmates might have been onto something, however, because she soon left college life and, in 1985, found a job as a dancing mermaid on *The Love Boat*. From 1986 to 1987, she was cast on *Capitol* as Angelica Clegg, a congressman's wife. But Hatcher didn't stick around for long; in 1987, she started to appear in several prime-time TV shows, such as *Night Court* and *L.A. Law*. By 1993, she landed her first major role—as Lois Lane on the series *Lois & Clark: The New Adventures of Superman*.

4. Christopher Reeve

Speaking of Superman...long before he was characterized personally and professionally as a "man of steel," Christopher Reeve played devilishly handsome and selfish Ben Harper on *Love of Life* from 1974 to 1976. His character was married to two women from the same town at the same time! His wives eventually exposed him for the cad that he was, and he ended up in prison. Perhaps leading a double life onscreen is why, in 1978, a casting director got the idea to make him a secretive superhero in *Superman*.

5. Demi Moore

For her first 19 years, her name was Demetria Guynes, but then she married musician Freddy Moore and took the name that most recognize today. In 1982, Demi beat out thousands of actors for the role of Jackie Templeton on *General Hospital*. She was an instant sensation as a sassy reporter who went to great lengths to get a scoop. She left daytime TV in 1983, eventually starring in feature films, such as *Ghost, Indecent Proposal,* and *A Few Good Men*.

6. Ray Liotta

The tough guy who later played a succession of gangsters, Liotta launched his career as lovable hero Joey Perrini on *Another World* from 1978 to 1981. A few years after Liotta's love-struck character left the soap, Robert De Niro suggested him for Martin Scorsese's disturbing film *GoodFellas* as mobster kingpin Henry Hill.

7. Marisa Tomei

After attending Boston University for a year, perky actor Marisa Tomei landed a role on *As the World Turns.* From 1983 to 1985, she played airhead Marcy Thompson. Her character accused a man of sexual harassment, then went on to marry a prince, Lord Stewart Cushing. He swept Marcy away to England where they lived happily ever after as Lord and Lady Cushing.

8. Cicely Tyson

This highly acclaimed actor got her start on *The Guiding Light* in 1966. She originated the role of nurse Martha Frazier. On the show, her husband, Dr. Jim Frazier, was played by Billie Dee Williams and later, James Earl Jones. Tyson was plucked from the hospital set when producers chose her for a film called *The Comedians.* Her cast mates in the film were an impressive lot: Richard Burton, Elizabeth Taylor, Alec Guinness, Peter Ustinov, and Lillian Gish. Throughout her career, Cicely Tyson has been known for portraying strong African American women.

9. Tommy Lee Jones

From 1971 to 1975, this future Oscar winner played a bad seed on *One Life to Live.* As Dr. Mark Toland, Jones portrayed a moody man married to a frigid wife. The combination was a recipe for disaster, until finally, he was murdered by a woman while he was running from the law.

10. Rick Springfield

In 1968, young Aussie singer/guitarist Rick Springfield (born Richard Springthorpe) was hired by a private promoter to visit military bases in Vietnam and entertain troops. By 1972, he lived in Hollywood, continued making music, and had branched out into acting. From 1981 to 1983, he played a sweetie pie named Dr. Noah Drake on *General Hospital,* breaking hearts all over the fictional town of Port Charles. He never stopped touring with his band, however, and his song "Jessie's Girl" won him a Grammy for Best Male Vocal Performance in 1982. Still touring and releasing CDs, Rick Springfield is another one of daytime TV's musical claims to fame.

11. Ricky Martin

This hottie was "Livin' La Vida Loca" in *General Hospital*'s Port Charles as Miguel Morez. As a fab example of typecasting, Martin was tapped to play a Latino singer. He had long, curly hair and steamed up the afternoons from 1994 to 1995. Today he's far from Port Charles; in fact, this Grammy Award-winning artist spends much of his free time working for children's charities.

12. Kathleen Turner

As a child, Mary Kathleen Turner traveled the world because her father was a U.S. foreign service officer. During that time, the Turner family lived in Canada, Cuba, London, Venezuela, and Washington, D.C. By age 23, she shed her first name and got her first big break on *The Doctors*. From 1978 to 1979, Kathleen played trampy Nola Dancy, a girl from the wrong side of the tracks who married someone from the right side. Then, in 1981, she debuted on the big screen as a sizzling temptress in *Body Heat*.

13. Larry Hagman

In 1957, more than 20 years before the entire nation pondered the question "Who shot JR?," a young Larry Hagman played Curt Williams on *Search for Tomorrow*. Then, from 1961 to 1963, he played a lawyer by the name of Ed Gibson on *The Edge of Night*. By 1965, Hagman was starring in *I Dream of Jeannie*. But once he put on his cowboy hat to play unscrupulous oilman JR Ewing on *Dallas* starting in 1978, all of his other characters seemed to fade away.

14. Susan Sarandon

Politically active and outspoken even as a teenager, Susan Sarandon landed a spot on the runway as a Ford model. But it was her role as Patrice Kahlman on the soap *A World Apart* that put her on the small screen from 1970 to 1971. She played a murderous drifter named Sarah Fairbanks on *Search for Tomorrow* in 1972, and by 1975, she had appeared in the cult classic *The Rocky Horror Picture Show*. Over the next 20 years, Sarandon was nominated for five Oscars before finally bringing one home in 1995 for her role in *Dead Man Walking*, which was directed by her partner Tim Robbins.

15. Meg Ryan

Before she was the queen of romantic comedies, Meg Ryan was tangled up in a love triangle on *As the World Turns.* From 1982 to 1984, the spunky actor portrayed good girl Betsy Stewart, who was in love with blue-collar Steve Andropolous. Her stepfather didn't approve, so Betsy married unscrupulous Craig Montgomery instead. But true love prevailed when Betsy left Craig and married Steve in May 1984. Their happiness didn't last, but so it goes in the soap world. Ryan's movie career took off when she left the show, and her starring role in *When Harry Met Sally* in 1989 solidified her place as a leading lady.

16 Favorite 1950s TV Shows

✳ ✳ ✳ ✳

1. *The Adventures of Ozzie and Harriet*
2. *The Donna Reed Show*
3. *Dragnet*
4. *The Ed Sullivan Show*
5. *Father Knows Best*
6. *Gunsmoke*
7. *Have Gun, Will Travel*
8. *The Honeymooners*
9. *I Love Lucy*
10. *I've Got a Secret*
11. *The Jack Benny Program*
12. *Leave It to Beaver*
13. *The Lone Ranger*
14. *Make Room for Daddy (The Danny Thomas Show)*
15. *The Milton Berle Show*
16. *You Bet Your Life*

18 Favorite 1960s TV Shows

1. *The Andy Griffith Show*
2. *Batman*
3. *The Beverly Hillbillies*
4. *Bewitched*
5. *Bonanza*
6. *Candid Camera*
7. *The Dick Van Dyke Show*
8. *Family Affair*
9. *Get Smart*
10. *Gilligan's Island*
11. *Gomer Pyle, U.S.M.C.*
12. *Green Acres*
13. *I Dream of Jeannie*
14. *Lassie*
15. *The Lucy Show*
16. *The Munsters*
17. *My Three Sons*
18. *The Twilight Zone*

"BUT WAIT... THERE'S MORE!" 11 of Ron Popeil's Greatest Gadgets

Before there was QVC, there was Ron Popeil, an inventor who became a multimillionaire by pitching labor-saving, albeit unusual, devices on TV with the catchphrase, "But wait... there's more!" Here are some of Popeil's famous and infamous products.

1. Veg-O-Matic

Popeil learned to be a pitchman from his father, Samuel, who was also an inventor and salesman of kitchen gadgets such as the Chop-

O-Matic, which later became Ron's Veg-O-Matic and together sold more than 11 million units. The Chop-O-Matic was introduced in the mid-1950s at the amazing low price of $3.98. Ron renamed it the Veg-O-Matic and pitched it as "the greatest kitchen appliance ever made...."

2. Solid Flavor Injector

Resembling a syringe with a large plastic "needle," this gadget is used to inject fillings such as dried fruit, small vegetables, nuts, chocolate chips, and candy into foods such as hams, roasts, cupcakes, and pastries. At just $14.95, it won't cost you a fortune to add a bit of flair and pizzazz to your food.

3. Smokeless Ashtray

The Smokeless Ashtray was a tiny device that promised to suck up the smoke that came from cigars and cigarettes before it filled the room, and in the 1970s, Ron sold more than a million of these contraptions at $19.95 each. With most smoking being done outside today, the Smokeless Ashtray has been replaced by something less expensive—wind.

4. Showtime Rotisserie and BBQ Oven

Introduced in 1998, the Showtime Rotisserie and BBQ Oven is by far Ron Popeil's most successful product to date. Originally available in three models, the Showtime Rotisserie has sold seven million units. Popeil's pitch for the Showtime Rotisserie, which sells for $159.80, is "Set it and forget it!," which has been repeated in infomercials so many times that it's impossible to forget.

5. Mr. Microphone

Launched in 1978, Mr. Microphone was a low-power FM modulator that turned radios into annoying precursors of the karaoke machine. The TV commercial featured Popeil's daughter and her boyfriend driving a convertible and using Mr. Microphone, which made one wonder why he didn't follow this invention up with Mr. Earplugs. Maybe it helped that he sold more than a million of them at $19.95.

6. Pocket Fisherman

Popeil advertised this device as "the biggest fishing invention since the hook...and still only $19.95." The handle was a mini tackle box containing a hook, line, and sinker...worms were up to you since it didn't come with a pocket shovel. The Pocket Fisherman was invented in 1963 by Ron's father after he was nearly injured by the tip of a fishing pole. Today's version sells for $29.95 and has a double-flex rod hinge that unfolds to a fully extendable position. Together, both versions of the Pocket Fisherman have sold more than two million units.

7. Inside-the-Shell Egg Scrambler

Not one of Popeil's best sellers, but here's how it works: A bent pin pierces the eggshell, rotates inside it, and creates perfectly scrambled eggs and yolk-free hard-boiled eggs. Only about 150,000 have sold at $19.95.

8. GLH Formula Number 9 Hair System

Got a bald spot? Ron Popeil can fix it with the GLH Formula Number 9 Hair System. Great Looking Hair isn't real hair but a spray that matches your hair color, thickens thinning hair, and covers bald spots. More than one million cans have sold for only $9.95 for the spray or $20 for the spray, shampoo, and finishing shield.

9. Electric Food Dehydrator

Introduced in 1965 at $59.95, Ron Popeil called it "the most famous food dehydrator in the world!" The sun might disagree with that claim, but the Electric Food Dehydrator, which brought Popeil back from semiretirement, currently comes with five trays and sells for $39.95.

10. Dial-O-Matic

If the Chop-O-Matic and Veg-O-Matic don't cut veggies small enough that kids can't recognize them, the Dial-O-Matic will. This food slicer debuted in the mid-1950s, preceding the modern food processor, and, at the original price of $3, took a much smaller slice out of the family budget. The Dial-O-Matic has sold two million units and is still available—now for $29.95—and can still turn hundreds of potatoes into french fries in minutes.

11. Pasta Maker & Sausage Machine

With this gadget, you can make ten different shapes of homemade pasta in just five minutes! You can even use it to make homemade sausage. Now retailing for $199.95, more than a million of these machines have sold since their debut in 1993.

21 Favorite 1970s TV Shows

✳ ✳ ✳ ✳

1. *Alice*
2. *All in the Family*
3. *The Brady Bunch*
4. *The Carol Burnett Show*
5. *Charlie's Angels*
6. *Good Times*
7. *Happy Days*
8. *Hawaii Five-O*
9. *The Jeffersons*
10. *Laverne & Shirley*
11. *Little House on the Prairie*
12. *Mary Tyler Moore*
13. *M*A*S*H*
14. *Maude*
15. *One Day at a Time*
16. *The Partridge Family*
17. *Sanford and Son*
18. *Starsky and Hutch*
19. *Three's Company*
20. *The Waltons*
21. *Welcome Back, Kotter*

TRAVELING SALESMEN
Celebrities Who Have Made Ads in Japan

❋ ❋ ❋ ❋

For decades, celebrities have been crossing the Pacific to make commercials in Japan. It's a quick, easy way for them to make a buck without harming their reps back in the States, thanks to secrecy clauses that prevent Japanese companies from disclosing the endorsements. But with the success of YouTube and similar sites, many of these commercials are now available worldwide on the Web. The spots make for hilarious viewing, and you can be sure that the stars are laughing all the way to the bank.

1. Harrison Ford

What do hiking near a volcano, dining at a sushi restaurant, sitting in a steam room, and jetting around on an airliner have in common? They all go great with Kirin beer, according to Harrison Ford. The man who turned both Han Solo and Indiana Jones into household names lent his visage to this refreshing lager in at least five different TV commercials, plus a print ad, during the mid-1990s.

2. Britney Spears

There are many sides to Britney Spears—pop star, mom, Paris Hilton's BFF, and, oddly enough, the face of Go-Go Tea. Brit appeared in ads for the iced tea beverage dressed as a '60s go-go girl, complete with white patent leather boots and some killer dance moves. The ads ran until early 2003, when the singer was "not a girl, not yet a woman."

3. Bruce Willis

After *Moonlighting,* but before he split with Demi Moore, Bruce Willis spent a lot of time in the Far East. In the early 1990s, the man who gave us four *Die Hard* films and lots of movies with numbers in their titles (*The Fifth Element, The Sixth Sense, The Whole Nine Yards*) pitched Maki jewelry stores, Georgia coffee drinks, Eneos gas stations, Subaru, and Post canned drinking water.

4. Jodie Foster

Jodie Foster appears to choose her movie roles carefully, opting for edgy roles that prick audience sensibilities: *The Silence of the Lambs, The Accused,* and *Panic Room,* to name a few. Her commercial résumé is a little less selective. From the mid-1990s to 2000, Foster pitched Keri beauty products, Pasona temp agency, Mt. Rainier iced coffee, and Honda, all the while smiling like she hadn't a care in the world. Clarice Starling, we hardly recognize ye.

5. Nicolas Cage

Maybe it happened while filming *Leaving Las Vegas* . . . or maybe *Honeymoon in Vegas.* Either way, at some point, Nicolas Cage was bit by the gambling bug, so much so that he felt the need to shill for Sankyo, the manufacturer of *pachinko* machines. Similar to slot machines, the devices can be found in casinos across Japan. Ads from the late 1990s feature a wild-eyed Cage so obsessed by his pachinko fever that he's having trouble functioning day to day!

6. Anne Hathaway

The Princess Diaries, a tale of an ugly duckling turned royal beauty, made its way into Japanese movie theaters in 2002. Shortly afterward, the film's star, Anne Hathaway, made her way into Japanese living rooms via commercials for the Lux line of hair and beauty products. Hathaway joins a lofty list of Lux lovelies, which includes Catherine Zeta-Jones, Penelope Cruz, and Charlize Theron. Hathaway's spots trade on her princess rep, with the actress dressed in ethereal white and appearing to float through life as weightless as her styling mousse.

7. Arnold Schwarzenegger

If Arnold Schwarzenegger is to be believed, inhaling a cup of Nissin instant noodles will provide you with enough strength to swing really heavy-looking bronze pots back and forth with ease. Or, you can melt away your stress with a can of Hop's Beer. Or tap into your superhero-worthy powers with a jolt of Vfuyy energy drink. The bodybuilder/actor/governor of California endorsed these Japanese products in commercial spots from the 1990s.

8. Ashley Judd

Ashley Judd is *thrilled* to be driving a Honda Primo, and she can barely contain her enthusiasm in the 2000 commercial that has her coining the phrase "Hondaful life." The actor, famous for roles in *De-Lovely* and *Kiss the Girls* and infamous for her family squabbles with sister Wynonna and mom Naomi, sports a bouncy, blonde 'do and catches the eye of everyone in these bubbly spots.

9. Sharon Stone

Many Americans weren't introduced to Sharon Stone until 1992's *Basic Instinct.* But Japanese audiences got a glimpse of the soon-to-be A-list actress in the late '80s when she appeared in ads for Vernal cosmetics. Dressed in a gray business suit, a brunette Stone looked sharp but offered not a hint of the upcoming sultry, villainous role that would forever seal her place in cinematic history.

10. Cameron Diaz

There's something about Aeon English Schools, a private institute with more than 300 schools in Japan, that made Cameron Diaz (as well as Celine Dion, Ewan McGregor, and Mariah Carey) want to sing their praises. In the Diaz spots (which aired in 2000 and 2001), the bubbly star of *Charlie's Angels* and *There's Something About Mary* looks fresh-faced and innocent as she repeats the word *believe* over and over in front of a series of different backgrounds. Aeon posters featuring Diaz's mug were also plastered around Japan during the same time.

11. Richard Gere

It's not cheap to be a Buddhist humanitarian, and Richard Gere is a famously generous one. Perhaps that's why he appears in ads for such entities as Mt. Rainier coffee drinks, Tokyo Towers real estate development, and Dandy House clothing. The actor has appeared in Dandy House commercials as recently as December 2006.

12. Madonna

Madonna is no stranger to endorsements, having appeared in Gap, H&M, and Versace ads in the United States. In Japan, the

"Material Girl" could be seen plugging Shochu rice beverages in ads that ran in 1995 and 1996. The spots show Madge slaying both a giant dragon and an evil wizard before enjoying a glass of the drink and announcing, "I'm pure." Okay...if you say so!

27 Favorite 1980s TV Shows

❋ ❋ ❋ ❋

1. *ALF*
2. *The A-Team*
3. *Cheers*
4. *The Cosby Show*
5. *Dallas*
6. *A Different World*
7. *Diff'rent Strokes*
8. *Dynasty*
9. *Facts of Life*
10. *Falcon Crest*
11. *Family Ties*
12. *The Golden Girls*
13. *Growing Pains*
14. *Knots Landing*
15. *L.A. Law*
16. *Magnum P.I.*
17. *Mama's Family*
18. *Matlock*
19. *Miami Vice*
20. *Moonlighting*
21. *Murder, She Wrote*
22. *Silver Spoons*
23. *Simon & Simon*
24. *thirtysomething*
25. *Trapper John, M.D.*
26. *Who's the Boss?*
27. *The Wonder Years*

"AND THE SURVEY SAYS..."
America's Longest-Running Game Shows

✳ ✳ ✳ ✳

Quiz shows first became popular in the age of radio, but when television was introduced, TV game shows became inextricably woven into American pop culture. Hundreds of game shows have come and gone since the first TV game show, Truth or Consequences, *hit the airwaves in 1950, but some, like those that follow, had the magic formula and ran for years.*

1. *You Bet Your Life*

This unique program was modeled after Groucho Marx's radio series of the same name, in which contestants answered questions for prize money. The audience was clued into the "secret word," but the contestant was not. If the contestant could answer the questions and come up with the secret word, a duck (a nod to Groucho's classic film *Duck Soup*) would descend from the ceiling and deliver $100 in prize money. Marx hosted the show during its original run from 1950 to 1961. Later versions hosted by Buddy Hackett and Bill Cosby were unable to match the success of the original.

2. *To Tell the Truth*

On this show, a team of celebrity panelists heard a story and then had to determine which of three contestants was associated with the story. Payoffs were based on the contestants' ability to fool the panel and weren't large by today's standards: Each incorrect guess from the panel paid the challengers $250 for a possible $1,000. But if the entire panel was correct, the challengers split $150. The show's original run lasted from 1956 to 1968, and the game that asked, "Will the real John Doe please stand up?" has enjoyed several reincarnations.

3. *Let's Make a Deal*

Monty Hall was the archetypal game show host in this long-running favorite that required contestants to have a little intuition and a lot of luck. The show involved contestants making a "deal" with Hall and selecting prizes that could be real or bogus. But what really made the show stand apart was the costumes that contestants wore. In the first days of the show, contestants wore everyday clothes until someone came to the show wearing a crazy costume to get the attention of producers, and immediately, a tradition was born. From then on, contestants on *Let's Make a Deal* wore nutty outfits in order to be singled out to participate. Several revivals have been attempted, but fans of the show seem to prefer reruns of the original, which ran from 1963 to 1977.

4. *Concentration*

The game show genre took a beating during the 1950s when it was revealed that several shows were rigged and contestants were given the answers in advance. Though they were later implicated in the quiz show scandals, producers Jack Barry and Dan Enright created a solid game called *Concentration,* which survived the tumult of the scandals, airing from 1958 to 1973. The game was based on two concepts: a children's game known as "Memory," and a word puzzle that was revealed when matching cards were removed from the board. The show survived in syndication for some time and enjoyed a revival in 1987 that lasted approximately five years.

5. *Hollywood Squares*

Mere mortals got a chance to play with celebrities in this game show based on tic-tac-toe. Nine Hollywood stars sit in separate, open-faced cubes that make up the board. The stars are asked questions by the host, and contestants judge whether or not their answers are true or false in order to put an *X* or *O* in the square. Prize winnings got larger and larger over the years, with one jackpot reaching $100,000. But the game was really a vehicle for the comedic banter between the host and the celebrities. Between the original version, which aired from 1966 to 1981, and its many reincarnations, *Squares* has featured celebrities such as Vincent Price, Joan Rivers, Whoopi Goldberg, Paul Lynde, Martin Mull, and ALF.

6. *I've Got a Secret*

An old parlor game, "Secret, Secret, Who's Got the Secret?," was the inspiration for this classic quiz show that originally aired from 1952 to 1967. The host introduced the contestant and asked them to whisper their "secret" into his ear. The secret was shown on-screen for at-home viewers, but a panel of celebrities had to try to guess the secret by asking questions. Each time a panelist guessed incorrectly, the player was paid $20, with a whopping $80 maximum prize. In recent years, the show was revived on the Game Show Network with larger payouts and secrets that are much racier than they were in the 1950s.

7. *What's My Line?*

In *What's My Line?*, four celebrity panelists tried to guess the occupation (or "line" of work) of a fifth, secret contestant by asking only "yes" or "no" questions. During the third round, panelists were blindfolded and challenged to guess the identity of a "Mystery Guest." The original run of the show (which paid players for appearances, since prize money never exceeded $50) ran from 1950 to 1967, but since then several revivals have been launched. Celebrity guests have included author Gore Vidal, actor Jane Fonda, and singer Bobby Darin.

8. *Truth or Consequences*

This show originally aired as a radio quiz show starting in 1940, then crossed over to television in 1950. The show asked contestants to answer obscure, often trick, questions, but if they couldn't answer, they had to suffer the "consequences"—often embarrassing or silly stunts. Bob Barker hosted the show from 1956 to 1975, but it never quite recovered after his departure. The show ran off and on for about 20 seasons from 1950 to 1978 and had a short-lived revival in the late '80s.

9. *Jeopardy!*

Answer: This game show was ranked first in the Nielsen ratings for quiz shows for more than 1,000 weeks. Question: What is

Jeopardy? With 27 Daytime Emmy Awards and 37 million viewers weekly, *Jeopardy* has dug its heels into television history. Current host Alex Trebek gives the answers to three contestants who buzz in to provide the questions. In 2004, contestant Ken Jennings set the record for consecutive games played during his unprecedented 74-game winning streak, earning more than $2.5 million before he stumbled. The current show has been on the air since 1984 and is a revival of the original, which ran from 1964 to 1975.

10. *Wheel of Fortune*

Since 1975, contestants have been spinning the wheel and risking bankruptcy to guess letters and complete the word puzzle on the board. Contestants can buy a vowel and vie to be the first to solve the puzzle. The bonus round allows winners to add cars, trips, and up to $1,000,000 in cash to their winnings. Before Pat Sajak and Vanna White took the reins in the early 1980s, Chuck Woolery and Susan Stafford hosted the show. Dubbed "America's game," *Wheel* frequently goes on tour across the country and features celebrity and charity versions of the show as well.

11. *The Price Is Right*

"Come on down!" Why does this relic from the 1970s still grab high daytime ratings more than 35 years after it debuted? Because with an agreeable host, contestants plucked from the audience, 80 different games like Plinko and Hi-Lo, and big prizes (motor homes, cars, trips, and furniture), there's something for everyone. The show, which debuted in 1972 and made Bob Barker a TV legend during his 35 years as host, is actually a revival of an earlier incarnation of the show, which aired from 1956 to 1965.

✳ ✳ ✳

"You have to learn the rules of the game. And then you have to play better than anyone else."
—Albert Einstein

16 Favorite 1990s TV Shows

✳ ✳ ✳ ✳

1. *Beverly Hills, 90210*
2. *ER*
3. *Frasier*
4. *Friends*
5. *Full House*
6. *Home Improvement*
7. *Mad About You*
8. *Married with Children*
9. *Murphy Brown*
10. *NYPD Blue*
11. *Roseanne*
12. *Saved by the Bell*
13. *Seinfeld*
14. *The Simpsons*
15. *Sisters*
16. *The X Files*

18 Memorable TV Theme Songs

A great TV theme song can tell you everything you need to know about a show in less than a minute. Better yet, if you can sing a few lines at work the next day and everyone joins in, you know you're on to something worth watching!

✳ ✳ ✳ ✳

1. "Theme from The Addams Family" (*The Addams Family*)

TV and film composer Vic Mizzy wrote the music and engaging lyrics that helped to describe the "creepy... kooky... mysterious... spooky... and all together ooky" Addams Family. The show takes a peek at the bizarre family: Gomez and Morticia, their children Pugsley and Wednesday, Cousin Itt, Uncle Fester, and servants Lurch and Thing, who all live together in a musty castle. The show lasted only two seasons, but it lives on in pop culture through reruns, cartoons, movies, and video games.

2. "Those Were the Days" (*All in the Family*)

Longing for a less complicated time, "Those Were the Days" was written by Charles Strouse and Lee Adams and was performed at the family piano by bigoted, blue-collar Archie Bunker and his screechingly off-key "dingbat" wife Edith. In the show, which aired from 1971 to 1979, staunchly conservative Archie is forced to live with a liberal when his "little goil" Gloria and her husband Michael move in with the Bunkers. The resulting discussions shed light on two sides of politics and earned Michael the nickname "Meathead."

3. "Generation" (*American Dreams*)

In this wholesome drama, the Pryor family faces the social and political issues of the 1960s, while teenager Meg Pryor and her friend Roxanne are regular dancers on *American Bandstand,* which sets the show to the sound track of the '60s. The theme song, "Generation," written and performed by Tonic's Emerson Hart, takes listeners back to a time when life was much simpler and safer. The show had an extremely loyal fan base, but poor time slots assigned by NBC resulted in low ratings, and the show was unexpectedly axed following the third season-ending cliffhanger, which left fans disappointed and longing for more.

4. "The Fishin' Hole" (*The Andy Griffith Show*)

When *The Andy Griffith Show* debuted in 1960, Sheriff Andy Taylor became one of TV's first single dads when his wife died and left him to raise their young son Opie in the small town of Mayberry. Aunt Bea came to town to help out, and Deputy Barney Fife helped keep small-town crime at bay. The result was an endearing slice of Americana that still lives on in syndication. The show's theme song was written by Earle Hagen and Herbert Spencer and is memorable but not for the lyrics—there are none! The melody is carried by a lone whistler (Hagen) and accompanies footage of Andy and Opie heading off together for some quality fishing time.

5. "Ballad of Jed Clampett" (*The Beverly Hillbillies*)

When hillbilly Jed Clampett struck oil while hunting on his land, he packed up his family and moved where the other rich people lived—Beverly Hills, of course! His beautiful and usually barefoot daughter Elly May attracted a lot of attention, as did pretty much everything about the Clampett family. Series creator Paul Henning wrote the "Ballad of Jed Clampett," which was performed by bluegrass musicians Flatt and Scruggs. The song made it to number 44 on the pop charts and to number one on the country charts.

6. "Theme Song from The Brady Bunch" (*The Brady Bunch*)

Series creator Sherwood Schwartz collaborated with composer Frank DeVol to come up with a theme song that describes what happens when a second marriage merges two families and six children under one roof. The song alone is memorable, but so is the opening sequence, which divided the screen into nine squares, one for each family member, including the housekeeper Alice. On the left, we saw the three daughters "... All of them had hair of gold, like their mother. The youngest one in curls." The right side introduced the three sons, who, with their father, made "... four men, living all together. Yet they were all alone." Who sang the song, you ask? After the first season, the cast members themselves!

7. "Where Everybody Knows Your Name" (*Cheers*)

Written by Judy Hart Angelo and Gary Portnoy (and sung by him, too), this comforting tune conjures up images of a place where the lonely and downtrodden can find a friend to lean on, where people can forget about their troubles for a while, and, yes, "where everybody knows your name." And that's exactly what *Cheers* did for 275 episodes from 1982 to 1993.

8. "Meet the Flintstones" (*The Flintstones*)

After two seasons without a theme song, show creators William Hanna and Joseph Barbera wrote lyrics for a tune by Hoyt Curtin. The show, which took place in the prehistoric town of Bedrock, was a parody on contemporary suburbia. There were no brakes on cars, just bare feet to slow things down. Cameras were primitive—birds feverishly chiseled slabs of rock to capture various images. And instead of a garbage disposal, people just kept a hungry reptile under the sink. Still, it was a "yabba-dabba-doo time!"

9. "I'll Be There for You" (*Friends*)

Written and performed by The Rembrandts, "I'll Be There for You" pretty much sums up the premise of this show about loyal friends who support each other through life's ups and downs. The intensely popular sitcom showed just how funny it is to be young, single, and living in New York City. Three guys and three girls formed a special bond as they roomed together, sometimes dated each other, and always entertained audiences worldwide. The song wasn't intended to be a full-length track, but eventually the band went back into the studio and recorded a longer version of the song, which topped U.S. charts and reached number two in the UK.

10. "Ballad of Gilligan's Isle" (*Gilligan's Island*)

All you have to do is listen to the theme song—it's all there! But here it is in a coconut shell: Five passengers went on a boating expedition that was supposed to last only three hours, but there was a storm, and the S.S. *Minnow* shipwrecked. The Skipper, his goofy first mate, and the passengers set up house on an island and made various futile attempts to be rescued. True *Gilligan's Island* aficionados know that there were two versions of the theme song, which was written by George Wyle and the show's creator Sherwood Schwartz. The first version specifically mentions five of the characters, then lumps the other two together, referring to them as "the rest." But Bob Denver (aka Gilligan) thought the song should be rewritten to include "The Professor and Mary Ann." Denver may have played the doofus on camera, but he used his star power to get equal billing for his fellow castaways . . . er, cast mates. He truly was everyone's "little buddy."

11. "Theme to Happy Days" (*Happy Days*)

Bill Haley and His Comets recorded a new version of their hit "Rock Around the Clock" for the theme song of the show about the middle-class Cunningham family and their life in Milwaukee in the 1950s and 1960s. After two seasons, the song "Theme to Happy Days," composed by Charles Fox and Norman Gimbel and performed by Truett Pratt and Jerry McClain, moved from the show's closing song to the opener. The song was released as a single in 1976 and cracked *Billboard*'s top five. The final season of the show featured a more modern version of the song led by Bobby Avron, but it was unpopular with fans.

12. "I Love Lucy" (*I Love Lucy*)

One of the most popular TV shows ever produced, *I Love Lucy* starred Lucille Ball as zany redhead Lucy Ricardo and Desi Arnaz as her husband, Cuban bandleader Ricky. Lucy and her reluctant neighbor and best friend, Ethel Mertz, were always involved in one harebrained scheme or another during this classic's six-year run. The show's theme song, written by Harold Adamson and Eliot Daniel, is most recognizable in its instrumental version, but it does have lyrics. During a 1953 episode in which Lucy believes everyone has forgotten her birthday, Ricky croons "I love Lucy, and she loves me. We're as happy as two can be...."

13. "Making Our Dreams Come True" (*Laverne & Shirley*)

Factory workers never had so much fun! Laverne and Shirley were two kooky girls who were introduced to TV audiences on *Happy Days* and ended up with their own hit show. They got into all kinds of trouble but always made it look like fun. The upbeat theme song was written by Charles Fox and Norman Gimbel and sung by Cyndi Grecco. The lyrics were empowering, but perhaps the most repeated line over the years was a mix of Yiddish and German words: "Schlemiel! Schlemazl! Hasenpfeffer Incorporated!"

14. "The Love Boat" (*The Love Boat*)

The Love Boat was just one of producer Aaron Spelling's offerings that dominated TV sets in the '70s and '80s. Love was definitely exciting and new every week when the *Pacific Princess* cruise ship set sail with a new set of passengers and a new set of challenges! Paul Williams and Charles Fox wrote the theme song, and for the first eight years, Jack Jones provided the vocals, but in 1985, Dionne

Warwick recorded her version for the show. With lyrics such as "Set a course for adventure, your mind on a new romance...," people were hooking up all over the Pacific seaboard.

15. "Love Is All Around" (*Mary Tyler Moore*)

Songwriter Sonny Curtis wrote and performed the empowering theme song for this trailblazing show about women's lib and the single life of spunky career woman Mary Richards. The opening sequence showed a fresh-faced Mary as she arrives in her new city and tosses her beret into the air out of the pure excitement of starting a new life. The original lyrics contemplated "...you might just make it after all," but after the first season, when it was clear that Mary would be a success, the lyrics were changed to "...you're gonna make it after all!" The bubbly and upbeat song has even been covered by Joan Jett & The Blackhearts and Sammy Davis, Jr.

16. "Theme from The Monkees" (*The Monkees*)

Here they come.... The original "prefab" four, The Monkees were a mix of zany actors and musicians cast as a rock band for the 1960s TV show of the same name. "Theme from The Monkees" was written by Bobby Hart and Tommy Boyce, and once the band members were cast, they recorded the song. The band was so successful that they went on tour and three of their songs reached number one on U.S. charts. The show only lasted two seasons, but The Monkees are now best known for their musical success and occasionally get together for reunion tours.

17. "Sunny Day" (*Sesame Street*)

Sesame Street was the first TV show to merge entertainment and education for the preschool set and is largely responsible for children starting kindergarten knowing their letters, numbers, and colors. The show, which airs in more than 120 countries, has won more than 100 Emmy Awards, making it the most award-winning TV series of all time. The cheerful and idyllic theme song was written by Joe Raposo, Jon Stone, and Bruce Hart, but the singers are all children. Or at least they were when the show debuted in 1969!

18. "A Little Help from My Friends" (*The Wonder Years*)

Set in the late 1960s and early 1970s, *The Wonder Years* chronicled the life of teenager Kevin Arnold as he grows up in suburbia in a middle-class family during this turbulent time. During the opening credits, the theme song, "A Little Help from My Friends," plays alongside "home movies" of Kevin and his family and friends. Hardly recognizable as the classic Beatles tune, Joe Cocker's cover of the song is much slower and in a different key but was reportedly loved by the Fab Four themselves.

22 Favorite TV Shows of the 2000s

❋ ❋ ❋ ❋

1. *Ally McBeal*
2. *The Amazing Race*
3. *American Idol*
4. *The Apprentice*
5. *CSI*
6. *Dancing with the Stars*
7. *Desperate Housewives*
8. *Everybody Loves Raymond*
9. *Fear Factor*
10. *Grey's Anatomy*
11. *King of Queens*
12. *Law & Order*
13. *Lost*
14. *The Office*
15. *Scrubs*
16. *Sex and the City*
17. *The Sopranos*
18. *Survivor*
19. *The West Wing*
20. *24*
21. *Who Wants to Be a Millionaire*
22. *Will & Grace*

Chapter 14
SCIENCE & NATURE
✳ ✳ ✳ ✳
History's Most Destructive Earthquakes

Every year, earthquakes cause thousands of deaths, either directly or due to the resulting tsunamis, landslides, fires, and famines. Quakes occur when a fault (where Earth's tectonic plates meet) slips, releasing energy in waves that move through the ground. Scientists measure the strength of tremors on the Richter scale, which assigns magnitude in numbers, like 6.0 or 7.2. A 5.0 tremor is equivalent to a 32-kiloton blast, nearly the explosive power of the atomic bomb dropped on Nagasaki in 1945! Going one whole number higher—such as from 5.0 to 6.0—reflects a tenfold increase in the amplitude of waves. Here are some of the most destructive earthquakes in recent history.

1. Southern Chile: May 22, 1960
The strongest earthquake ever recorded—9.5 on the Richter scale—was actually a succession of large quakes that struck southern Chile over the span of a few hours. A catastrophic tsunami ensued, severely ravaging the Chilean coast before rushing across the Pacific to pulverize Hawaii. In Chile, landslides, flooding, and the eruption of the Puyehue volcano less than two days later followed in the wake of the quake. All told, there were more than 5,700 deaths and $675 million in property damage in Chile, as well as Alaska, Hawaii, Japan, and the Philippines.

2. Alaska: March 28, 1964
The most powerful tremor in U.S. history—9.2 on the Richter scale—struck Prince William Sound in Alaska. The quake and the resulting tsunami, which reached more than 200 feet high at Valdez inlet, killed 125 people and caused $311 million in property damage.

3. Indonesia: December 26, 2004

This massive earthquake just off the west coast of Sumatra, and the tsunami that followed, killed at least 230,000 (and perhaps as many as 290,000) people in 12 countries—including about 168,000 in Indonesia alone. It registered 9.1 on the Richter scale and brought fatalities to countries all around the Indian Ocean. Scientists say the tremor was so strong that it wobbled Earth's rotation on its axis by almost an inch.

4. Missouri: December 16, 1811

The New Madrid fault—near where Missouri, Kentucky, Arkansas, and Tennessee meet—witnessed an 8.0 or greater magnitude quake nearly 200 years ago. The shaking spread so far that church bells reportedly rang in Boston, more than 1,500 miles away! It had dramatic effects on the area's geography, lifting up land to the point that the Mississippi River appeared to flow upstream. Fortunately, the sparsely populated area suffered only one death and minimal property damage.

5. Peru: May 31, 1970

A 7.9 magnitude quake just off the western coast of South America caused more than $500 million in damage and killed 66,000 Peruvians, with building collapses responsible for most of the deaths. Scientists say the South American tectonic plate continues to drift westward into the Pacific Ocean crustal slab, so additional serious earthquakes along the continent's coast are likely.

6. San Francisco: April 18, 1906

The Great San Francisco Earthquake—a 7.8 magnitude tremor—brought down structures across the Bay Area. In San Francisco, buildings crumbled, water mains broke, and streetcar tracks twisted into metal waves. But the majority of the 3,000 deaths and $524 million in property damage came from the massive post-tremor fire, which spread rapidly across the city in the absence of water to quell the flames. People as far away as southern Oregon and western Nevada felt the shaking, which lasted nearly a minute.

7. Pakistan: October 8, 2005

This earthquake—which registered 7.6 on the Richter scale—killed more than 80,000 people, injured almost 70,000, and destroyed thousands of structures. Landslides, rockfalls, and crumbled buildings left an estimated four million people homeless and cut off access to some areas for several days.

8. China: July 27, 1976

This quake—a 7.5 on the Richter scale—was one of many major tremors over the years along the "Ring of Fire," a belt of heavy seismic activity around the Pacific Ocean. It struck Tangshan, then a city of one million people, near China's northeastern coast. Official Chinese figures indicate around 250,000 deaths, but other estimates are as high as 655,000.

9. Southern USSR: October 5, 1948

This earthquake in Ashgabat, Turkmenistan, killed around 110,000 people, more than two-thirds of the city's population at the time. The 7.3 magnitude rumbling reduced much of the city to rubble and was one of the most devastating quakes to hit Central Asia.

10. Central California: October 18, 1989

The Loma Prieta quake—which struck the San Francisco area as game three of the 1989 World Series was just about to begin in Candlestick Park—killed 63 people and caused property damage of approximately $6 billion. At 6.9 on the Richter scale, it was the strongest shake in the Bay Area since 1906. Al Michaels, an ABC announcer in the ballpark for the game, was later nominated for an Emmy for his live earthquake reports.

11. Japan: January 17, 1995

This massive quake in Kobe, Japan, measured 6.9 on the Richter scale. It killed more than 5,000 people and caused in excess of $100 billion in property loss, making it the most costly earthquake in history. The staggering expense was largely due to the collapse of, or damage to, more than 200,000 buildings in the high cost-of-living area. Coincidentally, the Kobe quake—or the Great Hanshin

Earthquake, as it is most commonly known in Japan—occurred on the first anniversary of the Northridge tremor.

12. Southern California: January 17, 1994

The 6.7 magnitude Northridge tremor left 60 people dead and caused an estimated $44 billion in damage. The rumbling damaged more than 40,000 buildings in four of California's most populated and expensive counties: Los Angeles, Orange, Ventura, and San Bernardino. The earthquake, which was felt as far away as Utah and northern Mexico, luckily struck at 4:30 A.M., when most people were not yet populating the region's crowded freeways, office buildings, and parking structures, many of which collapsed.

15 Countries with the Greatest Oil Reserves

✳ ✳ ✳ ✳

Country	Proved Reserves (billion barrels)
1. Saudi Arabia	264.30
2. Canada	178.80
3. Iran	136.20
4. Iraq	112.50
5. Kuwait	101.50
6. United Arab Emirates	97.80
7. Venezuela	79.14
8. Russia	60.00
9. Libya	45.00
10. Nigeria	37.25
11. Qatar	27.40
12. Angola	25.00
13. United States	21.76
14. Mexico	14.70
15. Algeria	14.68

Source: CIA World Factbook, 2008

IT CAME FROM OUTER SPACE
10 Momentous Meteor Crashes

✳ ✳ ✳ ✳

Every day hundreds of meteors, commonly known as shooting stars, can be seen flying across the night sky. Upon entering Earth's atmosphere, friction heats up cosmic debris, causing streaks of light that are visible to the human eye. Most burn up before they ever reach the ground. But if one actually survives the long fall and strikes Earth, it is called a meteorite. Here are some of the more memorable meteor falls in history.

1. Arizona would be short one giant hole in the ground if it wasn't for a 160-foot meteorite landing in the northern desert about 50,000 years ago, which left an impact crater about a mile wide and 570 feet deep. Known today as the Barringer Crater, or Meteor Crater, the site is now a popular tourist attraction. Scientists believe the meteorite that caused the crater was traveling about 28,600 miles per hour when it struck Earth, causing an explosion about 150 times more powerful than the Hiroshima atomic bomb. The meteorite itself probably melted in the explosion, spreading a mist of molten nickel and iron across the surrounding landscape.

2. Michelle Knapp was idling away at her Peekskill, New York, home on October 9, 1992, when a loud crash startled her. When she ran outside to investigate, she found that the trunk of her red Chevy Malibu had been crushed by a football-size rock that passed through the car and dug a crater into her driveway. When Michelle alerted police, they impounded the stone and eventually handed it over to the American Museum of Natural History in Manhattan. Turns out the meteor was first spotted over Kentucky, and its descent was caught on more than a dozen amateur videotapes. As for Michelle's Malibu, it was purchased by R. A. Langheinrich Meteorites, a private collectors group, which has taken the car on a world tour of museums and scientific institutions.

3. In terms of casualties, a red Malibu is nothing compared to an entire population, but many scientists believe that a meteorite was responsible for the extinction of the dinosaurs. The theory holds that approximately 65 million years ago, a six-mile-wide asteroid crashed into Earth, causing a crater about 110 miles across and blowing tons of debris and dust into the atmosphere. Scientists believe the impact caused several giant tsunamis, global fires, acid rain, and dust that blocked sunlight for several weeks or months, disrupting the food chain and eventually wiping out the dinosaurs. The theory is controversial, but believers point to the Chicxulub Crater in Yucatan, Mexico, as the striking point of the meteorite. Skeptics say the crater predates the extinction of dinosaurs by 300,000 or so years. Others believe dinosaurs may have been wiped out by several distinct meteorite strikes, rather than just the widely credited Chicxulub impact. Scientists will likely be debating this one for centuries, or at least until another gigantic meteorite strikes Earth and wipes us all out.

4. The Tunguska Meteorite, which exploded near Russia's Tunguska River in 1908, is still the subject of debate more than 100 years later. It didn't leave an impact crater, which has led to speculation about its true nature. Most scientists believe that around 7:00 A.M. on June 30 a giant meteor blazed through the sky and exploded in a huge ball of fire that flattened forests, blew up houses, and scorched people and animals within 13 miles. Scientists continue to explore the region, but neither a meteorite nor a crater have ever been found. Conspiracy theorists contend that what actually hit Earth that day was an alien spaceship or perhaps even a black hole.

5. At 186 miles wide, Vredefort Dome in South Africa is the site of the biggest impact crater on Earth. And at an estimated two billion years old, it makes the Chicxulub Crater look like a spring chicken. Today, the original crater, which was caused by a meteorite about six miles wide, is mostly eroded away, but what remains is a dome that was created when the walls of the crater slumped, pushing up granite rocks from the center of the meteorite strike.

6. Second in size only to the Vredefort Dome, the Sudbury Basin is a 40-mile-long, 16-mile-wide, 9-mile-deep crater caused by a giant meteorite that struck Earth about 1.85 billion years ago. Located in Greater Sudbury, Ontario, the crater is actually home to about 162,000 people. In 1891, the Canadian Copper Company began mining copper from the basin, but it was soon discovered that the crater also contained nickel, which is much more valuable, so the miners changed course. Today, the International Nickel Company operates out of the basin and mines about 10 percent of the world's nickel supply from the site.

7. Santa had to compete for airspace on Christmas Eve 1965, when Britain's largest meteorite sent thousands of fragments showering down on Barwell, Leicestershire. Museums immediately started offering money for fragments of the rock, causing the previously sleepy town to be inundated with meteorite hunters and other adventurers from around the world. Decades later, the phenomenon continues to captivate meteorite enthusiasts, and fragments can often be found for sale online.

8. The Hoba Meteorite, found on a farm in Namibia in 1920, is the heaviest meteorite ever found. Weighing in at about 66 tons, the rock is thought to have landed more than 80,000 years ago. Despite its gargantuan size, the meteorite left no crater, which scientists credit to the fact that it entered Earth's atmosphere at a long, shallow angle. It lay undiscovered until 1920 when a farmer reportedly hit it with his plow. Over the years, erosion, vandalism, and scientific sampling have shrunk the rock to about 60 tons, but in 1955, the Namibian government designated it a national monument, and it is now a popular tourist attraction.

9. As Colby Navarro sat at his computer on March 26, 2003, he had no idea that a meteorite was about to come crashing through the roof of his Park Forest, Illinois, home, strike his printer, bounce off the wall, and land near a filing cabinet. The rock, about four inches wide, was part of a meteorite shower that sprinkled the Chicago area, damaging at least six houses and three cars. Scientists said that before the rock broke apart, it was probably the size of a car. Thank heaven for small favors.

10. The Ensisheim Meteorite struck Earth on November 7, 1492, in the small town of Ensisheim, France. A loud explosion shook the area before a 330-pound stone dropped from the sky into a wheat field, witnessed only by a young boy. As news of the event spread, townspeople gathered around and began breaking off pieces of the stone for souvenirs. German King Maximilian even stopped by Ensisheim to see the stone on his way to battle the French army. Maximilian decided it was a gift from heaven and considered it a sign that he would emerge victorious in his upcoming battle, which he did. Today, bits of the stone are located in museums around the world, but the largest portion stands on display in Ensisheim's Regency Palace.

Countries that Produce the Most Oil

✳ ✳ ✳ ✳

There are 83 million barrels of oil produced in the world every day. The following list breaks down production by country.

Country	Barrels per Day (millions)
1. Saudi Arabia	11.000
2. Russia	9.870
3. United States	7.460
4. Iran	3.956
5. China	3.725
6. Canada	3.310
7. Mexico	3.083
8. Norway	2.560
9. United Arab Emirates	2.510
10. Kuwait	2.440

Source: CIA World Factbook 2008

10 Catastrophic Hurricanes Since 1900

What begins as a thunderstorm off the west coast of Africa can become a hurricane by the time it reaches the Caribbean and the southeastern United States. Between 80 and 100 of these systems develop each year from June to November, but usually only a handful evolve into hurricanes that impact the United States. Check out some of nature's most destructive hurricanes.

1. The Great Labor Day Storm: September 1935

In little more than 24 hours, this storm went from a category 1 to a category 5, where it remained when it struck the Florida Keys, making it the first hurricane of such intensity to strike the United States. With wind speeds reaching 200 miles per hour and a 15-foot storm surge, this cataclysmic hurricane caused $6 million in damages. Of the more than 420 people killed in the storm, about 260 of them were World War I veterans who were in the region building bridges as part of President Roosevelt's New Deal. The flimsy camps that housed the veterans were no match for this wicked storm, and the train sent to rescue them was blown off the tracks.

2. Hurricane Camille: August 1969

With wind gusts exceeding 200 miles per hour and a 20-foot storm surge, Camille was the second category 5 hurricane to hit the United States. The massive storm struck along the mouth of the Mississippi River and flattened nearly everything along Mississippi's coastline. After pounding the Gulf Coast, Camille moved inland and caused heavy flooding and landslides in Virginia. In total, Camille caused more than $1.4 billion in damages and 259 deaths.

3. Okeechobee Hurricane: September 1928

Reaching category 5 strength when it slammed Puerto Rico, the storm then hit Palm Beach, Florida, with 150-mile-per-hour winds and little warning. Coastal residents were prepared, but 40 miles inland at Lake Okeechobee, the massive rainfall that accompanied

the storm crumbled a six-foot-tall mud dike around the lake.
The storm caused $100 million in damages and killed more than
1,800 people, but some estimates list the death toll as high as 4,000.

4. Hurricane Andrew: August 1992

The third category 5 storm to hit U.S. shores and the first severe
hurricane to hit southern Florida in 27 years, Hurricane Andrew
brought along 145-mile-per-hour winds (with gusts up to 170 miles
per hour) and a 17-foot storm surge. The day after Andrew ravaged southern Florida, it moved across to Louisiana, weakening
to category 3 status but still packing 120-mile-per-hour winds.
Andrew left 44 dead and caused $26.5 billion in damage, mostly
in Florida. Around 250,000 people were left homeless, more than
700,000 insurance claims were filed, and even the coral reefs off
the Florida coast sustained damage as far down as 75 feet.

5. Galveston, Texas: September 1900

Climatologist Isaac Cline dismissed the notion that a hurricane
could devastate the island city of Galveston, but when he noticed
unusually heavy swells from the southeast, he drove his horse and
buggy along the beach warning people to move to the mainland.
Unfortunately, perhaps due to Cline's initially cavalier attitude, less
than half the population evacuated, which led to between 8,000 and
12,000 deaths. The U.S. Weather Bureau ranked the storm a category 4 hurricane, with wind speeds measured at 100 miles per hour
before the measuring device blew away. Other records say winds
peaked around 145 miles per hour. The hurricane wiped out about
three-quarters of the city and caused nearly $20 million in damages.

6. Florida Keys and Corpus Christi, Texas: September 1919

This was the only Atlantic hurricane to form in 1919, but it was a
monster! With winds reaching 140 miles per hour, the category 4
storm originally made landfall in Key West, Florida, but continued
over the warm waters of the Gulf of Mexico and struck again in
Corpus Christi—now downgraded to category 3 but with a 12-foot
storm surge. The storm cost more than $22 million in damages and
killed between 600 and 900 people—many of them passengers on

ten ships lost in the Gulf of Mexico. Coincidentally, a boy named Bob Simpson survived the Corpus Christi leg of the storm, sparking his interest in hurricanes and eventually leading him to codevelop the Saffir-Simpson scale used to measure hurricane strength.

7. Hurricane Hugo: September 1989

The strongest hurricane to hit the United States since Camille, Hugo struck near Charleston, South Carolina, as a category 4 storm with winds surpassing 135 miles per hour and a 20-foot storm surge. Hugo was also responsible for an estimated 85 deaths and $7 billion in damage, making it the costliest hurricane at the time.

8. Hurricane Ivan: September 2004

Ivan was the fourth major hurricane of the busy 2004 season. At one time a category 5 storm, by the time Ivan struck at Gulf Shores, Alabama, it had weakened to category 3 status with wind speeds reaching 130 miles per hour. But Ivan was the storm that wouldn't die! After devastating much of the Florida panhandle, Ivan dumped water across the southeastern United States, then drifted over the Atlantic Ocean. Once back over the water, Ivan built up enough energy to loop around to the south, move across the Florida peninsula, and pick up steam over the Gulf of Mexico—again! The remnants of the storm intensified and made landfall as a tropical storm along the coast of Louisiana. When Ivan finally dissipated over Texas, the storm had left 121 people dead and had caused more than $19 billion in damages.

9. Hurricane Katrina: August 2005

The year 2005 was another busy year for hurricanes. Katrina, the fifth hurricane of the season, made landfall near Buras-Triumph, Louisiana, with winds reaching 125 miles per hour before devastating the entire Gulf Coast of Mississippi. But all eyes were on New Orleans, situated below sea level and surrounded by rivers and lakes. When Katrina made landfall slightly to the east, people in "The Big Easy" breathed a sigh of relief since it appeared that Mississippi had borne the major brunt of the storm. But that changed a few hours later when massive rainfall and a storm surge caused Lake Ponchartrain to flood. When the city's levee system was breached in several places, 80 percent of New Orleans was left under water. The U.S. government was severely criticized for its delay in sending aid. Katrina's wrath took more than 1,800 lives and hundreds are still missing. With more than $81 billion in damages, Katrina was the most expensive natural disaster in U.S. history.

10. The New England Hurricane: September 1938

Normally, hurricanes thrive on the warm, tropical waters along the southeastern coast of the United States. But this storm had other plans, striking the northeastern coast instead. With winds gusting at more than 100 miles per hour, the eye of this hurricane struck Long Island, New York, but winds and massive rainfall wreaked havoc in Massachusetts, Connecticut, and Rhode Island, and caused damage in Montreal as well. Dubbed the "Long Island Express," the storm killed 700 people, injured 700 more, and caused $306 million in damages. It also brought a 12- to 16-foot storm surge that destroyed more than 8,000 homes and 6,000 boats

Countries with the Worst Drinking Water

❉ ❉ ❉ ❉

Country	Daily Amount of Organic Water Pollutant (kg)
1. China	6,088,663
2. United States	1,805,861
3. India	1,519,842
4. Russia	1,388,061
5. Japan	1,184,699
6. Germany	966,669
7. Indonesia	732,965
8. Brazil	629,406
9. France	564,565

Source: World Development Indicators Database

9 Accidental Inventions

❋ ❋ ❋ ❋

We tend to hold inventors in high esteem, but often their discoveries were the result of an accident or twist of fate. This is true of many everyday items, including the following surprise inventions.

1. Fireworks

Fireworks originated in China some 2,000 years ago, and legend has it that they were accidentally invented by a cook who mixed together charcoal, sulfur, and saltpeter—all items commonly found in kitchens in those days. The mixture burned and when compressed in a bamboo tube, it exploded. There's no record of whether it was the cook's last day on the job.

2. Potato Chips

If you can't eat just one potato chip, blame it on chef George Crum. He reportedly created the salty snack in 1853 at Moon's Lake House near Saratoga Springs, New York. Fed up with a customer who continuously sent his fried potatoes back, complaining that they were soggy and not crunchy enough, Crum sliced the potatoes as thin as possible, fried them in hot grease, then doused them with salt. The customer loved them, and "Saratoga Chips" quickly became a popular item at the lodge and throughout New England. Eventually, the chips were mass-produced for home consumption, but since they were stored in barrels or tins, they quickly went stale. Then, in the 1920s, Laura Scudder invented the airtight bag by ironing together two pieces of waxed paper, thus keeping the chips fresh longer. Today, chips are packaged in plastic or foil bags or cardboard containers and come in a variety of flavors, including sour cream and onion, barbecue, and salt and vinegar.

3. Saccharin

Saccharin, the oldest artificial sweetener, was accidentally discovered in 1879 by researcher Constantine Fahlberg, who was working at Johns Hopkins University in the laboratory of professor Ira

Remsen. Fahlberg's discovery came after he forgot to wash his hands before lunch. He had spilled a chemical on his hands and it, in turn, caused the bread he ate to taste unusually sweet. In 1880, the two scientists jointly published the discovery, but in 1884, Fahlberg obtained a patent and began mass-producing saccharin without Remsen. The use of saccharin did not become widespread until sugar was rationed during World War I, and its popularity increased during the 1960s and 1970s with the manufacture of Sweet'N Low and diet soft drinks.

4. Corn Flakes

In 1894, Dr. John Harvey Kellogg was the superintendent of a sanitarium in Battle Creek, Michigan. He and his brother Will were searching for wholesome foods to feed patients that also complied with the strict vegetarian diet of the brothers' Seventh Day Adventist beliefs. Will accidentally left some boiled wheat sitting out, and it went stale by the time he returned. Rather than throw it away, the brothers sent it through rollers, hoping to make long sheets of dough, but they got flakes instead. They toasted the flakes, which were a big hit with patients, and patented them under the name Granose. The brothers experimented with other grains, including corn, and in 1906, Will created the Kellogg's company to sell the corn flakes. On principle, John refused to join the company because Will lowered the health benefits of the cereal by adding sugar.

5. Slinky

In 1943, naval engineer Richard James was trying to develop a spring that would support and stabilize sensitive equipment on ships. When one of the springs accidentally fell off a shelf, it continued moving, and James got the idea for a toy. His wife Betty came up with the name, and when the Slinky made its debut in late 1945, James sold 400 of the bouncy toys in 90 minutes. Today, more than 250 million Slinkys have been sold worldwide.

6. Microwave Ovens

The microwave oven is a standard appliance in most American homes, but did you know it has been around since the late 1940s?

In 1945, Percy Spencer was experimenting with a new vacuum tube called a magnetron while doing research for the Raytheon Corporation. He was intrigued when the candy bar in his pocket began to melt, so he tried another experiment with popcorn. When it began to pop, Spencer immediately saw the potential in this revolutionary process. In 1947, Raytheon built the first microwave oven, the Radarange, which weighed 750 pounds, was 5½ feet tall, and cost about $5,000. When the Radarange first became available for home use in the early 1950s, its bulky size and expensive price tag made it unpopular with consumers. But in 1967, a much more popular 100-volt, countertop version was introduced at a price of $495.

7. Silly Putty

It bounces, it stretches, it breaks—it's Silly Putty, the silicone-based plastic clay marketed as a children's toy by Binney & Smith, Inc. During World War II, while attempting to create a synthetic rubber substitute, James Wright dropped boric acid into silicone oil. The result was a polymerized substance that bounced. It took several years to find a use for the product, but finally, in 1950, marketing expert Peter Hodgson saw its potential as a toy, renamed it Silly Putty, and a classic toy was born! Not only is it fun, Silly Putty also has practical uses—it picks up dirt, lint, and pet hair; can stabilize wobbly furniture; and is useful in stress reduction, physical therapy, and in medical and scientific simulations. It was even used by the crew of *Apollo 8* to secure tools in zero gravity.

8. Play-Doh

One smell most people remember from childhood is the odor of Play-Doh, the brightly-colored, nontoxic modeling clay. Play-Doh was accidentally invented in 1955 by Joseph and Noah McVicker while trying to make a wallpaper cleaner. Toy manufacturer Rainbow Crafts marketed it a year later. More than 700 million pounds of Play-Doh have sold since then, but the recipe remains a secret.

9. Post-it Notes

A Post-it note is a small piece of paper with a strip of low-tack adhesive on the back that allows it to be temporarily attached to documents, walls, computer monitors, and just about anything else. The idea for the Post-it note was conceived in 1974 by Arthur Fry as a way of holding bookmarks in his hymnal while singing in the church choir. He was aware of an adhesive accidentally developed in 1968 by fellow 3M employee Spencer Silver. No application for the lightly sticky stuff was apparent until Fry's idea. The 3M company was initially skeptical about the product's profitability, but in 1980, Post-it notes were introduced around the world. Today, they are sold in more than 100 countries.

Countries that Consume the Most Oil

✳ ✳ ✳ ✳

The world consumes about 82.6 million barrels of oil a day, nearly as much as is produced on a daily basis. Here's how the top oil consumers stack up.

Country	Barrels per Day (millions)
1. United States	20.800
2. China	6.930
3. Japan	5.353
4. Russia	2.916
5. Germany	2.618
6. India	2.438
7. Canada	2.290
8. South Korea	2.130
9. Brazil	2.100
10. Mexico	2.078
11. Saudi Arabia	2.000
12. France	1.999
13. United Kingdom	1.820
14. Italy	1.732

Source: CIA World Factbook 2008

Chapter 15
MONEY & BUSINESS

✳ ✳ ✳ ✳

How the Top 9 Fast-Food Chains Stack Up

Americans spend more money on fast food than on movies, music, books, magazines, and newspapers combined. The rapid growth of this $240 billion industry over the last 30 years has been the result of economic shifts that have forced more women to work outside the home. Here are the top nine fast-food chains and how they stack up worldwide.

1. Domino's Pizza

In 1960, brothers Tom and James Monaghan started the first Domino's Pizza in Ypsilanti, Michigan, when they purchased a pizza store called DomiNick's for $500. A year later, Tom became the restaurant's sole owner when James traded his share of the business for a Volkswagen Beetle. Tom renamed the store Domino's Pizza, and it soon became one of the world's leading pizza chains with more than 8,500 stores in 55 countries. Serving in excess of one million customers each day, Domino's reached $5.4 billion in global sales in 2007.

2. Arby's

Founded in Ohio in 1964 by Forest and Leroy Raffel, the name Arby's is a play on R.B., an abbreviation for Raffel Brothers and also for roast beef, the restaurant's specialty. Always a bit ahead of the times, in 1991, Arby's became the first fast-food chain to introduce a light menu, adding three sandwiches and four salads, all of which were under 300 calories and 94 percent fat free. Then in 1994, the chain banned smoking in all of its restaurants. Arby's currently employs more than 26,000 people at 3,700 stores worldwide and brings in $1.26 billion annually.

3. Taco Bell

Glen Bell opened the first Taco Bell in Downey, California, in 1962. Two years later, the first franchise was granted, and in 1969, Taco Bell went public on the stock market. Today, sales total more than $6.2 billion. Taco Bell maintains more than 6,000 restaurants worldwide, employing 143,000 workers.

4. Wendy's

Dave Thomas opened the first Wendy's—named for his daughter—in Columbus, Ohio, in 1969. In 1970, Thomas introduced the drive-thru window, an innovation that allowed customers to purchase food without leaving their cars. The chain's passion for customer service and quality products has remained unchanged throughout the years. Today, with annual sales of $2.16 billion, Wendy's has more than 6,000 restaurants and 44,000 employees.

5. Pizza Hut

In 1958, brothers Dan and Frank Carney of Wichita, Kansas, founded Pizza Hut. Now this restaurant chain specializes in American-style pizza along with side dishes such as buffalo wings, bread sticks, and garlic bread. Pizza Hut is the world's largest pizza chain, operating more than 12,800 stores in 97 countries and employing 140,000 people. With $5.3 billion in annual sales in the United States alone, the company rakes in more dough than its nearest competitors—Domino's and Papa John's—combined.

6. Subway

Almost everyone recognizes Jared Fogle as the poster boy for Subway's healthy, low-fat diet. He lost 245 pounds in a year by eating two Subway sandwiches per day and walking. Subway was founded in 1965 by 17-year-old college freshman Fred DeLuca and family friend Dr. Peter Buck. Now there are more than 30,000 Subway restaurants in 87 countries, employing more than 150,000 people. With worldwide sales totaling more than $11.3 billion annually, Subway serves nearly 2,800 sandwiches and salads in the United States every 60 seconds. If all the sandwiches made by Subway in a year were placed end to end, they would wrap around the world an estimated six times.

7. KFC

Kentucky Fried Chicken was the brainchild of Harland Sanders, who opened his first restaurant during the Great Depression in a gas station in Corbin, Kentucky. In the 1930s, Sanders developed his secret recipe of 11 herbs and spices, which has been touted as one of the best-kept secrets in the world and to this day is locked in a vault in Louisville. Colonel Sanders, as he was known, sold his empire in 1964 for $2 million. Today, KFC is a $10.3 billion franchise with more than 14,000 restaurants in 105 countries. The company employs 750,000 people who serve more than a billion "finger lickin' good" chicken meals each year.

8. Burger King

In December 1954, James McLamore and David Edgerton opened the first Insta Burger King in Miami, Florida. The restaurant was based on an assembly line production system inspired by a visit to the McDonald brothers' hamburger stand. Today, Burger King has more than 11,500 restaurants in 73 countries. With worldwide revenues of $2.46 billion, the chain employs more than 340,000 employees and serves 11 million customers a day.

9. McDonald's

Originally founded by Dick and Mac McDonald as a barbecue drive-in in the 1940s, the McDonald's Corporation now boasts total revenues of more than $23 billion. Known for its signature french

fries, the corporation trains more new workers annually than the U.S. Army, and an estimated one in eight Americans has worked for McDonald's. In 1968, McDonald's operated about 1,000 restaurants worldwide, but today it has more than 30,000.

HAPPY DAYS, INDEED
Comparison Shopping: 1957

✳ ✳ ✳ ✳

*Maybe Father knew best in 1957, but he probably didn't have
a clue about how much Mother forked over at the grocery store
for his tuna noodle casserole. He made about $4,494 a year, paid
about $19,000 for his house, $2,500 for his Ford, and roughly
25 cents a gallon to fill 'er up. Let's see how deep Mother had
to dig into her pocketbook at the grocery store checkout.*

1. Campbell's Tomato Soup

It's no wonder Campbell's tomato soup has always been a family
favorite. People have been wallowing in its creamy comfort for
generations. To make it even more soothing, in 1957 a can only set
you back a dime! Today, it's still an affordable form of therapy, and
it costs only a buck.

2. Canned Corn

The "Ho Ho Ho, Green Giant" jingle wasn't born until 1959, but
cooks in 1957 reached for a can of corn with his jolly green likeness
for about 14 cents per 27-ounce can. Today, 95 cents will get you a
15-ounce can.

3. Gum

Gum chompers had a few choices back in 1957. There was Juicy
Fruit, Wrigley's Spearmint, and Dubble Bubble, to name a few.
You could pretty much chew until your jaw hurt at just 19 cents for
6 packs (30 pieces). Today, in addition to the dental bills, it costs
about $1.19 for a 6-pack of gum.

4. Iceberg Lettuce

Iceberg lettuce used to rule the refrigerator's produce bin—it only
cost 19 cents per head in 1957! Salad makers these days reach for
romaine, red leaf, and endive, just to name a few. Iceberg still has
its loyal followers, but they can now plan on paying $1.49 per head.

5. Broccoli

In 1957, when the word *fiber* was mostly used to discuss fabrics, a bunch of broccoli only cost 23 cents. Today's health conscious crowd pays around $1.79 per bunch to munch this super food.

6. Nabisco Saltines

Nabisco saltines can settle an upset stomach, and, at 25 cents for a 16-ounce package in 1957, that's better than medicine. But today, the same size box will set you back $2.69.

7. Ground Beef

To make that delicious meatloaf, Mother shelled out 30 cents for a pound of hamburger in 1957. Today, we pay considerably more for our ground beef—$4.09 per pound!

8. Syrup

In 1957, you could douse a stack of flapjacks with pure Vermont maple syrup because it cost only 33 cents for 12 ounces. At $9.36 for 12 ounces of the real stuff today, we have to go a little lighter on the sap. But these days it's much less expensive to grab an imitation. You can get 12 ounces of Aunt Jemima for $1.89.

9. Tang

Tang Breakfast Crystals were launched in America in 1957 for around 50 cents a jar. In 1965, the *Gemini 4* astronauts were first given this powdered vitamin C powerhouse on their space mission. Today, anyone can get Tang for $3.39 for a 12-ounce canister.

10. Eggs

In 1957, a dozen eggs cost a mere 55 cents. For those who aren't quite ready to pour an omelette from a pint-size container of artificial eggs, you can still crack the good old-fashioned, incredible, edible egg for $2.99 a dozen.

11. Pot Roast

Pot roasts brought families to the table most Sundays in 1957, and it cost 69 cents a pound for that roast. Today, it's harder to get busy

families together, but when they do, the cook can expect to pay
$4.59 per pound.

12. Butter

When they weren't cooking with lard or shortening, American
women of 1957 opted for butter at 75 cents a pound. These days,
we're more likely to count fat grams and opt for margarine or other
butter substitutes. In any case, at about $3.99 a pound, we don't pay
with just our arteries to enjoy good old-fashioned butter today.

13. TV Dinner

A Swanson TV dinner cost just 75 cents in 1957. With classics
like *Wagon Train* and *American Bandstand* shown in 39.5 million
homes, TV trays were popping up all over the place. Today, a frozen
chicken and corn tray will set you back $2.99.

14. Milk

Back in 1957, milk was $1 per gallon. Today, we have a lot more
choices when standing in the dairy aisle, but whether whole, 2 percent, 1 percent, skim, or soy, milk sets us back about $3.49 when it's
not on sale.

9 Strange Things Insured by Lloyds of London

✳ ✳ ✳ ✳

*Average people insure average things like cars, houses,
and maybe even a boat. Celebrities insure legs, voices, and some
things you might not want to examine if you're a claims adjuster.
Here are a few unusual things that the famous Lloyds
of London has insured over the years.*

1. Before rock 'n' roll, a popular type of music in England in the 1950s
was skiffle, a type of folk music with a jazz and blues influence
played on washboards, jugs, kazoos, and cigar-box fiddles. It was so
big at the time that a washboard player named Chas McDevitt tried
to protect his career by insuring his fingers for $9,300. It didn't do

him much good because skiffle was replaced by rock 'n' roll, washboards by electric guitars, and McDevitt by McCartney.

2. Representing the Cheerio Yo-Yo Company of Canada, 13-year-old Harvey Lowe won the 1932 World Yo-Yo championships in London and toured Europe from 1932 to 1935. He even taught Edward VIII, the Prince of Wales, how to yo-yo. Lowe was so valuable to Cheerio that the company insured his hands for $150,000!

3. The famous comedy team of Bud Abbott and Lou Costello seemed to work extremely well together, especially in their famous "Who's on First?" routine. But to protect against a career-ending argument, they took out a $250,000 insurance policy over a five-year period. After more than 20 years together, the team split up in 1957—not due to a disagreement but because the Internal Revenue Service got them for back taxes, which forced them to sell many of their assets, including the rights to their many films.

4. While playing on Australia's national cricket team from 1985 to 1994, Merv Hughes took out an estimated $370,000 policy on his trademark walrus mustache, which, combined with his 6'4" physique and outstanding playing ability, made him one of the most recognized cricketers in the world.

5. In 1957, world-famous food critic Egon Ronay wrote and published the first edition of the *Egon Ronay Guide to British Eateries*. Because his endorsement could make or break a restaurant, Ronay insured his taste buds for $400,000.

6. In the 1940s, executives at 20th Century Fox had the legs of actress Betty Grable insured for $1 million each. After taking out the policies, Grable probably wished she had added a rider to protect her from injury while the insurance agents fought over who would inspect her when making a claim.

7. Rock legend Bruce Springsteen is known to his fans as The Boss, but Springsteen knows that he could be demoted to part-time status with one case of laryngitis. That's why in the 1980s he insured his famous gravelly voice for $6 million. Rod Stewart has also insured his throat and Bob Dylan his vocal cords to protect themselves from that inevitable day when they stop blowin' in the wind.

8. From 1967 to 1992, British comedian and singer Ken Dodd was in *The Guinness Book of Records* for the world's longest joke-telling session—1,500 jokes in three and a half hours. Dodd has sold more than 100 million comedy records and is famous for his frizzy hair, ever-present feather duster, and extremely large buckteeth. His teeth are so important to his act that Dodd had them insured for $7.4 million, surely making his insurance agent grin.

9. During the height of his career, Michael Flatley—star of *River-dance* and *Lord of the Dance*—insured his legs for an unbelievable $47 million. Before becoming the world's most famous Irish step dancer, the Chicago native trained as a boxer and won the Golden Gloves Championship in 1975, undoubtedly dazzling his opponents with some extremely fast and fancy footwork.

America's Top 10 Most Dangerous Jobs

❉ ❉ ❉ ❉

You may hate your job, but is the threat of death or injury always hanging over your head? The order may change from year to year, but these are typically the most dangerous jobs in America.

1. Fisher
2. Pilot
3. Logger
4. Iron/Steel Worker
5. Refuse/Recyclable Materials Collector
6. Farmer/Rancher
7. Electrical Power Installer/Repairer
8. Roofer
9. Sales, Delivery, and Other Truck Driver
10. Agricultural Workers

12 Items that Would Require a Name Change to Sell in American Stores

✳ ✳ ✳ ✳

The meanings of many foreign words get lost in translation when converted into English. But the following products would probably benefit from a name change if they want to be successful in the United States.

1. Aass Fatøl

On those rare hot days, Norwegians like to quench their thirst with a cold bottle of Aass Fatøl beer. The word *fatøl* appears on many Scandinavian beer labels and means "cask." This beer comes from the Aass Brewery, the oldest brewery in Norway. If you'd like to get some Aass, it's imported in the United States.

2. Ass Glue

Ass glue is made from fried donkey skin and is considered a powerful tonic by Chinese herbalists, who use it to fortify the body after illness, injury, or surgery. If you have a dry cough, a dry mouth, or are irritable, you can find ass glue at most Chinese herb shops.

3. Big Nuts

Big Nuts is a chocolate-covered hazelnut candy from the Meurisse candy company in Belgium. For those who like candy that makes a statement, Big Nuts is available online.

4. Cream Collon

Glico's Cream Collon is a tasty cookie from Japan. The small cylindrical wafers wrapped around a creamy center actually do resemble a cross section of a lower intestine filled with cream. An ad says to "Hold them between your lips, suck gently, and out pops the filling." Yum! Glico's Cream Collon can be ordered on the Internet.

5. Dickmilch

Dairy cases in Germany are the place to find *dickmilch*, a traditional beverage made by Schwalbchen. In German, *dickmilch* means "thick milk" and is made by keeping milk at room temperature until it thickens and sours. Known as sour milk in the United States, it's a common ingredient in German and Amish baked goods.

6. Fart Juice

While it may sound like an affliction caused by drinking it, Fart Juice is a potent potable in Poland. Made from the leftover liquid from cooking dried beans, this green beverage could pass for a vegetable juice and is probably a gas to drink, but it's not available in the United States.

7. Golden Gaytime

Street's Golden Gaytime is toffee-flavored ice cream dipped in fine chocolate and crunchy cookie pieces and served on a stick. Also available in a cone, Golden Gaytime is one of many Street's ice cream treats sold in Australia. One memorable advertising slogan remarks: "It's so hard to have a Gaytime on your own."

8. Kockens Anis

If you think *anis* sounds funny, you'll laugh even harder when you see Kockens Anis in Swedish grocery stores. Anis is aniseed, a fragrant spice used in baking, and Kockens is the brand name. While aniseed is found in most U.S. grocery stores, don't ask for the Kockens brand because it's not available and could get you coldcocked.

9. Mini-Dickmann's

Mini-Dickmann's, a German candy made by Storck, is described as a "chocolate foam kiss." Available in milk, plain, or white chocolate, Mini-Dickmann's are only an inch and a half long. Too embarrassed to be seen with a box of Mini-Dickmann's? Try Super-Dickmann's, the four-inch variety. Both sizes are available from Storck USA.

10. Pee Cola

If you're asked to take a cola taste test in Ghana, one of the selections may be a local brand named Pee Cola. The drink was named after the country's biggest movie star Jagger Pee, star of *Baboni: The Phobia Girl*. Don't bother looking for a six-pack of Pee to chug because it's not available in the United States.

11. Piddle in the Hole

Take a Piddle in the Hole at a pub in England and you'll be drinking a beer from the Wyre Piddle Brewery. Made in the village of Wyre Piddle, the brewery also makes Piddle in the Wind, Piddle in the Dark, and Piddle in the Snow. Before you run out for a Piddle, you should know that it's only available in the UK.

12. Shito

Shito is a spicy hot chili pepper condiment that, like ketchup in the United States and salsa in Mexico, is served with most everything in Ghana. There are two versions: a spicy oil made with dried chili pepper and dried shrimp; and a fresh version made from fresh chili pepper, onion, and tomato. Shito appears as an ingredient in Ghanaian recipes but hasn't found a market in the United States.

8 Unforgettable Ad Campaigns

✳ ✳ ✳ ✳

Some commercial messages last only for the 30 seconds that they exist in real time, while others linger with us for decades. Here are some amusing ads that have stood the test of time.

1. Volkswagen: "Think Small" (1959)

In 1959, art director Helmut Krone and copywriter Julian Koenig came up with this "less is more" message geared toward car buyers. Like the VW Beetle, the ads were simple and uncluttered, featuring photos of the car against a plain background. Can you sell a car with a headline that reads "Lemon"? Sure! In the ad, Volkswagen was pointing out that the car in the photo didn't make it off the assembly line because one of the many inspectors found a blemish. "We pluck the lemons; you get the plums," was the slogan.

2. Nike: "Just Do It" (1988)

When ad exec Dan Wieden met with a group of Nike employees to talk about a new ad campaign, he told them, "You Nike guys... you just do it." The result was one of the most effective taglines in advertising history. During the first ten years of this award-winning campaign, Nike's percent of the sport shoe market shot up from 18 to 43 percent. Today, the Nike name is so recognizable that it doesn't even need to appear in the advertising. Only the iconic "swoosh" is needed.

3. Miller Lite Beer: "Tastes great, less filling" (1974)

This campaign peppered with ex-jocks contained more than 200 commercials, and its lively debate entertained sports fans for nearly two decades. Is Miller Lite good because of the taste or because you can drink a ton of it and still have room for nachos? We may never know. But during the first five years of the campaign, sales of Miller Lite took off from just under 7 million barrels a year to more than 31 million barrels, breaking the all-time record for beer makers. A guy's gotta be full after that!

4. McDonald's: "You deserve a break today" (1971)

In 1970, Needham, Harper & Steers successfully pitched an upbeat, catchy melody to McDonald's, but they struggled with the lyrics. Noticing that the word *break* continuously surfaced in focus groups, copywriter Keith Reinhard finally wrote the perfect lyrics for the jingle. Within the next few years, global sales jumped from $587 million to $1.9 billion. *Advertising Age* named the song the top jingle of the 20th century.

5. Federal Express: "Fast Talker" (1982)

These memorable ads are breathtaking...literally. You might gasp for air when watching the TV spots. When writer Patrick Kelly and art director Mike Tesch discovered John Moscitta, Jr., who could speak more than 500 words per minute, they knew he would be perfect for ads for the overnight delivery service. When director Joe Sedelmaier put his quirky spin on the concept, the spots were discussed around watercoolers across the country.

6. Coca-Cola: "The pause that refreshes" (1929)

With the advent of the Great Depression, corporate America worried that sales would suffer. Not so with Coca-Cola, whose ads depicted carefree people and an idealized view of American life when real life was rather dreary. During the first year of this campaign, sales actually doubled! The economy may have been depressed, but "the pause that refreshes" appears to have been just what Americans needed to lift their spirits.

7. Clairol: "Does she... or doesn't she?" (1956)

"...Only her hairdresser knows for sure." When there's only one female employee in the copywriting department, you give her a shot at the product geared toward women. Shirley Polykoff, who coined the phrase that jump-started the home hair-coloring industry, felt that a woman had the right to change her hair color without everybody knowing about it. The campaign lasted for 15 years, and Clairol's sales increased by 413 percent in the first six years!

8. Apple Computer: "1984" (1984)

This is the TV spot that made the Super Bowl about more than just football. Based on George Orwell's book *1984*, the commercial pitted the new Macintosh computer against the totalitarian control of Big Brother and the Thought Police (repre-
sented by other computer companies). Depicting an apocalyptic view of the future, the ad opened with a zombielike crowd fixated on a huge screen, then an Amazon woman entered and hurled a hammer into the screen, shattering it. The ad's creators, Lee Clow and Steve Hayden, won every advertising award that year for this venerable commercial.

✳ ✳ ✳

*"Many a small thing has been made large
by the right kind of advertising."*

—Mark Twain, *A Connecticut Yankee in King Arthur's Court*

Chapter 16
THIS & THAT

9 Ironic Twists of Fate

Throughout history, people have made bold proclamations that were not only incorrect but many times contradicted their own actions. Here are a few examples.

1. "Take Me Out to the Ball Game"

Next to the national anthem, the song most associated with the game of baseball is "Take Me Out to the Ball Game," an early-20th-century song usually played during the seventh-inning stretch. Ironically, it was written by two men who had never attended a baseball game. Jack Norworth wrote the words in 1908, after seeing a sign that said, "Baseball Today—Polo Grounds." Albert Von Tilzer added the music. The song gained popularity in vaudeville acts, and now it's played at nearly every baseball game in the country.

2. Clark Gable

William Clark Gable was a high school dropout with big ears who eventually became known as the "King of Hollywood." In 1924, Gable's friendship with Lionel Barrymore helped him land a screen test at MGM. Producer Irving Thalberg thought Gable's screen test was awful and referred to his ears as "batlike." In spite of that, he was signed to a contract and went on to make a number of hit movies for the studio. When MGM head Louis B. Mayer decided that Gable was getting difficult to work with, he loaned the actor to the Columbia studio. Ironically, Gable won an Academy Award for his 1934 performance in the Columbia film *It Happened One Night*.

3. Ludwig van Beethoven

German composer Ludwig van Beethoven is generally regarded as one of the greatest composers in history and was a dominant figure in the transitional period between the Classical and Romantic eras in Western music. Around age 28, Beethoven developed a severe case of tinnitus and began to lose his hearing. His hearing loss did not affect his ability to compose music, but it made concerts increasingly difficult. At the premiere of his Ninth Symphony, he reportedly had to be turned around to see the applause of the audience because he could not hear it. In 1811, after failing to play his own Piano Concerto No. 5, he never performed in public again.

4. Tom Seaver

In 1966, baseball pitcher Tom Seaver signed with the New York Mets and was assigned to a minor league team in Florida. After seeing Seaver pitch, Chicago Cubs scout Gordon Goldsberry said, "He won't make it." On the contrary—when Seaver was called up by the Mets in 1967, he had 18 complete games with 16 wins, including two shutouts. Seaver was named the National League Rookie of the Year and went on to a 20-year career with 311 wins, 3,640 strikeouts, and a 2.86 ERA. Nicknamed "Tom Terrific," Seaver was elected to the Baseball Hall of Fame in 1992.

5. James Dean

In 1955, actor James Dean advised teens about the dangers of speeding and drag racing in a two-minute televised public service announcement. Dean talked about how he used to "fly around quite a bit" on the highways, but then he took up track racing, and after that he became "extra cautious" on the highways. He also warned, "The life you save may be *mine*." On September 30, 1955, Dean was pulled over for speeding in his Porsche 550 Spyder on his way to a race in Palm Springs, California. Later that afternoon, an oncoming vehicle crossed into Dean's lane, and the two cars collided head-on. Dean was pronounced dead at the hospital.

6. Television

Darryl F. Zanuck was an actor, writer, producer, and director who helped develop the Hollywood studio system in the 1920s. He also cofounded Twentieth Century Pictures in 1933. In 1946, television was in its infancy, but the movie industry was worried. When asked his thoughts, Zanuck said, "Television won't be able to hold on to any market it captures after the first six months. People will soon get tired of staring at a plywood box every night." Of course, television thrived, but it did not bring an end to movies.

7. Gus Grissom

Virgil "Gus" Grissom was America's second man in space aboard the *Liberty Bell 7*. After landing in the Atlantic, a hatch on the space capsule opened prematurely, and Grissom nearly drowned before being rescued by helicopter. To prevent this from happening again, Grissom recommended to NASA designers that the hatch on the three-man *Apollo* capsule be made more difficult to open. Ironically, while testing the *Apollo* capsule before its first flight, Grissom was killed in a fire along with fellow astronauts Ed White and Roger B. Chaffee when the new hatch proved too difficult to open.

8. Charles Justice

In 1900, Charles Justice was serving time in prison in Columbus, Ohio. While performing cleaning duties in the death chamber, he thought of a way to improve the restraints on the electric chair. Justice suggested that metal clamps replace the leather straps, allowing the inmate to be secured more firmly and minimizing the problem of burnt flesh. These changes were made, and Justice was later paroled. But he was later convicted of murder and sentenced to death. In an ironic twist of fate, on November 9, 1911, justice was served and the inmate found out firsthand how well those metal clamps worked on the same electric chair he had improved.

9. The Beatles

On January 1, 1962, Paul McCartney, John Lennon, George Harrison, and Pete Best auditioned at Decca Records, performing 15 songs in just under an hour. The songs included some Lennon–McCartney originals and covers of other songs, but their performance was mediocre. In fact, producer Mike Smith flatly rejected them saying, "We don't like their sound. Groups of guitars are on their way out." The Beatles went on to sign with producer George Martin at EMI Records and proved Smith extraordinarily wrong.

18 Odd Things You Can Buy in Japanese Vending Machines

✳ ✳ ✳ ✳

Japan seems to have a yen for selling unusual products via vending machines—they sell more than any other country. Aside from the usual candy, gum, and cans of soda, here are some of the more obscure items available for purchase in Japanese vending machines.

1. Fresh eggs
2. Bags of rice in various sizes
3. Fishing line, fish hooks, and bait
4. Toilet paper in small packets—most public restrooms in Japan charge a fee for toilet paper
5. Fresh flowers
6. Frequent flyer miles—Japan Air Lines (JAL) has a machine that reads a credit card and boarding pass and issues frequent flyer miles
7. Beer in cans or two-liter jugs
8. Film and disposable cameras
9. Pornographic magazines
10. Designer condoms
11. Batteries
12. Live rhinoceros beetles—a popular pet for Japanese children
13. Kerosene—for home space heaters
14. Dry ice—sold at supermarkets for keeping frozen food cold until the customer gets home
15. Sake in preheated containers
16. Cups of hot noodles
17. Fortunes—found at shrines and temples
18. Umbrellas—for both rain and shade

TYPHOID MARY HAD NOTHING ON THE REST OF THE YEAR
Going Back in Time: 1907

✳ ✳ ✳ ✳

In 1907, Americans had a life expectancy of just 45.6 years for men and 49.9 for women. Even worse, this was the year that typhoid, an abdominal disease spread through water and food supplies, ravaged the nation. But alas! Public health officials discovered that 47 people stricken with the disease were all from families that employed a cook named Mary. With "Typhoid Mary" safely quarantined, these were the highlights of that year.

1. An Economic Boom

Industrial capitalism was on the rise in 1907 and with it came lots of jobs. New businesses created a need for more clerical help and a new "white collar" mentality was born. More workers received a salary instead of an hourly wage. Retail jobs also flourished and women were working outside the home more than ever before.

2. The First Electric Washing Machine

By 1907, U.S. power companies were growing in technology and scale. As a result, life became a little easier for housewives, especially when the Thor washing machine was introduced by Hurley Machine Company of Chicago. To go with the Thor, a company in Düsseldorf, Germany, came up with the first household detergent in the same year. It was called Persil.

3. The Beginnings of UPS

Seattle entrepreneur James E. Casey was only 19 in 1907 when he borrowed $100 to create a delivery service he called the American Messenger Company. He and his friends ran errands and delivered packages and food. Most deliveries were done on foot, with longer trips made via bicycle. A Model T Ford was added six years later, and by 1919, the company had expanded beyond Seattle and was renamed United Parcel Service.

4. The Creation of Mother's Day

After her mother died, Anna Jarvis started a letter-writing campaign in support of the celebration of mothers everywhere. A minister in Grafton, West Virginia, obliged and dedicated the second Sunday in May specifically to the late Mrs. Jarvis. Ironically, the woman who is credited with creating what we now know as Mother's Day never became a mother herself. Her entire life was dedicated to caring for others: first her elderly mother and then her blind sister. Jarvis never married and, in 1948, died a pauper.

5. Swimming Without a Skirt is a Police Matter

When Australian long-distance swimmer Annette Kellerman decided to swim at Boston's Revere Beach in a one-piece bathing suit—*without* a skirt—she was arrested. The charge? Indecent exposure, of course! The 22-year-old wasn't the only one under scrutiny. Even infants were required to wear complete bathing costumes in the land of the free until a quarter of a century later.

6. The "Monobosom" and Other Fashionable Styles

Ladies of the early 20th century certainly didn't show much skin. However, they were very creative in enhancing their fully clothed silhouettes. The hourglass figure was highly coveted, but if you weren't a full-bodied woman by nature, you simply had to work harder. Corset strings were pulled so tightly that the hips were forced back and the chest thrust forward creating a "monobosom." But things loosened up a tad after dark. To show off their fine jewelry, women of 1907 wore low sweetheart necklines often accented with feather boas.

7. And Now for the Tresses

In 1907, America was at war against tuberculosis, which killed hundreds of people from the 1880s to the 1950s. To complement their pale complexions, survivors opted for masses of ringlets, thanks to the invention of the waving iron in the 1870s. Hair coloring was frowned upon, but the brave went for it anyway, using herbs, rust, and other concoctions. To promote hair growth, petroleum jelly, castor oil, and gallic acid were also part of the beauty arsenal.

8. No One Wanted Their MTV

A lucky few enjoyed phonographs in 1907, but the most common way to hear a new song was by piano. People would trade, borrow, and collect the sheet music to their favorite songs. A popular choice was George M. Cohan's "You're a Grand Old Rag" from his hit Broadway musical *George Washington, Jr.* The song quickly spread beyond New York City and became a staple in piano benches across the country. Eventually, Cohan changed the title to "You're a Grand Old Flag," and the song remains a national treasure.

9. A Movie for a Nickel

Way before the TV network and even before the Ryan and Tatum O'Neal film, the word *nickelodeon* meant a small neighborhood theater where people would gather to see a movie. The cost? A nickel, of course! These theaters held about 200 chairs and featured live piano music before each show. Movies were comedic sketches, animal acts, or vaudeville acts that lasted around 15 minutes each.

10. The Invention of the Paper Towel

The paper towel was created by a crafty teacher in Philadelphia who found a way to keep her students from perpetuating a cold epidemic. Instead of sharing the same cloth towel, she cut some paper into individual squares. The Scott Paper Company, which was already making toilet paper, got wind of the story. Ironically, the company had an entire railroad car full of paper that was too thick to be used in the bathroom. Arthur Scott came up with a way to copy the teacher's design on a bigger scale. It didn't take long before he was selling the idea as a product called the Sani-Towel.

11. The Chicago Cubs Win the World Series!

The World Series was only four years old in 1907. What's more, Ty Cobb was merely 20. But youth was on the side of the Chicago Cubs as they won the World Series, beating Cobb and his Detroit Tigers four games to none. The Series wasn't without its share of drama—the first game was called because of darkness.

Countries that Use the Most Cell Phones

✳ ✳ ✳ ✳

Country	Number of Cell Phones (millions)
1. China	547
2. India	296
3. United States	255
4. Russia	170
5. Brazil	121
6. Japan	107
7. Germany	97
8. Pakistan	88
9. Indonesia	82
10. Italy	79

Source: CIA World Factbook 2008

Countries with the Most Internet Users

✳ ✳ ✳ ✳

Country	Number of Internet Users (millions)
1. China	253.0
2. United States	223.0
3. Japan	88.1
4. India	80.0
5. Brazil	50.0
6. Germany	42.5
7. United Kingdom	40.2
8. South Korea	35.6
9. Italy	32.0
10. France	31.3

Source: CIA World Factbook 2008

LOST AT SEA
10 Items that Were Buried with the *Titanic*

When the opulent passenger liner RMS Titanic *was built in 1912, it was declared by* Shipbuilder *magazine to be "practically unsinkable." Unfortunately, the word* practically *turned out to be key. On the* Titanic's *maiden voyage from Southampton, England, to New York City, it hit an iceberg and sank in just three hours. Of the 2,229 passengers and crew onboard, only 713 survived. The ship has been a source of fascination ever since, partly because of the many stories associated with its sinking, but also because of the huge wealth that went down with the ship and remains on the ocean floor to this day. Here are some of the people and cargo that were onboard that fateful day*

1. Passengers

The *Titanic* carried 1,316 passengers (325 in first class, 285 in second class, and 706 in third class) of which 498 survived. Around two-thirds of first-class passengers survived, compared to around one-quarter of those in third class, mainly because, at some point, the gates to the third-class quarters were locked, denying those passengers access to lifeboats. Some of the more famous first-class passengers included millionaire Benjamin Guggenheim and his manservant, who both helped women and children into lifeboats before changing into their best clothes and preparing to "die like gentlemen," which they did. Also in first class was Lady Duff Gordon, a dress designer whose clientele included the British royal family. She and her husband survived, but they were later accused of bribing crew members to not allow more people into their lifeboat, which had been only half full. John Jacob Astor IV, the world's richest man at the time, was also onboard. He assisted his pregnant wife, Madeleine, onto a lifeboat but was not allowed to board himself because officers were applying the principle of "women and children first." Madeleine survived, but John went down with the ship.

2. Lifeboats

Famously, the *Titanic* had an inadequate number of lifeboats for the number of people it carried. In fact, it had just 20, with a total capacity of 1,178 people—about half the number of people onboard. The ship had been designed to hold 32 lifeboats (still not enough for everyone), but the owner, White Star Line, had been concerned that too many boats would spoil its appearance.

3. Crew

The *Titanic* had around 900 crew members, of whom 215 survived. These staff included the deck crew (responsible for sailing the ship), the engineering department (who kept the engines running), the victualing department (responsible for passenger comfort), restaurant staff, and musicians. As the ship was sinking, its two bands came together on the deck and played to keep the spirits of the passengers up. None of the band members survived.

4. Art

Perhaps unsurprisingly, considering the wealth of many of its passengers, the *Titanic* was carrying a number of works of art, all of which were lost when the ship sank. The most spectacular of these was a jeweled copy of *The Rubáiyát,* a collection of about 1,000 poems by the 11th-century Persian mathematician and astronomer Omar Khayyám. The binding of this incredibly luxurious book contained 1,500 precious stones, each set in gold. It had been sold at auction in March 1912 to an American bidder for £405, or around $1,900—15 years' worth of wages for a junior crew member on the *Titanic.*

5. Linen

The restaurants, cafés, kitchens, and bedrooms of the *Titanic* required so much linen that White Star Line built a large laundry close to the docks at Southampton, so that each time the ship docked, the dirty linen could quickly be unloaded and cleaned for the next voyage. The 200,000 individual items (not including items belonging to passengers) included 18,000 bedsheets, 6,000 tablecloths, 36,000 towels, and 45,000 table napkins.

6. Freight

One important function of the *Titanic* was to carry transatlantic mail. When the ship sank, there were 3,364 bags of mail and between 700 and 800 parcels onboard, contents unknown. Other cargo claimed as lost included 50 cases of toothpaste, a cask of china headed for Tiffany's, five grand pianos, and 30 cases of golf clubs and tennis rackets for A.G. Spalding. However, contrary to popular myth, the *Titanic* was not carrying an ancient Egyptian mummy that was believed to have cursed the ship.

7. Food

With all those people onboard, it's not surprising that the ship contained incredible quantities of food. There were 75,000 pounds of fresh meat, as well as 15,000 pounds of fish, 25,000 pounds of poultry, and 2,500 pounds of sausage. Among other items, the ship carried 40 tons of potatoes and 1,750 pounds of ice cream—that's the weight of a full-grown elephant.

8. Drink

Passengers needed something to wash down all that food, so the *Titanic* carried 15,000 bottles of ale and stout, 1,000 bottles of wine, and 850 bottles of spirits, plus 1,200 bottles of soft drinks and mixers, such as lemonade, tonic water, and orange juice.

9. Tableware

Serving all that food and drink required 57,600 items of crockery, 29,000 pieces of glassware, and 44,000 pieces of cutlery. The cutlery alone would have weighed more than 4,000 pounds!

10. Passenger Facilities

The sinking of the *Titanic* also meant the loss of some of the most opulent facilities ever seen on a cruise liner, such as the first-ever onboard heated swimming pool, a Turkish bath, first- and second-class libraries, and a veranda café with real palm trees. The ship also had a Marconi wireless radio station to send and receive telegrams and a 50-phone switchboard complete with operator. The

Titanic even had a state-of-the-art infirmary and operating room staffed by two physicians. All of this was lost when the ship sank.

DO YOU KNOW HOW FAST YOU WERE GOING?
Speed Records for 13 Land and Water Vehicles

When it comes to speed, most people don't even think about it until a police officer asks if they know how fast they were going. But speed records are kept for just about everything that goes. Here are some records for the world's fastest vehicles on land and sea.

1. Fastest Long-Distance Sailing Ship

According to the World Sailing Speed Record Council, the fastest long-distance sailing ship is the *Groupama 3,* a 105-foot-long trimaran piloted by French skipper Franck Cammas and crew. They set the record on a transatlantic trip in 2007, crossing the Atlantic at an average speed of 29 knots (about 33 miles per hour) and completed the trip in 4 days, 3 hours, 57 minutes, and 54 seconds. Another Frenchman, Bruno Peyron and the crew of the *Orange II* set the round-the-world sailing record on March 16, 2005, circling the globe (27,000 nautical miles) in 50 days, 16 hours, and 20 minutes, with an average speed of 17.89 knots (around 20 miles per hour).

2. Underwater Speed Records

Official underwater speed records—usually achieved by military submarines—are not kept due to the secrecy surrounding the capabilities of these warships. But in 1965, the USS *Albacore,* a Gato-class submarine, was clocked at 33 knots (38 miles per hour), an unofficial underwater speed record. Claims of higher speeds have been made by submarine manufacturers but have not been officially measured. Russia's Akula-class submarine allegedly can travel submerged at 35 knots (approximately 40 miles per hour), while the Alfa-class submarine it replaced was said to reach 44.7 knots (approximately 51.4 miles per hour) for short periods.

3. Sailing Speed Record

The fastest sailing vessel, and the smallest, is the sailboard, a surfboard with a sail attached. Champion windsurfer Antoine Albeau of France holds the world sailing speed record of 49.9 knots (about 57 miles per hour), set on a 1,000-meter canal in Les Saintes Maries de la Mer, France, on March 5, 2008. Albeau broke Irishman Finian Maynard's record of 48.7 knots (about 56 miles per hour), set in April 2005.

4. Fastest Lawn Mower

Most kids hate mowing the lawn, but that might change if their parents bought them this riding mower. On July 4, 2006, at the Bonneville Salt Flats, Bob Cleveland drove his specially-built lawn mower at an average speed of just over 80 miles per hour. Cleveland assembled the mower himself, using a Snapper lawn tractor with a 80-horse power Briggs & Stratton V-twin modified engine and other custom accessories. At the time he set the record, Cleveland was an eight-time champion in the National Lawn Mower Racing Series.

5. Fastest Steam-Powered Vehicle

Probably the longest-running speed record belongs to a steam-powered vehicle, the Stanley Steamer. Between 1902 and 1927, these steam-powered automobiles were produced for the public by the Stanley twins—Francis and Freelan—through their Stanley Motor Carriage Company. In 1906, a Stanley Rocket driven by Fred Marriott set the world land speed record for all automobiles, reaching 127.7 miles per hour at the Daytona Beach Road Course in Florida. While the land speed record has been broken by cars with internal combustion or jet-powered engines, the Stanley Steamer still owns the record for steam-powered cars.

6. Fastest Roller Coaster

While it never leaves the park, the Kingda Ka roller coaster at Six Flags Great Adventure amusement park in Jackson, New Jersey, is recognized as the world's fastest roller coaster. Opened in 2005, the Kingda Ka is a hydraulic launch rocket coaster that reaches its top speed of 128 miles per hour in just 3.5 seconds. Its 456-foot-tall tower is also the world's tallest for a coaster. Built by the Swiss ride manufacturer Intamin, the Kingda Ka uses an over-the-shoulder safety restraint system to keep riders in their seats, but there's no guarantee it will keep their lunch in their stomachs.

7. Bicycle Speed Records

Bicycles require human power to move forward, but that doesn't mean they can't move fast. The record for the fastest speed achieved on a regular (upright) bicycle belongs to Fred Rompelberg, who, in 1995, reached a speed of 166.944 miles per hour while being paced by a motor vehicle, which substantially reduced his wind resistance. The official record for an unpaced upright bicycle is 51.29 miles per hour over 200 meters set by Jim Glover in Vancouver in 1986. Recumbent bicycles—those funny-looking bikes where the rider sits in a reclined position with legs extended forward—are aerodynamically faster than conventional bicycles. Canadian cyclist Sam Whittingham set the recumbent bicycle speed record on October 5, 2002, reaching 81 miles per hour over 200 meters with a running start and no pace vehicle.

8. Fastest Electric (Battery-Powered) Vehicle

Electric cars are usually thought to be slow, but not the Buckeye Bullet. This electric (battery-powered) vehicle, designed and built by engineering students at Ohio State University, holds both the U.S. and international land speed records, which have different sets of rules. To set the international record, an electric car must run a 1-kilometer course twice in opposite directions within a one hour time period. On October 13, 2004, at the Bonneville Salt Flats, driver Roger Schroer set the new international land speed record of 271.737 miles per hour. To set the U.S. record, the vehicle had to be impounded for four hours between two qualifying runs so that it couldn't be repaired, adjusted, or tampered with. On October 15, 2004, the Buckeye Bullet, driven again by Schroer on the same course, set the U.S. land speed record at 314.958 miles per hour.

9. World's Fastest Speedboat

The world's fastest speedboat was actually built in the backyard of the man who set the record. On October 8, 1978, at Blowering Dam, Australia, motorboat racer Ken Darby captained the *Spirit of Australia* to a world record average speed of 318.75 miles per hour, breaking his own record of 290.313 miles per hour set the previous year. Darby designed and built the *Spirit of Australia* himself, using balsa wood, fiberglass, and a military surplus engine he bought for only $69. This is a dangerous sport—no other speedboat racer has clocked in at more than 300 miles per hour and survived.

10. Fastest Diesel-Powered Vehicle

The word *diesel* used to conjure up images of smelly buses and slow-moving trucks, but that picture changed on August 23, 2006, when the JCB DIESELMAX diesel-powered car driven by Andy Green averaged 350 miles per hour over two runs at the Bonneville Salt Flats. On the first run, he hit 365.779 miles per hour. The JCB DIESELMAX was built by the British company JCB, which normally makes diesel-powered backhoes, loaders, and other types of construction equipment.

11. Fastest Person on Two Wheels

The fastest person on two wheels is motorcycle racer Chris Carr. On September 5, 2006, at the Bonneville Salt Flats in Utah—the site of many land speed records—Carr broke the motorcycle land speed record with an average speed of 350.8 miles per hour over two passes on a fixed-length course in two opposite-direction runs. Of the two passes, Carr's fastest was 354 miles per hour. He was riding the Number Seven Streamliner, a specially designed bike with a turbocharged V4 engine.

12. World's Fastest Trains

In the category of trains with wheels, the French TGV, a high-speed train, is the fastest in the world. On April 3, 2007, under test conditions, the high-speed train consisting of two engine cars and three double-decker passenger cars set the record of 357.2 miles per hour. In the category of magnetic levitation trains—where the cars float above a guidance track using powerful electric magnets—the Japanese JR-Maglev three-car train set a record of 361 miles per hour on December 2, 2003. But, without people onboard—and with rockets attached—railed vehicles can go much faster. On April 30, 2003, an unmanned four-stage rocket sled (a small railroad car with rockets strapped to it) reached a speed of 6,462 miles per hour at Holloman Air Force Base in New Mexico.

13. Land Speed Record

The land speed record was set on October 15, 1997, by Andy Green, a British fighter pilot in the Royal Air Force. On Black Rock Desert, a dry lake bed in northwestern Nevada, Green's Thrust-SSC jet-propelled car reached a speed of 763.035 miles per hour, making him the first driver to reach supersonic speed (761 mph) and break the sound barrier. Green broke his own record of 714.144 miles per hour, which was set on September 25, 1997. The ThrustSSC is powered by two after-burning Rolls-Royce Spey engines—the same engines used in the Phantom jet fighters Green flew for the RAF. The jet engines powering the ThrustSSC burn 4.8 gallons of fuel per second and get about 0.04 miles per gallon.

10 Autos that Are Stolen Most Often

❋ ❋ ❋ ❋

1. 1995 Honda Civic
2. 1991 Honda Accord
3. 1989 Toyota Camry
4. 1997 Ford F150 Series
5. 1994 Chevrolet C/K 1500 Pickup
6. 1994 Acura Integra
7. 2004 Dodge Ram Pickup
8. 1994 Nissan Sentra
9. 1988 Toyota Pickup
10. 2007 Toyota Corolla

Source: National Insurance Crime Bureau, 2008

17 Silly and Humorous Book Titles

✳ ✳ ✳ ✳

1. *Across Europe by Kangaroo* by Joseph R. Barry
2. *Be Bold with Bananas* by Crescent Books
3. *The Devil's Cloth: A History of Stripes* by Michel Pastoureaut
4. *Fancy Coffins to Make Yourself* by Dale L. Power
5. *The Flat-Footed Flies of Europe* by Peter J. Chandler
6. *How to Avoid Huge Ships* by John W. Trimmer
7. *How to Be a Pope: What to Do and Where to Go Once You're in the Vatican* by Piers Marchant
8. *How to Make Love While Conscious* by Guy Kettelhack
9. *How to Read a Book* by Mortimer J. Adler and Charles Van Doren
10. *Lightweight Sandwich Construction* by J. M. Davies
11. *The Making of a Moron* by Niall Brennan
12. *101 Super Uses for Tampon Applicators* by Lori Katz and Barbara Meyer
13. *101 Uses for an Old Farm Tractor* by Michael Dregni
14. *Scouts in Bondage* by Michael Bell
15. *Superfluous Hair and Its Removal* by A. F. Niemoeller
16. *Suture Self* by Mary Daheim
17. *Underwater Acoustics Handbook* by Vernon Martin Albers

FINS, HULA HOOPS, AND A BOY NAMED BEAVER
A Nostalgic Look Back on 1957

✳ ✳ ✳ ✳

Life in America in 1957 was much simpler. Everybody loved Lucy and Father always knew best. Make yourself a root beer float, sit on the davenport, and take a look back at life in 1957.

1. Welcome to Babyville.
After World War II, people were settling down and getting back to the business of creating the American dream. Record numbers of

babies were born between 1946 and 1964, and, even today, this generation is referred to as the "Baby Boomers." By 1957, everybody on the fast track was moving out to the suburbs. Doctors, lawyers, teachers, and cops led a mass exodus to the land of lawn mowers and charcoal grills. With all the new babies being born, it's no wonder that suburbia became known as "Babyville."

2. It was a small world, after all.

In 1957, during the height of the Baby Boom, the Census Bureau reported that there were 171,984,130 people in the United States, and 2,889,768,830 in the entire world. Today, there are 6.6 billion people in the world, including more than 300 million Americans.

3. Does this price include the white picket fence?

The American dream was a whole lot cheaper in 1957. You could buy your very own house for about $12,200. A custom built, split-level cost a little more—around $19,000. For those who weren't quite ready to buy, rent was only about $90 a month!

4. It's all relative.

Those house prices look pretty good, but what was the average household income in 1957? On average, people made around $4,500 a year. If you sold cars, you made $7,000 to $10,000 a year. A secretary made about $3,900 a year. So, could you afford to own?

5. All eyes toward the sky.

In July 1957, American John Glenn set a new transcontinental speed record. The navy test pilot flew a supersonic jet from California to New York in just 3 hours, 23 minutes, and 8.4 seconds.

6. What's a Sputnik?

Before astronauts, space missions flew without a crew. The first of these, *Sputnik*, came from the Soviet Union. *Sputnik* technically wasn't a satellite, it was a 184-pound basketball-size bundle of radio transmitters that took only 98 minutes to orbit Earth. When it was launched on October 4, 1957, during the height of the Cold War, the United States was caught completely by surprise and the "Space Race" was on!

7. You know what they say about the size of a man's fin.

General Motors and Ford were duking it out with their "Olds vs. Edsel" wars. Ford's Edsel included such forward-thinking features as lights that reminded drivers that it was time to service the engine. Chevrolet opted to put their money into advertising. This is the year that had Dinah Shore singing "See the USA in your Chevrolet" on radio and TV spots. Whatever people chose to drive, the average cost of a car was only $2,749. Brace yourself—gasoline was only about 25 cents a gallon!

8. Rabbit ears were popping up all over the place.

In 1957, there were 47,200,000 TV sets in America; the RCA Victor model cost $78. What was everybody watching? Top shows included *Gunsmoke, The Danny Thomas Show, I Love Lucy,* and *The Ed Sullivan Show.*

9. What's with all the hips?

Music lovers had plenty of choices in the year when rock 'n' roll took over the charts. Songs like Sam Cooke's, "You Send Me" and Jimmie Rodgers's "Honeycomb" were popular, but the true sensation of the year was Elvis Presley. He rocked teens across the country with hits like "All Shook Up" and "Jailhouse Rock." You could buy a 45-rpm record (that's the little one) for 79 cents or an album (the big one) for about three bucks. The only problem was that a hi-fi record player cost $79.95.

10. Lennon and McCartney meet for the first time.

In 1957, a chance meeting at a church in Liverpool would forever change the face of rock music. On July 6, The Quarrymen, a skiffle group led by singer and guitarist John Lennon, performed a gig at the Woolton Parish Church. Among those in attendance was a young musician named Paul McCartney. The two future Beatles were introduced by a mutual friend, and McCartney helped Lennon set up for the gig. Lennon was so impressed with McCartney's musical abilities that he invited him to join the group. The Quarrymen eventually became The Beatles, and the rest is music history.

11. This black and white had nothing to do with TV.

In the interest of school desegregation, President Eisenhower sent army troops to keep the peace at Central High School in Little Rock, Arkansas, so that nine black students could attend the formerly all-white school. These kids are forever stamped in history as the Little Rock Nine.

12. Who's Dick Clark?

People started bopping in the middle of the family room in 1957 when ABC began airing *American Bandstand*, hosted by Dick Clark. Teens danced to the hits of the day, and each week a different band performed. After each song, Clark would interview the teens and have them rate the song for its "danceability." The first nationwide audience poll ranked Patti Page as *American Bandstand*'s favorite female vocalist of the year. The show went off the air in 1989.

13. Teen idols were "dreamy."

Teenage girls had plenty of swooning to do thanks to the many teen idols of the late 1950s. Ricky Nelson rocked and rolled on his family's hit TV show, *Ozzie and Harriet*, and people tuned in every week just to see if he'd sing. And Pat Boone cut such a wholesome image in his white patent leather shoes that even parents couldn't object. In 1957, he topped the charts with "Love Letters in the Sand."

14. The Braves win the World Series!

But they weren't from Atlanta. In 1957, they were the Milwaukee Braves. In 1957, the Braves, led by Hank Aaron, beat Mickey Mantle and the New York Yankees to win the World Series. But it wasn't easy—it took all seven games.

15. Baseball moves to California.

Due to aging stadiums and slumping ticket sales, the archrival Brooklyn Dodgers and New York Giants moved west following the 1957 season. The Dodgers played one final game at Ebbets Field on September 24, 1957, before moving to Los Angeles. The stadium remained without a team and was eventually torn down in 1960. On September 29, 1957, the Giants played their last game at the Polo

Grounds, before heading to San Francisco. The stadium was vacant until the Mets moved in for the 1962 and 1963 seasons. It was demolished in 1964.

16. "Fashion Forward" had nothing to do with Paris.

In 1957, American women had houses to clean, children to rear, and parties to plan. With cardigans, pearls, knee-length skirts, and heels, a lady always looked good. Teenage girls opted for bobby socks, saddle shoes, and poodle skirts. Females young and old even wore pants from time to time, especially pedal pushers or Capri pants. For hip young fellas, a leather jacket or a letterman sweater was a must.

17. And the Oscar goes to . . .

. . . *The Bridge on the River Kwai,* for Best Picture. Alec Guinness also won the Oscar for Best Actor for his role in the movie. Joanne Woodward claimed her statue for Best Actress in *The Three Faces of Eve.* Other favorites were *An Affair to Remember, 12 Angry Men,* and that kid who swivels his hips in a movie called *Jailhouse Rock.* With the average price of a movie ticket at just 50 cents, you could afford to see them all!

Countries that Consume the Most Beer

✳ ✳ ✳ ✳

Country	Gallons per Person per Year
1. Ireland	41.0
2. Germany	31.4
3. Austria	28.0
4. Belgium	26.0
Denmark	26.0
5. United Kingdom	25.6
6. Australia	23.5
7. United States	22.5
8. Netherlands	21.1
9. Finland	20.9

"Goodbye" in 21 Different Languages

✳ ✳ ✳ ✳

1. Afrikaans .... Totsiens
2. Chinese (Cantonese) .... Joi gin
3. Chinese (Mandarin) .... Zai jian
4. Danish .... Farvel
5. Dutch .... Vaarwel
6. English .... Goodbye
7. French .... Au revoir
8. German .... Auf Wiedersehen
9. Greek .... Adio
10. Hawaiian .... Aloha
11. Hungarian .... Viszontlátásra
12. Irish Gaelic .... Slán
13. Italian .... Arrivederci/ciao
14. Japanese .... Sayonara
15. Polish .... Do widzenia
16. Portuguese .... Adeus
17. Russian .... Do svidaniya
18. Scottish Gaelic .... Beannachd leibh
19. Spanish .... Adiós
20. Swedish .... Adjö
21. Welsh .... Ffarwél